TRACKS
FOR
FIGHTING VEHICLES

Prepared by

E.W.E. MICKLETHWAIT M.A. F.C.I.P.A.

from material collected from many sources and with the co-operation of members of the staffs of the Ministry of Supply, certain firms and the School of Tank Technology.

Exclusive facsimile edition

This is a facsimile of the wartime edition of this book, with the original blemishes and printing anomalies.

Copyright © 2020 Tank Archives Press

All rights reserved. No part of this publication may be reproduced or stored in a retrieval system or transmitted, in any form or by any means, electronic, mechanical, photocopying, recording or otherwise, without prior permission in writing from Tank Archives Press.

To request permission, write to the editor at at the address below.

ISBN: 978-1-951171-00-1

Published by:
Tank Archives Press
PO Box 181802
Coronado
CA 92178
USA

Editor: Bruce Oliver Newsome, PhD.

Acknowledgements

The Editor wishes to thank the following:

David Willey
(Curator, The Tank Museum)

Sheldon Rogers
(Archives Assistant, The Tank Museum)

Ian Hudson
(Research Assistant, The Tank Museum)

Karley List (Intern)

AUTHOR'S NOTES

At some points, especially in Parts II and III, the reader may be tempted to ask "So what?" He may feel the subject has been left in the air. It has. And there it will remain until somebody does some experimental work to establish the fundamental background of the subject. There is a limit to the amount of theory that can be developed by calculation without experiment, and the author feels that the limit is approached (if not exceeded) in this book.

ACKNOWLEDGMENT

Much of the material in this book is "home made" by the recipe of taking a track and applying to it the laws of mechanics. The raw material for this process, as well as other material embodying history or experience, has been collected from such a variety of sources - books, reports, conversations etc. - that it seems impracticable to make detailed acknowledgment. As far as possible footnotes are included in the text indicating the sources of specific items of information, but the author would like to make this general acknowledgment to all who have assisted him knowingly or otherwise.

CHAPTER, SECTION AND PAGE NUMBERING

To allow flexibility for later amendments this book is in loose-leaf form and is arranged in numbered chapters and sections rather than numbered pages. The sections are numbered consecutively through each chapter, and identified by the chapter number followed by the section number separated by a dot. Thus Section 4.5 means the 5th section in Chapter 4 whilst 4.15 means the 15th section in Chapter 4. To help in finding a section the section numbers are printed at the head of each page.

The diagrams or tables in any one section are indicated by the section number followed by a letter. Thus Figure 4.15b, is the second figure in Section 4.15 and can easily be found.

PREFACE

This book has been prepared by the School of Tank Technology in accordance with its policy of compiling a series of text books on various aspects of tank engineering. Hitherto there has been hardly any technical literature devoted to tanks, because the engineers actively engaged in tank design and development have been too busy to write and consequently, except in a few centres where there has been some continuity of thought, many new-comers to the subject have had perforce to approach their problems without any acquaintance with past experience.

Textbooks are usually written by persons who are already acknowledged authorities on the subject. Under present circumstances this has not been possible, because all those with such qualifications are fully employed and are unable to devote the necessary time to the preparation of a book. Therefore, the course has been adopted of asking an engineer of experience in patent and other work to study the literature, reports and specimens available at the School of Tank Technology, to discuss matters with specialists, and then to commit the results of his researches to paper in an easily assimilable form.

The enquiring mind is at once struck by the lack of accepted theory dealing with the fundamental facts affecting the design and use of tracks and this has led the author to make some theoretical explorations into the matter. Some of these have been tentatively covered by others and some are original; but almost all await substantiation by practical experiment. The book is therefore divided into parts. The first is a survey of development and practice intended for reference and for the use of students and others approaching the subject for the first time, while Parts II and III contain the excursions into theory.

To have submitted drafts of this book to all those who might have made useful suggestions would have caused great delay, and so the course has been adopted of publishing a limited edition in the hope that those who can, will correct or supplement the information given. The School of Tank Technology will welcome comments and new material which will be sifted and, in due course, incorporated in a new edition. It is particularly hoped that any readers in the United States or Dominions will give us the benefit of their experience as different schools of thought may have grown up abroad.

School of Tank Technology.
July, 1944.

Colonel.
Commandant.

CONTENTS.

Section 0.0   Index to Part I
Section 0.1   Index to Part II
Section 0.2   Index to Part III
Section 0.3   Glossary

PART I

PAST AND PRESENT PRACTICE

Chapter 1. GENERAL HISTORICAL DEVELOPMENT OF TRACKED VEHICLES.
1. The invention of tracks
2. Attachments to wheels, Boydell's Girdle, Tipping's Plates, Diplock's Pedrail.
3. Earliest practical use of tracks
4. The invention of the tank
5. Arduous performance requirements of earliest heavy tanks
6. Medium or Whippet tanks
7. Post 1918 experimental designs
8. The Vickers Medium tank
9. Light tanks
10. A.9 and 10 and early Valentine
11. A.13 and later Cruisers
12. Infantry tanks

Chapter 2. MAIN TYPES OF TRACK AND THEIR BROAD FUNCTIONS
1. Types of track
2. The flexible pin jointed type
3. Rubber bushed tracks
4. Continuously flexible or endless band type
5. Irreversible types, the elastic girder and rigid girder types
6. Main functions of the track
7. Providing multi-wheel drive from a single axle
8. Increasing the area of ground which contributes adhesion
9. Distribution of the pressure due to the weight of the vehicle to reduce sinkage and rolling resistance
10. Providing a ramp for obstacle crossing

Chapter 3. POSSIBLE FORMS OF PIN-JOINTED TRACK LINKS
1. Essential Characteristics
2. Ground engaging surfaces for support and adhesion
3. Wheel paths and guiding surfaces
4. Driving surfaces for taking the sprocket drive
5. Hinges
6. Pin retention. Split pin with or without castellated nut, S-pin.
7. Floating pins, solder and lead plug
8. Anvil and sleeve
9. Bent banana
10. Welded plates
11. Rivetted pin end
12. Circlip
13. Wedge and flat
14. Skoda inclined guide
15. Pin retention, concluding remarks

Chapter 4. HISTORICAL DEVELOPMENT OF TRACK LINKS

1. Historical development
2. Early designs
3. Last war tank tracks

Contents contd.

4. Post 1918 experimental designs
5. Vickers Medium tanks, Built up tracks
6. Stamped tracks. Vickers Medium tanks, Matilda etc.
7. Views of the Mechanical Warfare Board 1930-31
8. S. of D.'s welded stamped design
9. Carden Loyd tracks
10. Direct descendents of the Carden Loyd track
11. Vickers 6-ton tractor, Dragon Medium Mark IV., and Tank Infantry Mark 1 (A.11.)
12. Lubricated mud-sealed tracks
13. A.9, A.10 and early Valentine tracks
14. A.13. E.1.
15. A.13
16. Back to the dry pin
17. Single spud box section designs
18. Single spud ribbed designs
19. Skeleton designs. German tracks
20. The tracks of the German half-tracked carrier
21. Rubber and rubber jointed tracks
22. American tracks
23. Russian tank tracks
24. Track Data.

CHAPTER 5 MATERIALS AND MANUFACTURE

1. Introductory.
2. Manganese Steel.
3. Malleable Cast Iron.
4. Carbon Steel.
5. Historical and General.
6. The Rearmament Expansion.
7. Wartime Production.
8. German Tank Materials.
9. An Example of the Manufacture of Manganese Steel Links. Preparing the Metal.
10. Melting the Metal.
11. Casting the Manganese Steel Links.
12. Heat Treatment of Manganese Steel Links.
13. Some other Materials and Processes.

0.1

PART II

THEORETICAL AND CONTROVERSIAL SUBJECTS

Chapter 11. REQUIREMENTS

1. Introductory – Incompleteness of existing theory
2. Requirements for modern tracks
3. Ease of manufacture
4. Strength and reliability
5. Long life
6. Obstacle crossing performance
7. Adequate support and adhesion under the widest possible range of conditions
8. Low rolling resistance
9. Silence
10. Detail points

Chapter 12. TRACK TENSION, AND TRACK SLACK

1. Introductory
2. Relation of tension to shape of a flexible band for various forms of loading
3. Two straight lines: Point loading
4. Circular arc: Radial loading uniform along curve e.g. centrifugal force
5. Parabola: Vertical loading uniform along horizontal
6. Catenary: Vertical loading uniform along the curve. Level span
7. Tension and slack in inclined span of Catenary
7.1 Appendix. The Catenary (inclined span)
7.2 Appendix.
7.3 Appendix.
8. Tension and slack in terms of sag in a span of the track. The Cromwell
9. Tension and slack in inclined span. The Cromwell
10. Tension and slack in terms of sag. Pz.Kpfw.III.
11. Track tension. Its distribution round the track.
12. Effect of suspension movement on track tension.
13. Upward force on front and rear road wheels due to track tension
14. Sprung idler or sprocket and compensated idler or sprocket arrangements.
15. Relation between tractive effort and adhesion on the level and on a slope.
16. Track tension due to a hump.
17. Obstacle crossing. Effect of tensions.
18. Track tension due to mud packing.
19. Track tension. Experimental data
20. Track tension. Concluding remarks. Tension not limited by adhesion or tractive effort.

Chapter 13. STRENGTH OF TRACKS

1. Introductory
2. Bending of track pins
3. Stresses in lugs of track links under tension
4. Reverse bend.
5. Bending moment about horizontal axes in track links
6. Twisting
7. Bending about vertical axis

Chapter 14. DESIGN FACTORS AFFECTING TRACK LIFE.

1. Wear of sole plate or spud face
2. Pitch increase of tracks relative to sprocket
3. Sprocket pitch, pitch polygon, and pitch circle
4. Shapes of sprocket teeth

Contents contd.

5. Meshing of tracks and sprockets
6. Overpitched track. Slack
7. Overpitched track. Driving
7.1 Appendix
8. Overpitched track. Braking.
9. Underpitched track. Slack
10. Underpitched track. Driving
11. Underpitched track. Braking
12. Correctly pitched track. Driving, slack and braking.
13. Sprocket tooth design: Reversibility, strength
14. Wrap, test.

Chapter 15. ROLLING RESISTANCE ON HARD GROUND. VIBRATION & NOISE

1. Relation of Power/Weight Ratio to speed rolling resistance and slope-climbing performance.
2. Factors contributing to rolling resistance
3. Transmission and sprocket losses.
4. Rolling friction of wheels.
5. Rolling resistance test results, hard ground and non-driven track.
6. Track joint friction
7. Power loss due to finite pitch of track. Scrub.
8. Leading and trailing spuds
9. Power loss and noise due to vibration and hammering
10. Kinetic energy loss due to hammering on sprockets etc.
11. Slap.
12. Comparison with actual track behaviour.
13. Longitudinal acceleration due to sprocket tooth action.

0.2

PART III.

SOIL MECHANICS IN RELATION TO TRACKS.

Chapter 21. MECHANICAL PROPERTIES OF SOILS.
1. Its importance.
2. Soil as an engineering material.
3. Characteristics of soils.
4. Size of soil particles.
5. Shape of soil particles.
6. Moisture content.
7. Arrangement of particles.

Chapter 22. SOILS ACTUALLY ENCOUNTERED.
1. Introductory.
2. Shingle.
3. Sand.
4. Windblown Sand.
5. Volcanic soil.
6. Laterite.
7. Loam.
8. Loess.
9. Clay.
10. Ice.
11. Snow.
12. General remarks.

Chapter 23. ADHESION AND SHEARING STRENGTH OF SOILS.
1. Introductory.
2. Elementary laws of friction. Coefficient of friction.
3. Adhesion factor.
4. Shearing of soils: Coulomb's equation.
5. Shearing of soil in plane inclined at $(45° - \phi/2)$ to horizontal.
6. Conditions for shear in horizontal plane or plane inclined at $(45° - \phi/2)$.
6.1. Appendix.
7. Application to spud distribution; limit to increase of adhesion by adding spuds.
8. Adhesion by combination of shearing and surface friction. depending on spud design.
9. Relation between adhesion and mean ground pressure.
9.1. Appendix. Relation between adhesion factor, internal friction, cohesive strength and mean ground pressure.
10. Effect on adhesion of disturbance of the ground as by rocking or snaking of track links.
11. Practical spud design.
12. Shape of spuds.

Chapter 24. BEARING CAPACITY OF SOIL
1. What happens when a soil is loaded.
2. Apparatus for recording relation of sinkage to pressure.
3. Curves relating sinkage to pressure.
4. Formulae for bearing capacity in terms of internal friction, cohesion and surcharge.
4.1. Appendix. Bearing capacity of soils, stress distribution - Introductory.
4.2. Appendix. Mohr's circle diagram for two dimensional stress system
4.3. Appendix. Application of Mohr's stress circle to soil.
4.4. Appendix. Vertical penetration by shear of soil.
4.5. Appendix. Equilibrium of elementary sector. Radial lines shown to be slip lines.
4.6. Appendix. Lines of principal stress.
4.7. Appendix. Magnitude of stresses.

Contents contd.

- 4.8. Appendix. Rough loaded area.
- 5. Terzaghi's approximate formula for yield by shear.
- 5.1. Appendix.
- 6. Figures for bearing capacities.

Chapter 25. GROUND PRESSURE.

- 1. Mean ground pressure. The so-called soft and hard ground pressures.
- 2. Ground pressure with slack track.
- 3. Maximum ground pressure and sinkage. Above the yield point.
- 4. Effect of track tension on sinkage.
- 5. Effect of sizes and numbers of wheels.
- 6. The effect of track links of finite length.
- 7. Track slack due to bowing on soft ground.
- 8. Maximum ground pressure and total load below the yield point.
- 9. The first wheel.
- 10. The next wheel.
- 11. Effect of numbers and sizes of wheels on maximum ground pressure below the yield point.
- 11.1. Appendix.
- 12. Varying the number of wheels keeping the total weight constant.
- 13. Varying the number and radius of wheels inversely.
- 14. "Squashed earth", rolling resistance, power below yield point. An example.
- 15. "Squashed earth" power beyond the yield point, an example.
- 16. Available test results, for soft ground.
- 17. "Squashed earth" power for rigid girder track.
- 18. Diametral pressure, effect of shape of track ground contact area, above yield point.
- 19. The short wide track and the long narrow track.

GLOSSARY

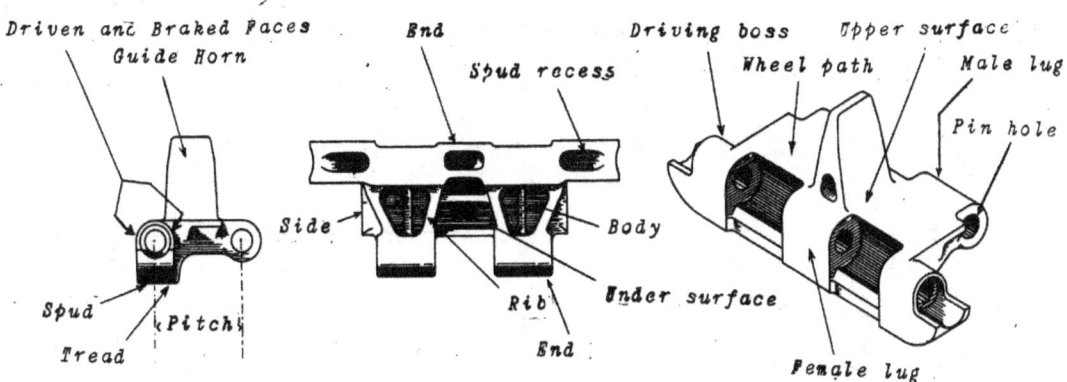

FIG. 0.3a

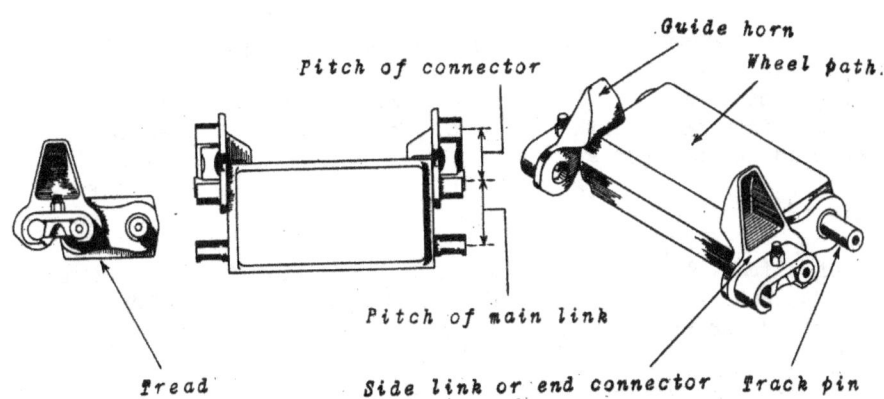

FIG. 0.3b

ADHESION. The grip which a track or wheel obtains on the ground whether by surface friction, or by digging in and tending to shear the ground or by a combination of the two.

ADHESION FACTOR. The ratio between the maximum tractive effort which a vehicle can exert, as limited by track slip, and the total normal force exerted by the vehicle on the ground. Where adhesion is obtained only by surface friction, the adhesion factor is the same as the co-efficient of friction.

BACK BEND. Of track. See REVERSE BEND.

BAR. See SPUD.

BODY. Of a track link. The portion of the link between the male and female lugs. (See Fig. 0.3a).

BOW RADIUS. The minimum radius to which a length of track, lying free on the ground, can be curved about a vertical axis.

BRAKED FACE. Of a track link. The face of a lug that takes the reverse driving or braking pressure from the sprocket. (See Fig. 0.3a).

CONTINUOUSLY FLEXIBLE TRACK. A track such as an endless rubber band which can flex at any point in its length.

DRAWBAR PULL. The force exerted at the drawbar by a vehicle which is either towing another or connected to an anchorage.

DRIVEN FACE. Of a track link. The face of a lug that takes the driving pressure from the sprocket. (See Fig. 0.3a).

DRIVING BOSS. Of a track link. A projection for engaging the sprocket to take the drive. (See Fig. 0.3a).

ELASTIC GIRDER TRACK. An irreversible track in which adjacent links are interlocked by elastic components, such as rubber buffers, to limit reverse bend.

ENDLESS RUBBER BAND TRACK. A continuously flexible track comprising an endless band of rubber, possibly reinforced with steel cables.

ENDS. Of a track link. The edges of a link which are connected to the neighbouring links. (See Fig. 0.3a).

FEMALE LUGS. Of a track link. The lugs on the end of the link which are greater in number. (See Fig. 0.3a).

FLEXIBLE TRACK. A track that can flex in either direction about horizontal transverse axes.

GROUND PRESSURE. The pressure exerted by a track on the ground under any given circumstances. The mean ground pressure, often referred to simply as the ground pressure, is the weight of the vehicle divided by the area of track in contact with the ground, or track contact area, generally measured in lbs. per sq. in.

GROUSER. See SPUD.

GUIDE HORN. Of a track link. The upstanding projection or projections which locate the wheels on the wheel path and transmit the side thrust to the track when steering. (See Fig. 0.3b).

HALF TRACKED VEHICLE. See SEMI-TRACKED VEHICLE.

IDLER. The wheel round which the track passes at the end of its contour, opposite to the sprocket. Sometimes called the track adjusting wheel, as it is generally employed for adjusting the track tension.

IRREVERSIBLE TRACK. A track that can flex freely only in one direction (i.e. that required to pass round sprocket etc.), about horizontal transverse axes.

JOINTED TRACK. A track comprising rigid links connected by joints at which the flexing takes place.

KNUCKLING. The ability of a track joint to flex between desired angular limits without fouling.

LATERALLY FLEXIBLE TRACK. A track which is capable of flexing about vertical axes so that it can lie in a curve on the ground. See BOW RADIUS.

LENGTH OF TRACK ON GROUND. On hard ground is usually taken to be equal to the distance between the centres of the front and rear load carrying wheels.
On soft ground it depends upon the sinkage and is taken to be the actual length of ground contact projected on a horizontal plane. See also TRACK CONTACT AREA.

LINK. Of a track. Each of the rigid units which are flexibly connected to form a jointed type of track. Also known as plate and shoe.

LUGS. Of a track link. A series of projections through which the pin passes to form a pin joint or hinge of alternate lugs from each of the two links so connected.

0.3

MALE LUGS. Of a track link. The lugs on the end of the link which are fewest in number. To secure a symmetrical joint one of the two link ends of any joint will practically always have one more lug than the other. (See Fig. 0.3a).

OVERPITCHED TRACK. A track whose pitch is greater than that of the sprocket, e.g. a track whose pitch has increased due to wear.

PIN JOINTED TRACK. A track in which the flexing takes place in sliding pin joints or hinges.

PIN RETAINER. The device which keeps the track pin in position.

PIN HOLE. Of a track link. The hole which receives the pin in a lug or set of lugs. (See Fig. 0.3a).

PITCH. 1. Of a track link. The distance between corresponding points of neighbouring track joints. Some tracks have two different pitches, for example the pitch of the main links and the pitch of the side links or connectors. (See Fig. 0.3b).

    2. Of sprocket. See SPROCKET PITCH.

PITCH CIRCLE. Of sprocket. See SPROCKET PITCH CIRCLE.

PITCH POLYGON. Of sprocket. See SPROCKET PITCH POLYGON.

PLATE. See LINK.

REFLEX ANGLE. Of track. See REVERSE BEND.

RETURN WHEEL. The wheel or wheels which support the top run of the track between sprocket and idler. Also known as top roller or return roller.

REVERSE BEND. Flexing of a track in the direction opposite to that which it assumes when passing round the sprocket. The angle of reverse bend is the angle between successive links when flexed to the full extent in the reverse direction. Known also as back bend and reflex angle.

RIB. Of a track link. A projecting ridge extending from the male lugs to the female lugs to provide strength. (See Fig. 0.3a).

RIGID GIRDER TRACK. An irreversible track in which adjacent links interlock to form a rigid girder, thus preventing reverse bend.

ROAD WHEEL. The wheels which normally run on the track and support the weight of the vehicle. Sometimes called bottom roller or bogie wheel.

ROLLER PATH. See WHEEL PATH.

ROLLING RESISTANCE. The sum of all the resistances to the motion of a vehicle except air resistance and gradient resistance. The losses in transmission between engine and sprocket are usually included.

RUBBER BUSHED TRACK. A jointed track incorporating rubber bushes which permit flexing by shear, i.e. relative rotation between the inner and outer cylindrical surfaces of the rubber.

RUBBER JOINTED TRACK. A track in which the joints employ rubber in the form of either blocks or bushes.

SEMI-TRACKED VEHICLE. A vehicle in which some wheels (usually the front steered wheels) run without tracks while others run on tracks.

SIDES. Of a track link. The edges which constitute the sides of a wrap or length of track. (See Fig. 0.3a).

SOLE PLATES. See SPUD.

SPROCKET. The wheel to which power is transmitted from the transmission and from which it is passed on, by direct engagement, to the track.

SPROCKET PHENOMENA. Circumstances and occurences associated with the engagement of a track and sprocket.

SPROCKET PITCH. The distance between corresponding points of neighbouring teeth on the pitch circle. In cases where one link spans two teeth, the pitch of the sprocket is the distance between corresponding points on alternate teeth.

SPROCKET PITCH CIRCLE. The circle on which lie the axes of the track pin joints of a track passing round the sprocket. It is generally reckoned that the speed of a tank in ft. per sec. is equal to the circumference of the pitch circle in ft. multiplied by the rotational speed of the sprocket in revolutions per second.

SPROCKET PITCH POLYGON. The polygon at the corners of which lie the axes of the pin joints of a track passing round a sprocket.

SPUD. A projection extending transversely across the underside of a track link to dig into soft ground and improve adhesion. When made in detachable units are known as spuds or grousers. May also be called bar or sole plate. (See Fig. 0.3a).

SPUD RECESSES. Recesses formed in the under surface of the spud of certain tracks. (See Fig. 0.3a.).

TOE AND HEEL. Projections similar to a pair of spuds on a track link but extending only a part of the way across the latter. Usually the heel is in the middle of the width of the link and the toe comprises two side portions with a gap between them corresponding to the heel.

TOP ROLLER. See RETURN WHEEL.

TRACK. The endless band or chain which passes round the wheels on each side of a tracked vehicle and on which the wheels run. See also:- Continuously flexible, Elastic girder, Endless rubber band, Flexible, Irreversible, Jointed, Laterally flexible, Pin jointed, Rigid girder, Rubber bushed, Rubber jointed.

TRACK ADJUSTING WHEEL. See IDLER.

TRACK BEHAVIOUR. The terms track behaviour and track performance together include all details of the manner in which a track functions. The distinction between them is that performance characterises the results achieved, including points such as efficiency and life, whilst behaviour characterises phenomena such as track ride whether or not these have any effect on the performance.

TRACK COMPONENTS. The following terms are employed to describe various components of tank tracks. See also:- Body, Braked face, Driven face, Driving boss, Ends, Female lugs, Guide horn, Link, Lugs, Male lugs, Pin retainer, Pin-hole, Rib, Sides, Spud, Spud recesses, Toe and heel, Track-pin, Tread, Under surface, Upper surface, Web, Wheel path.

TRACK CONTACT AREA. On a hard surface is normally the area of the spud faces; on a soft surface it is the overall length of track in contact with the ground multiplied by the overall width of track.

TRACK FLAP. See TRACK RIDE.

TRACK LINK. See LINK.

TRACK PERFORMANCE. See TRACK BEHAVIOUR.

TRACK PIN. A steel spindle which fits into the hole in the male and female lugs to form a hinge. (See Fig. 0.3b).

TRACK RIDE. The oscillations of the top run of the track, after leaving the sprocket, with the vehicle in forward motion. They are caused by variations in ground and vertical movement of the road wheels or bogies. Applied to a vehicle in reverse, the term describes the oscillations of the track between the driving sprocket and the nearest road wheel or bogie. Synonymous expressions track flap and serpentine effect.

TRACK SHOE. See LINK.

TRACK TENSIONER. See IDLER.

TRACKED VEHICLE. A vehicle in which the wheels on each side run on a track. Sometimes called a tracklayer.

TRACTIVE EFFORT. The force tending to propel a vehicle forward, measured at the pitch line of the sprocket.

TRACTIVE RESISTANCE. See ROLLING RESISTANCE.

TREAD. The pattern on the surface of the track which engages the ground. (See Fig. 0.3b).

UNDER SURFACE. Of a track link. The lower face when the link is on the ground. (See Fig. 0.3a).

UNDERPITCHED TRACK. A track whose pitch is less than that of the sprocket, as is usual in the case of a new track.

UPPER SURFACE. Of a track link. The upper face when the link is on the ground. (See. Fig. 0.3a).

WEB. Of a track link. A horizontal strengthing piece.

WHEEL CUM TRACK VEHICLE. A vehicle in which the weight can be transferred from a set of wheels running on tracks to other wheels running without tracks, and vice versa.

WHEEL PATH. The surface of the track on which the wheels run. Also known as roller path. (See Fig. 0.3a).

WRAP. Of track. A length of track comprising an arbitrary number of links. Tracks are often issued in wraps to facilitate handling.

WRAP DIAGRAM. A diagram of a wrap fitted to a sprocket indicating the measurements corresponding to the pitch tolerances.

WRAP TEST. An arbitrary test in which a wrap of track is fitted to a sprocket to determine whether the average pitch lies within specific limits.

PART 1

CHAPTER 1

GENERAL HISTORICAL DEVELOPMENT OF TRACKED VEHICLES

1.1 THE INVENTION OF TRACKS.

For many centuries vehicles have run on wheels. Wheels are simple, robust, efficient and long wearing, and can be steered without loss of power or complicated mechanism. There are, however, conditions in which load bearing wheels tend to sink into the ground or driving wheels fail to obtain a driving grip and it is therefore not surprising that the advent of the mechanical age was accompanied by suggestions for providing wheels with various attachments to prevent them from sinking into the ground or enable them to obtain an improved driving grip.

Probably the earliest reference to what we know as tracks appeared as long ago as February 15th, 1770. Richard Lovell Edgeworth, in his British Patent Specification No. 953/1770 proposed "making portable railways to wheeled carriages, so that several pieces of wood are connected to the carriage, which it moves in regular succession in such manner that a sufficient length of railway is constantly at rest for the wheels to roll upon, and that when the wheels have nearly approached the extremity of this part of the railway their motion shall lay down a fresh length of rail in front...." Thus the germ of the idea of an endless chain track is very far from being of recent origin, although over a hundred years elapsed before any serious attempts seem to have been made to apply the idea commercially.

1.2 ATTACHMENTS TO WHEELS, BOYDELL'S GIRDLE, TIPPING'S PLATES, DIPLOCK'S PEDRAIL.

In the meantime there was considerable development of a class of scheme in which an individual wheel carried and successively laid on the ground a series of feet or plates. Among these may be mentioned Boydell's girdle, Tipping's plates, and Diplock's pedrail. Figure 1.2a shows a view of a Boydell Traction engine which appeared about the middle of the last century.

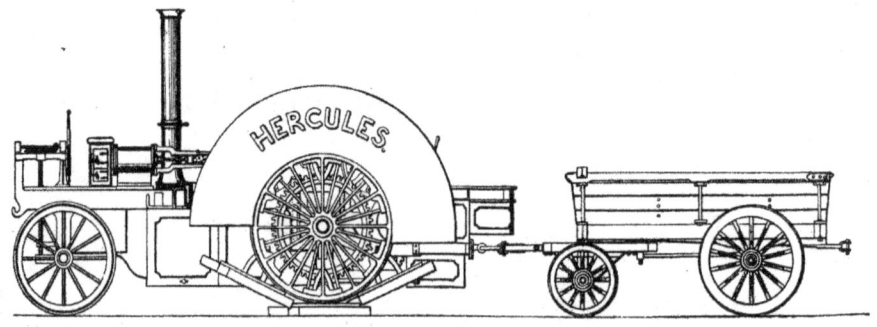

FIG. 1.2a. A BOYDELL TRACTION ENGINE

Figure 1.2b shows a set of Tipping's plates used on a carriage for launching lifeboats by carrying them across soft beaches, (1) and Figure 1.2c shows a similar device used on guns in the last war. Figure 1.2d shows a view of Diplock's pedrail. Diplock considered that earlier schemes made a mistake in attempting in effect to lay down a rail and cause rollers to run along it and his idea was to lay down a series of rollers, each on a foot, and cause the rail to run over them. A number of pedrails were constructed about the beginning of the present century and in 1905 one of them, shown in Figure 1.2d, took part in War Office trials at Aldershot.

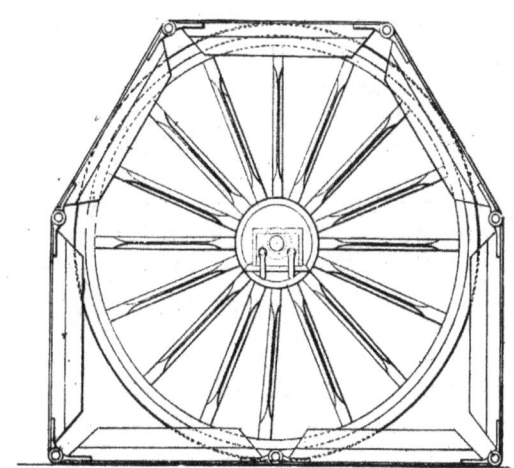

FIG. 1.2b
TIPPING'S PLATES

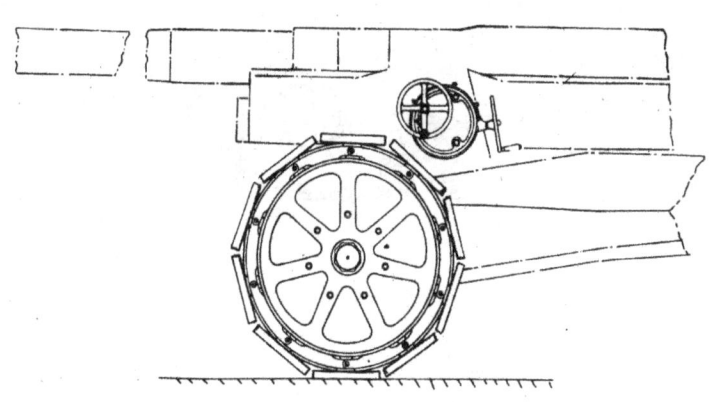

FIG. 1.2c
GIRDLE USED ON GUNS
IN THE
1914-18 WAR

FIG. 1.2d
DIPLOCK'S PEDRAIL

(1). See Johnson, Lt.Col. P.H., "The Mechanical Requirements of the Royal National Lifeboat Institution." Proc. I. Mech. E. Feby. 1941.

1.3 EARLIEST PRACTICAL USE OF TRACKS.

Towards the end of the last century the patent literature shows a revival of attention to the chain track idea and in the earlier years of the present century these also found their way to practical construction. Among these were that invented by Mr. A.O. Lombard of the Lombard Steam Log Hauler Company of U.S.A. shown in Figure 1.3a, and the tractor developed by Mr. David Roberts of Richard Hornsby & Sons at the instigation of the War Office. Figure 1.3b shows one of these tractors which after appearing in War Office trials and the Royal review in 1908 was inspected by King Edward and later by King George V., at that time Prince of Wales. It is said that during these trials in 1908 Major Donoghue of the Mechanical Transport Committee suggested fitting the vehicle with a gun and bullet proof shields to make it a fighting machine and not merely a tractor, but if this is the case nothing seems to have come of it.

A number of other chain track tractors were being developed at about the same time but enough has been said to indicate that the caterpillar or chain track was already well known and used at the beginning of the 1914-18 war. (1).

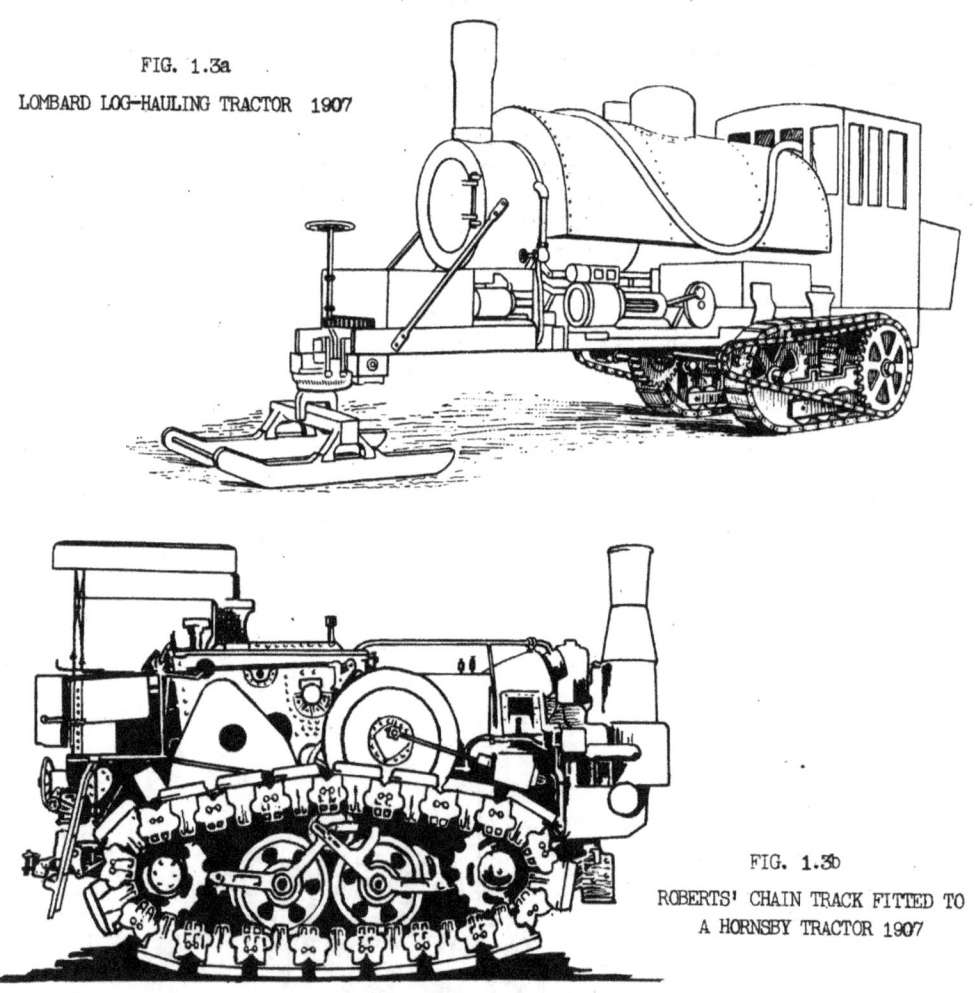

FIG. 1.3a
LOMBARD LOG-HAULING TRACTOR 1907

FIG. 1.3b
ROBERTS' CHAIN TRACK FITTED TO A HORNSBY TRACTOR 1907

(1) For fuller details of the History of tracked vehicles prior to the 1914-18 war see:-
Legros, L.A. "Traction on Bad Roads or Land", Proc. 1. Mech. E. 1918. pp 55 - 158.
"The Evolution of the Chain-track Tractor," the Engineer, Vol. 124, pp. 111-112, 134-136, 156-159, 181-184, 202-205, 221-224 and 241-244.
Young, C.F.T., "The Economy of Steam Power of Common Roads", London 1860.
Diplock, B.J., "A New System of Heavy Goods Transport", London 1902.

1.4 THE INVENTION OF THE TANK.

The story of the invention of the first tank is far from straightforward. Various forms of armoured fighting vehicles such as chariots were of course known and used from the very earliest times, and among the many machines designed and built by Leonardo da Vinci was an armoured fighting vehicle. But such schemes lacked the two main characteristics of the modern tank, the engine and the tracks.

In 1903 H.G. Wells published in the Strand Magazine a story called "The Land Ironclads" in which he described a battle of the future (as it then was) dominated by huge ironclads propelled by steam engines on a number of large pedrails. But before the idea was brought down to earth in a workable machine, it was reinvented several times and many difficulties had to be overcome. In fact, a number of trials were carried out with various designs before the appearance of "Mother", the first tank which met the requirements specified at the time. (1)

1.5 ARDUOUS PERFORMANCE REQUIREMENTS OF EARLIEST HEAVY TANKS.

In this connection it is worth emphasizing the arduous obstacle crossing performance conditions which the first heavy tanks were called upon to fulfil. With a continuous front stretching from the sea, the war was reaching a condition of stalemate in which no advance was made except after the most intense bombardment and even then it usually halted after a few hundred yards, until the guns could be brought up to undertake a fresh pounding. As a result the fighting was localised on a belt of country honeycombed with trenches and to make matters worse the ground was reduced to a morass of mud and craters by days, weeks or years of shelling. A rumour is also said to have got about that the Germans were proposing to erect concrete walls as a substitute for waterlogged trenches.

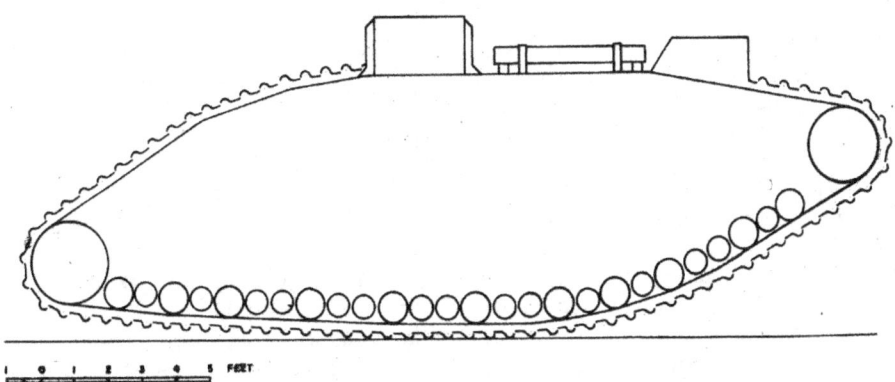

FIG. 1.5a. MK.V OUTLINE

As a result the officially specified obstacle consisted of a parapet 4ft. 6ins. high with a face sloped at 45°, followed by a gap 5ft. wide, but the test course in Hatfield Park also included a parapet 5ft. 6ins. high with a 4ft. 6ins. gap, and a parapet 4ft. 6 ins. high with a 9ft. gap.

(1.) For further details of the evolution of the first tank see:-
History of the Ministry of Munitions (official) Vol. XII. Part III Tanks. 1920.
Tennyson D'Eyncourt, Sir Eustace, "Account of the British Tanks used in the War" (Engineer - Sept. 12. 1919).
Stern, Sir Albert, "Tanks".
Halstead, Ivor, "The Truth about our Tanks".
Encycl. Britannica, "Tanks".
Murray Wilson, G."Fighting Tanks".

The factors which determine the obstacle crossing performance of a vehicle are briefly referred to in Section 2.10 and it is sufficient here to point out that the requirements put forward for the heavy tanks necessitated firstly great length and secondly a track contour which at its foremost point was at a considerable height above the ground so that the front of the tank would not merely butt against a vertical obstacle but would tend to climb up and over it. It was to meet this last condition that Sir William Tritton and Lt. W.G. Wilson evolved the familiar rhomboidal shape with the tracks passing right over the top of the vehicle, as shown in Figure 1.5a.

1.6 MEDIUM OR WHIPPET TANKS

This last feature was not incorporated in the Medium, Mark A and B or Whippet Tanks of which the general level of the track contour was considerably lower. The tracks and suspension were in other respects similar to those of the Heavy tanks. In particular neither the Heavy tanks nor the Medium tanks of the 1914-18 war incorporated any springs in the suspension, that is to say, the axles carrying the wheels which ran on the track and supported the weight were rigidly fixed and could not move up and down relatively to the hull.

Another characteristic was that a large number of wheels were provided very close together. In fact the Heavy Mark V had 26 wheels (Fig. 1.5a.) at each side, whilst the Mark V++ had no less than 33, and the Medium B had 23, so that the track was backed up by wheels almost continuously throughout its length. In fact on the Medium B the close spacing was carried to the extent of overlapping the wheels as on the latest German tanks. As a result reverse bending was impossible and the track preserved a more or less rigid contour in accordance with the arrangement of the wheels.

1.7 POST-1918 EXPERIMENTAL DESIGNS.

Before the end of the 1914-18 war experimental work had already begun on various new projects including the Medium D, an amphibious tank which was provided with a sprung suspension. The idea of a sprung suspension for a tracked vehicle was not new in itself and French tanks, as well as some of the early tractors, had sprung suspensions, but the application of this feature to tanks may be regarded as the parting of the ways as regards British track design and the main functions which the tracks of the original tank were designed to fulfil. The speed which can in practice be achieved on a machine with rigid suspension is strictly limited, and a demand for speeds higher than those of the early tanks (the Heavy Mark V would do 4.6 miles per hour in fourth gear, whilst the Medium Mark B was capable of 6.1 miles per hour) rendered sprung suspension a sine qua non. In fact every tank put into service in any country since 1918 has had sprung suspension. As speed has increased still further the tendency has been for the absorption and wheel deflection permitted by the springs to be increased. Moreover as a result of the difficulty of providing suspension mechanism for a large number of wheels, especially if the absorption is great, the general tendency has been towards a decrease in the number of wheels for a given weight of tank, especially in designs intended for the highest speeds.

About and shortly after 1918 a number of unconventional tracks were designed or tried out largely with the object of securing increased efficiency by what was known as horn steering. The most usual method of steering a tank is to employ some combination of gears, clutches and brakes which locks one track or causes it to move more slowly than the other so that the tank scrambles round in a more or less sharp curve. This of course, necessitates skidding of the tracks and wastes a good deal of power, as well as imposing heavy loads on the suspension and transmission.

With horn steering the track is constructed so that it can flex laterally and the horn which supports the front part of its outline is hinged so that it can be moved to one side or the other with the object of laying the track in a curve. At the time this form of steering came to nothing but something rather similar has been adopted more recently on carriers and the Tetrarch and Harry Hopkins light tanks.

About 1921 economy broke out and the staff for research into these projects was drastically curtailed. At the same time it was clearly desirable to produce some tanks of newer design than the wartime models but it was felt that these experimental projects would not be ripe for production for a number of years.

1.8 THE VICKERS MEDIUM TANK.

Accordingly it was decided in 1922 to produce a tank and a tractor which embodied the lessons learnt with wartime models but were less dependent on untried features. The results were the Vickers Light tank, subsequently known as the Medium tank Mk. 1, and the Dragon Mk. 1, subsequently the Medium Dragon Mark 1. (1)

The tracks and suspension (and indeed the whole chassis) were almost identical in the tank and the dragon.

The Medium tank, shown in Figure 1.8a, had sprung suspension, the twelve wheels on each side being carried on tubular telescopic struts containing helical springs. This arrangement cushions the shocks occasioned by traversing uneven ground at high speed, and also enables the load to be shared more evenly between the wheels on irregular ground.

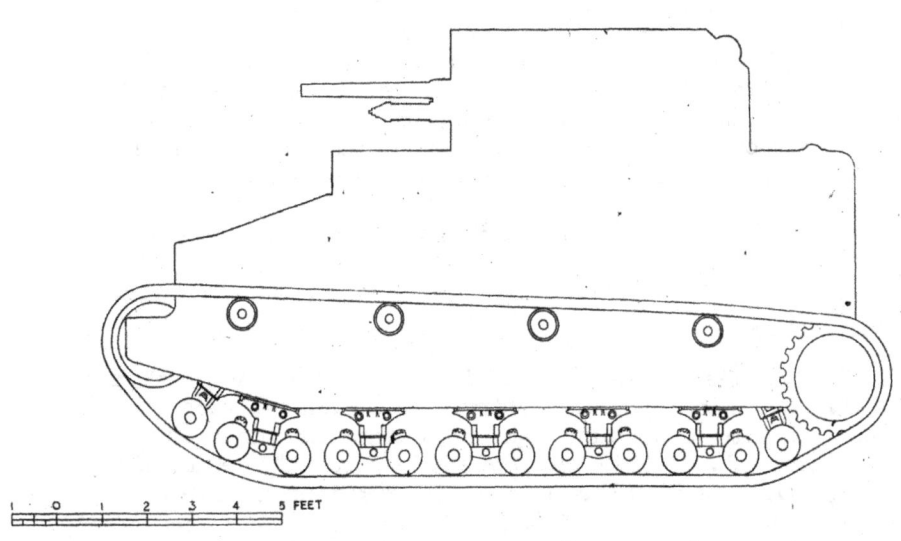

FIG. 1.8a. VICKERS MEDIUM TANK MK. 1A. OUTLINE

1.9 LIGHT TANKS.

The Vickers Medium tanks remained standard service equipment till shortly before the present war, the main development in the inter-war breathing space being the introduction of very light tanks by Martel and by Carden Loyd. These started as minute "tankettes" of about 2 tons or less and gradually grew to the light tank Mk. VIC. of some 5 tons, comparable in weight with the French Renault light tanks of the 1914-18 war.

(1) For fuller details see:-
Martel, Lt. Col. G. Le Q., "In the Wake of the Tank" Chaps. 7 and 8.

1.10 **A.9 and 10. and VALENTINE**

In 1934 design was started (by Sir John Carden of Vickers to a War Office Specification) on the A.9, a vehicle of about 7 tons, armoured to the 14 mm standard, and with a speed of not less than 25 m.p.h., for use within the Tank Brigade either as a fighting tank or as a close support tank. At the same time the A.10, a very similar tank, but weighing 15 tons, armoured to the 1" standard and having a speed of 10 m.p.h. was designed for close co-operation with Infantry formations. These tanks ultimately became much more alike both in weight and speed (12 - 14 tons and 19 - 20 m.p.h) and were known as Cruiser tanks, Marks I and II. When, late in 1937, Vickers were asked to produce an Infantry tank, they produced a shortened thickened up version of A.10, which became Tank Infantry Mk. III or Valentine.

1.11 **A.13 AND LATER CRUISERS.**

In 1936 a British Military Mission (including General Wavell and Colonel Martel) attended manoeuvres of the Russian Army and among the Russian tanks they saw a type known as the B.T. which was constructed on an American Christie type chassis and gave a remarkable performance as regards speed, due to its high power-weight ratio, and its suspension which included four large road wheels on each side with independent springing of great absorption.

A similar chassis was obtained from America and formed the basis of the A.13.E.1. and A.13.E.2., which, however, had 14 mm armour, a fighting turret and a lengthened hull, besides numerous other changes. This tank, developed by Nuffield Mechanisation & Aero Ltd., later became the Cruiser Mk.III and may be regarded as the ancestor of modern British Cruiser Tanks. In the Mk. IV the armour was increased to 30 mm by simply adding armour to the Mk. III but a complete redesign was considered necessary which incidentally effected considerable reduction of height. Redesign by the Mechanisation Board in conjunction with the L.M.S. Railway Co., produced the Mk. V. or Covenanter while Mechanisation & Aero preferred their own redesign and produced the Mk. VI. or Crusader (with 5 wheels each side).

From the latter have developed the Cavalier, Centaur and Cromwell.

1.12 **INFANTRY TANKS.**

In 1936 the design was also put in hand of a special tank known as the A.11.E.1 intended to lead infantry assaults on positions where "the heaviest possible protection" (which at that time meant 60 mm of armour) "was essential." This tank, which subsequently became the Infantry Tank, Mark I, or Matilda I, was only required to have a speed of 5 miles per hour and a weight of some 10 tons.

Late in the same year construction was started on a heavier type of tank, the A.12.E.1, to which the name Matilda was subsequently transferred. It was about this time that the classification of tanks as Light, Cruiser, or Infantry tanks began to be recognized, and these three types were clearly formulated in the Annual Report of the Mechanisation Board for 1937.

In November 1939 a demand was made for an Infantry tank similar in general lines to the Matilda, but longer, to improve trench crossing ability, and also capable of surmounting a vertical obstacle five feet high and with armour to the 60 mm standard. This was known as the A.20 and from it developed the A.22, subsequently known as the Churchill.

CHAPTER 2.

MAIN TYPES OF TRACK AND THEIR BROAD FUNCTIONS

2.1 TYPES OF TRACK.

There are a number of different functions which the track of a tracked vehicle may perform, but in many cases it is necessary for various reasons to adopt a compromise in which it fulfils some of these functions only partially or not at all. The extent to which any particular function is fulfilled will depend to a large extent on factors outside the control of the track designer and in particular on the characteristics of the suspension, such as the number and size of the weight-carrying wheels, the spacing between them, the absorption and wheel deflection permitted by the springs, and generally on the contour of the track. These factors in turn will be determined by the general design of the vehicle and in particular the speed at which it is required to operate on various types of ground, and the extent to which it must be capable of negotiating soft ground, and obstacles of various sorts, referred to generally as its performance. It will, of course, also depend to a very large extent on the type of track adopted, but here again the choice will be largely governed by the performance required. Hence before examining the functions which a track may be intended to fulfil and the extent to which it actually does so, it will be desirable to refer to a number of different main types of track, namely:-

(a) The flexible pin jointed type of either short pitch or long pitch, dry pin or lubricated pin type.
(b) The rubber bushed type.
(c) The continuously flexible or endless band type.
(d) Irreversible types. The rigid girder and elastic girder types.

2.2 THE FLEXIBLE PIN-JOINTED TYPE.

The great majority of tank tracks in every country except America are of the flexible pin-jointed type. The track consists of a chain formed of a number of rigid links each connected to its neighbour by a hinged joint. This joint is usually formed like a door hinge by one or more lugs in one link fitting between lugs on the neighbouring link and connected together by a pin passing through them. Very often all the links are identical but some tracks are made up of two different sorts of link which occur alternately in the length of the track, which is then referred to as having a two-piece link.

The characteristics of a track depend to a considerable extent on its pitch, that is to say the distance between corresponding points of neighbouring joints, and a track with a very long pitch could almost be regarded as a separate type from one of very short pitch, but for the fact that tracks may have any intermediate pitch from the shortest (which in current types is about $1\frac{3}{4}$ inches) to the longest (which in tank tracks seldom if ever exceeds 8 or 10 inches).

It will be realised that when any pin-jointed track bends its shape does not conform to a smooth curve but to a polygon. In the case of a very short-pitched track provided it is not bent too sharply this polygonal shape differs only slightly from a smooth curve but in the case of a long pitched track the difference is considerable. The effects of this are discussed in later chapters.

A further sub-division which may be referred to is the distinction between dry pin and lubricated types of track. In practically all current tank tracks the pin is completely without any lubrication and the conditions of operation of the hinge are at best that of friction between clean dry metal surfaces and more often between surfaces separated by an abrasive layer of sand or grit either wet or dry. To improve these conditions a number of designs have in the past been produced in which the pin is lubricated and seals are provided to keep out dirt and keep in lubricant. As discussed later such types have not come into general use.

2.3 RUBBER BUSHED TRACKS

The rubber bushed type of track is similar to the flexible pin jointed type except that the pin is surrounded by a rubber bushing and the pivotal movement of the hinge takes place not by sliding between two metal surfaces but by distortion of the rubber. The rubber consists of a thick walled tube with its inner surface bonded so that it is obliged to turn with the pin while its outer surface is obliged to turn with the link. Consequently the pivotal movement takes place by rotation of the outer surface of the rubber relatively to the inner surface.

2.4 CONTINUOUSLY FLEXIBLE OR ENDLESS BAND TYPE

This type of track does not consist of a series of rigid links connected by joints but of a continuous band which is flexible at practically any point in its length. The band may be formed of rubber which to provide tensile strength is reinforced in various ways as by means of fabric or steel cables. A lot of work was done by M. André Kégresse on this type of track, and the American half-tracked vehicles employ tracks of this type developed by the Goodrich Company.

2.5 IRREVERSIBLE TYPES. THE ELASTIC GIRDER AND RIGID GIRDER TYPES.

In the types referred to above the track can bend either way i.e. to a convex or a concave curve. In the rigid girder track the links interlock with one another so that the track can bend to a convex curve, as it must when passing round the ends of its contour, but cannot bend to a concave curve. With a short pitched pin jointed track or a continuously flexible track it is obvious that the pressure on the ground is greatest underneath each wheel, since the track can bow upwards to a greater or less extent between successive wheels. With a rigid girder track such upward bowing is prevented and consequently the portion of track between two wheels presses on the ground in exactly the same way as a rigid plate or girder. This type of track cannot of course be used with a sprung suspension which allows individual wheels to move up and down since the girder would be over-loaded in passing over hard obstacles or hard uneven ground, and consequently its application has hitherto been confined to very slow moving vehicles, for example tracked trailers made by Messrs. Roadless Traction Ltd. for taking lifeboats across beaches into the water and similar vehicles made in America by the Athey Truss Wheel Company for various purposes such as log trailers.

As pointed out above the use of an irreversible type of track rules out the possibility of having independently sprung wheels. But it has been suggested (1) that the bogie wheel bearings of each track should be mounted on a rigid unit and the whole unit should be resiliently connected to the hull. In this way the whole of the hull would be sprung and only the individual track units would be unsprung, the advantages of the rigid girder track being retained. No steps have however been taken to try out this scheme.

The elastic girder track is similar in principle to the rigid girder track but in this case the joints incorporate rubber blocks which tend to make the track take up a moderate convex curvature. The normal load on the track just about flattens it out so that as in the rigid girder track the pressure is distributed on the ground between the wheels

(1) Townshend E.R. British Patent Application No. 6955 of 1943.

but at the same time there is a certain amount of flexibility to allow the track to adapt itself to slight irregularities on hard ground.

2.6 MAIN FUNCTIONS OF THE TRACK

We are now in a position to examine briefly the main functions which a tank track may fulfil. Briefly these include:-

(a) Providing multi-wheel drive from a single axle, i.e. the equivalent of a locomotive coupling rod, to ensure that the whole area of ground on which the weight of the tank is supported contributes its quota to the tractive effort i.e. the force which propels the tank forward.

(b) Increasing the area of ground upon which a grip is obtained to drive the tank forward, so as to increase the tractive effort on certain types of ground.

(c) Distributing the pressure due to the weight of the vehicle over as large an area of ground as possible, so as to keep down the maximum pressure exerted on the ground and prevent the ground being squashed down more than is essential, thereby reducing the rolling resistance, i.e. the force which opposes the movement of the tank.

(d) Improving obstacle-crossing performance by providing the equivalent of a ramp for helping the vehicle to mount an obstacle, and by bridging the gap between wheels and thereby preventing individual wheels from dropping too far into trenches etc.

(e) To produce an even and smooth roller path along which the road wheels can run with the minimum of resistance.

In some vehicles such as the heavy tanks of the 1914-1918 war the track fulfils all these functions to a very complete extent, but in many modern vehicles other requirements, and particularly the need for speed and therefore sprung suspension, have rendered a compromise necessary. It is therefore important to examine how any particular track performs each of these functions and the extent to which it does so.

2.7 PROVIDING MULTI-WHEEL DRIVE FROM A SINGLE AXLE.

It is well-known that in any given conditions there is a limit to the frictional or driving force that can be exerted by any one wheel. Consequently if there is a danger of the wheels slipping this danger will be reduced by increasing the number of wheels to which a drive is transmitted since if each wheel contributes its quota to the total forward force a greater force can be provided. For example in the case of a railway locomotive a pair of coupling rods are provided which compel all the driving wheels to rotate simultaneously. If the coupling rods were removed the drive would only be transmitted to one pair of wheels. Similarly in the case of a tank the track transmits the drive from the final drive unit to all the wheels so that the whole of the weight of the tank contributes its quota of frictional force to make up the tractive effort.

Undoubtedly this is a considerable advantage of a track as may be realised by comparing the transmission and suspension of an ordinary tank with that of a vehicle such as the German 8-wheeled armoured car (a relatively light vehicle.) The use of a track eliminates the complication involved in transmitting the drive to a wheel which is not only sprung but also steered, and moreover it does this for all the wheels of the vehicle, of which there are seldom less than ten (carriers are an exception) and may be over sixty.

2.8 INCREASING THE AREA OF GROUND WHICH CONTRIBUTES ADHESION

The maximum driving force or adhesion which can be provided by a particular piece of ground depends largely on the load applied to it. If this were the only component of adhesion the area of ground gripped would not affect the tractive effort obtained for a given weight of tank, since the same tractive effort could be obtained from a small area heavily loaded as from a large area lightly loaded i.e. having the same weight spread over it. On most types of ground, however, there is an additional component of adhesion which does not depend on the loading and is consequently increased by increasing the area over which the load is distributed. This matter is discussed more fully in Chapter 23.

2.9 DISTRIBUTION OF THE PRESSURE DUE TO THE WEIGHT OF THE VEHICLE TO REDUCE SINKAGE AND ROLLING RESISTANCE.

It is obvious that the area of ground with which a track makes contact is very much greater than that with which the wheels would make contact. Consequently if the pressure due to the weight of the vehicle could be uniformly distributed over the whole of this area the provision of a track would very much reduce the intensity of pressure (for example in pounds per square inch). This in turn would reduce the tractive resistance or rolling resistance (i.e. the resistance to forward movement of the vehicle) since the work done in squashing down the ground must be provided by the engine and will represent a certain (very considerable) resistance to forward movement.

Actually the term "ground pressure" is customarily used in connection with tanks to signify the mean ground pressure on the whole area of track in contact with the ground, i.e. the weight of the tank divided by the area of both tracks. But if the pressure is much greater than this at one point the ground will be squashed down to a corresponding maximum depth, and, as the point of maximum pressure moves along, each point in the ground will be squashed down to this depth, and the depth will not be reduced merely because the pressure is less at other points. Hence in considering how far the ground is squashed down the mean ground pressure is of no consequence whatsoever and what we need to get at is the maximum pressure.

The extent to which a uniform distribution of pressure is actually achieved varies very widely between one vehicle and another and it is essential to realise that the mere provision of a track does not automatically distribute the pressure uniformly over the whole area of track in contact with the ground.

In the case of a continuously flexible or very short pitched track, the track may be compared with a carpet which is unrolled in front of the vehicle and rolled up again when the vehicle has passed over it. Provided the carpet is flexible, there is no essential reason why it should press on the ground at any point except the area underneath a wheel.

On very soft ground where the wheels sink in to a great depth a certain amount of pressure distribution will be obtained as a result of the tension in the track if this is considerable. But with a given tension a flexible track can only exert a lateral pressure if it is curved and if actual figures are worked out under typical conditions it will be found that the distribution of pressure due to tension is only substantial when the ground sinks to a considerable depth and even then perhaps 80% of the track-ground contact area may be supporting no appreciable weight.

In the case of a rigid girder track which forms a rigid bridge between neighbouring wheels very complete distribution of pressure can be achieved on reasonably flat soft ground with very little sinkage and it is claimed that this form of track gives a very greatly reduced rolling resistance on soft ground, a claim that is in agreement with the calculations made in Chapter 25. In the case of a flexible pin-jointed track of long pitch the effect of the rigid links is to produce something between the continuously flexible track and the rigid girder track and on certain types of tank a long pitched track has been adopted in order to improve performance on soft ground by reducing the rolling resistance.

It is sometimes not fully realised that the mean ground pressure may bear little relationship to the actual maximum ground pressure which will determine the extent to which the ground is squashed down and the rolling resistance resulting from this cause, and certainly no effort appears to have been made to establish an improved basis for comparison or to investigate the factors upon which the rolling resistance on soft ground actually depends or how it could be reduced.

It is obvious that to squash down two strips of ground, each about a foot wide and many miles long, to a depth varying from an inch or two to a foot or more, must require an enormous quantity of energy and this energy can only come from the engine of the vehicle via the transmission. Consequently the cross-country speed that can be maintained with a given size of engine and transmission largely depends on the maximum ground pressure as does the cross-country range with a given load of fuel. In fact as the distribution of ground pressure is widely regarded as being one of the most important functions of a track it is somewhat surprising that the extent to which the load is in fact distributed over the area of track in contact with the ground has not been more thoroughly investigated. The matter is considered in more detail in Chapter 25.

2.10 PROVIDING A RAMP FOR OBSTACLE CROSSING.

The function of assisting obstacle crossing is closely bound up with that of providing a drive to all the wheels. Perhaps the lowest standard of obstacle crossing performance is that of a four-wheeled vehicle with two-wheel drive and no tracks, since the vehicle is very liable to lose adhesion and the wheels are likely to sink into holes or trenches so that the vehicle becomes bellied, or so that the front wheel abuts against a vertical face which it cannot mount. The situation is considerably improved by transmitting a drive to all the wheels since the whole of the weight of the vehicle then contributes its quota to the adhesion, and any wheel coming up against an obstruction has at least some tendency to climb over it. If the number of wheels is increased the performance is better still, since if one wheel or pair of wheels comes to a trench the weight of the vehicle may be taken on the other wheels so that the one pair of wheels is suspended above the bottom of the trench and has a good chance of mounting the far side. If now a track is provided even with no sprocket or idler the performance is slightly increased still further since the track to some extent tends to bridge the gap between one wheel and the next and may also wrap itself round the edge of an obstacle to help the vehicle to climb up on to it.

The addition of a front idler or sprocket extends the upwardly inclined front portion of the track to a greater height and thereby provides the equivalent of an extended ramp up which the vehicle may climb on to an obstacle. Provision of a rear sprocket or idler in addition further improves the performance in circumstances where there is a tendency for the back of the vehicle to fall into a trench.

The conditions governing the obstacle crossing performance of a tank are more a matter of general design and suspension arrangements than of track design and will not be discussed in this work. (1).

(1) See also Kühner, Kurt, Das Kraftfahrzeug im Gelände. V.D.I. Zeitschrift. 24 Aug. 1935.
Merritt H.E. The Design of High Speed Track Vehicles. Proc. I.A.E. 1939.

It is however worth commenting here that the height of the maximum obstacle which can be surmounted is governed by the length of the tank as much as, if not more than, by the height of the front sprocket or idler.

Briefly it may be said that for climbing a vertical step if the length and factors such as the centre of gravity of the tank, and the characteristics of the suspension, have been determined, there is a certain optimum height for the foremost point of the track. This will normally be at the same level as the axis of the front sprocket or idler and if this level is below the optimum level referred to the step-climbing performance will be reduced but if it is above the optimum level the performance will not be increased since the limiting factor will then be the length of the tank.

These considerations clearly have an influence on the contours of the tracks of various vehicles. Figure 2.10a shows a number of these contours together with a note of the approximate step-climbing performance of each vehicle. It is virtually impossible ever to assess step-climbing performance with great accuracy but from the rough figures given it will be observed that in general high step-climbing performance necessitates a long track outline and a relatively high front sprocket or idler.

For most modern tanks a very big step-climbing and trench-crossing performance is considered unnecessary, firstly because modern defence systems do not present a continuous front honeycombed with trenches, and secondly because such performance is useless not only against the anti-tank gun and the anti-tank mine, which are designed to damage the tank, but also against obstacles such as coffins, pimples and dragons' teeth which are designed to tip the tank over sideways or cause it to belly.

CHAPTER 3.

POSSIBLE FORMS OF PIN-JOINTED TRACK LINKS.

3.1. ESSENTIAL CHARACTERISTICS

Before proceeding (in chapter 4) to trace the historical development of the various forms of track link that have been used in practice, it will be convenient to give the reader a background by outlining the essential structural features that must be possessed by pin jointed track links, and the various alternative forms that each of these characteristics may take. Reference may also be made to the illustrated glossary at Section 0.3.

It will be obvious that all track links must have certain features in common, inasmuch as these features are dictated by the functions which the track has to fulfil. Thus, all links must possess the following:-

a) A surface to rest on the ground to give support, which may provide:-

b) A surface to engage the ground to give adhesion whether by friction or by digging-in and tending to shear the ground.

c) A wheelpath for the load bearing wheels to run on.

d) Guiding faces to keep the wheels on the tracks.

e) Driving surfaces for example on trunnions, openings, or teeth, to take the drive from the sprocket.

f) A hinge for connecting it to the next link.

3.2 GROUND ENGAGING SURFACES FOR SUPPORT AND ADHESION

It is clear that the track link must afford a surface on which the upward pressure of the ground can act to support the load.
This surface will offer a certain measure of adhesion even if it is completely flat and in some cases this adhesion has been relied upon as sufficient for normal running. (Fig 3.2a)

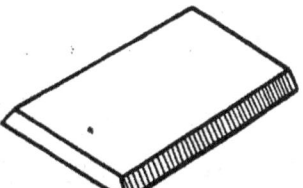

FIG. 3.2a. FLAT UNDERSURFACE

In other cases the supporting surface has not been completely flat but has had in it various forms of grooves or recesses formed either on purpose to improve adhesion or because the link could not be made otherwise. In particular, if a track link is formed by stamping, it is very much easier to push up projections on its upper surface if recesses are formed in its underface (Fig 3.2b) In the same category with tracks having recesses in their under side one may mention tracks having irregular projections, that is, anything other than a straight bar or spud extending transversely across the track, e.g. a chevron, (Fig 3.2c)

FIG. 3.2b. RECESSED UNDERSURFACE

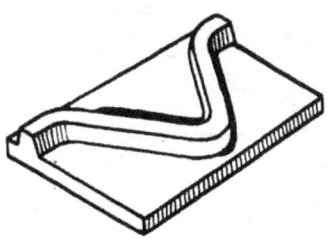

FIG. 3.2c. CHEVRON

3.3.

The adhesion provided by a flat surface is generally not sufficient in many conditions, and is not much improved by recesses which are liable to become filled with earth. Accordingly, the majority of links have formed on them one or more transverse spuds to dig into the ground and improve adhesion. (Fig. 3.2d)

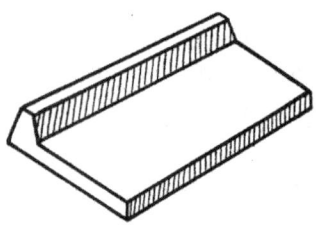

FIG. 3.2d
SINGLE SPUD, FLAT FACE

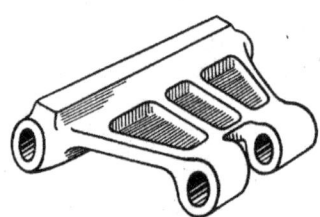

FIG. 3.2e
SINGLE SPUD, RECESSED FACE

Examples of tracks having a single transverse spud and a series of ribs standing out from the adjacent under surface of the link are very many and in fact this is the commonest form of ground engaging surface of modern tracks.

In some cases of ribbed under surfaces, the spaces between the ribs are closed by a flat portion constituting the upper surface of the track link, generally the surfaces on which the wheel or wheels run. (Fig. 3.2e) In other cases the gap between the ribs may extend right through the track and either form a cavity extending into the interior of a hollow guide horn or a hole going completely through the track. In the latter case the link may assume a more or less skeleton form. (Fig 3.2f).

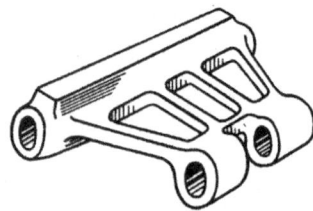

FIG. 3.2f
SINGLE SPUD, SKELETON

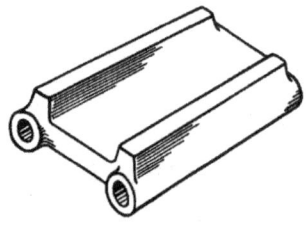

FIG. 3.2g
DOUBLE SPUD, FLAT FACE

In some tracks each link is provided with two spuds, one near each end. (Fig. 3.2g)

3.3 WHEEL PATHS AND GUIDING SURFACES

The wheel paths or rail surfaces on which the wheels run, and the guiding surfaces by which the wheels are kept on the track, are largely determined by the type of load-carrying wheels employed. Clearly there must be a surface for each wheel to run on which is smooth, and of adequate width to take the tyre of the wheel. If twin wheels are used, there must be a wheel path for each tyre.

Where flanged wheels are used, the edge of the wheel path may be relied on for guiding (Fig. 3.3a) but with unflanged wheels the guiding surfaces must be afforded by up-standing projections or guide horns on the track links.

The hinge joint must be designed so that the wheel passes smoothly from one link to the next.

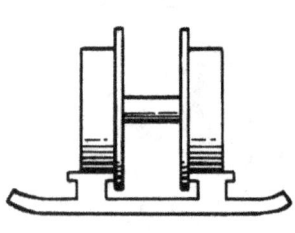
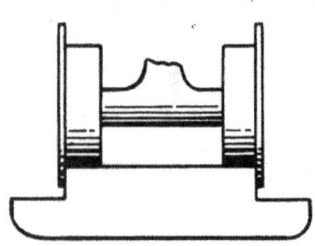

FIG. 3.3a
FLANGED WHEELS

In the case of a single wheel there must be two guide horns, one on each side, whereas with two wheels the opposite faces of a single guide, projecting between the wheels, may serve the purpose.

Occasionally there are two guide horns for three or four wheels.

The form of guide may vary. (Fig 3.3b): In one case trouble was experienced with throwing of tracks which had a very rounded form of guide and a guide with higher, straighter sides was substituted. In other cases the guide is in the form of a steep pyramid or wedge or even a narrow arch whose sides are almost vertical.

Care must be taken that the surfaces of wheel paths and guides are not such as to damage the road wheel tyres. On early designs the edges of the guide horns were relatively sharp whereas later designs use a more rounded horn.

Holes in the roller path such as sprocket tooth holes, are liable to damage the tyres even if they have slightly rounded edges.

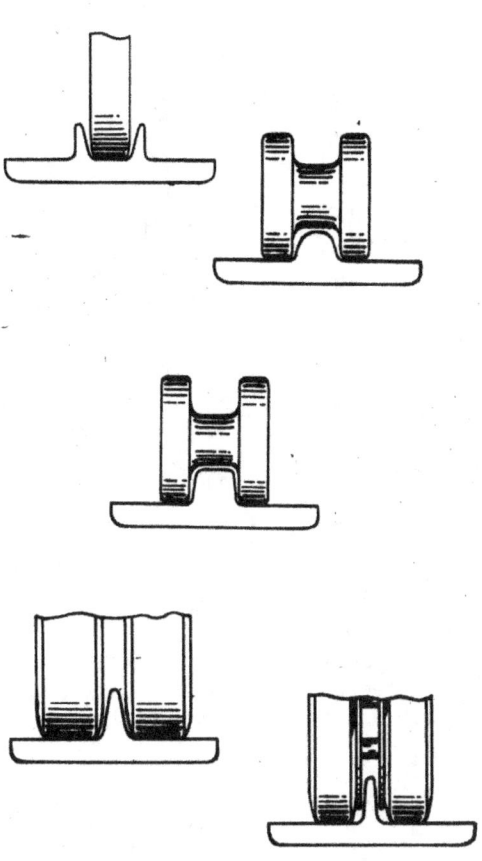

FIG. 3.3b
TYPES OF GUIDE HORN

3.4 DRIVING SURFACES FOR TAKING THE SPROCKET DRIVE

The form of the surfaces for taking the sprocket drive is again to a large extent determined by the type of sprocket and whether single or twin sprocket drive is employed. In some cases the bosses or trunnions which engage the sprocket teeth are formed only on the upper part of the track link (Fig 3.4a) whereas in other cases the sprocket teeth appear through holes in the under surface of the link.

With regard to the longitudinal position of the boss or trunnion this may either be between adjacent pins (Fig 3.4b) or it may surround one of the pins.

More often one of the pin bosses constitutes the trunnion and the sprocket tooth extends through an adjacent gap. In the case of a single sprocket the middle boss will naturally be employed, (Fig. 3.4c)

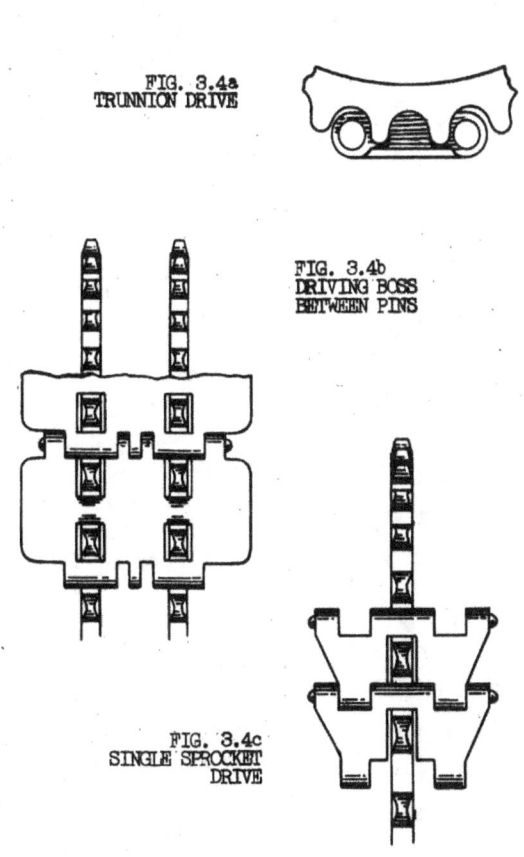

FIG. 3.4a
TRUNNION DRIVE

FIG. 3.4b
DRIVING BOSS
BETWEEN PINS

FIG. 3.4c
SINGLE SPROCKET
DRIVE

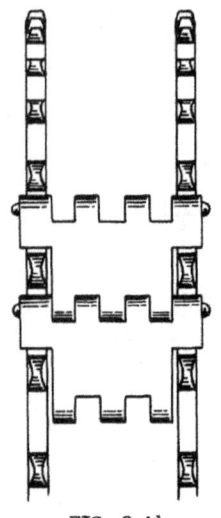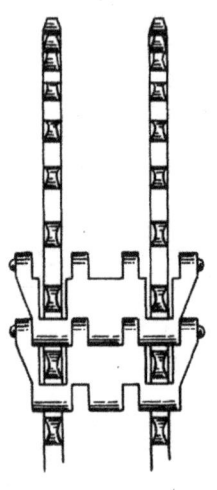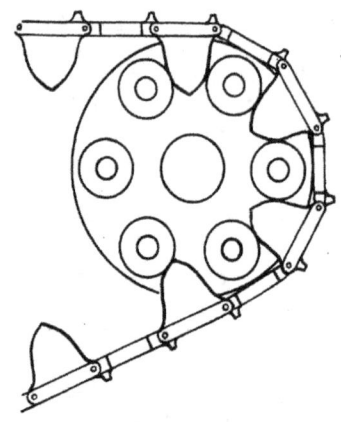

FIG. 3.4d
EXTERNAL SPROCKET DRIVE

FIG. 3.4e
INTERNAL SPROCKET DRIVE

FIG. 3.4f
ROLLER SPROCKET

whereas with twin sprocket drive if the spacing of the sprockets is equal to the width of the track, the outermost bosses may constitute the trunnions, (Fig 3.4d) whilst if the spacing of the sprockets is less than the total width of track a pair of inner bosses may be used as the trunnions. (Fig 3.4e).

Mention should also be made of the roller type of sprocket which requires teeth on the track links (for example the guide horns) to enter between the rollers and take the drive (Fig 3.4f)

3.5 HINGES

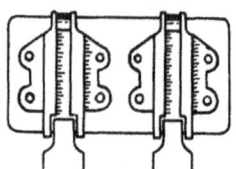

FIG. 3.5a. CHAIN LINKAGE

In certain early tracks of what is termed the built up type the hinge between one link and the next formed part of a separate chain to which the sole plate or shoe was secured by rivets (Fig 3.5a). In general each chain would have one lug projecting from one link between a pair of lugs on the neighbouring link so as to give what is referred to as a 1-2 linkage, i.e. a linkage having one lug on one link knuckling between two lugs on a neighbouring link (Fig 3.5b).

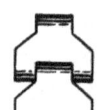

FIG. 3.5b. 1-2 LINKAGE

Similarly a 2-3 linkage comprises two lugs on one link interleaving between three lugs on the next link. (Fig. 3.5c).

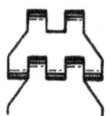

FIG. 3.5c. 2-3 LINKAGE

With later designs, the hinge lugs and the sole or shoe of the link are made in a single piece.

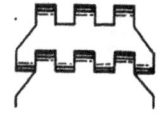

FIG. 3.5d. 3-4 LINKAGE

Note:- The built-up type is sometimes referred to as a chain type track while the single piece type is referred to as a link type. This nomenclature does not seem particularly apt as most people regard a chain as nothing more than a series of links.

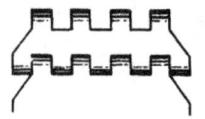

FIG. 3.5e MULTISHEAR LINKAGE

Single piece links having a 2-3 linkage are extremely common today and many examples could be quoted. Tracks with a 3-4 linkage (Fig 3.5d) are also common while those having more than a 3-4 linkage, e.g. a 4-5 linkage are usually referred to as multishear links. (Fig. 3.5e)

The tracks referred to above comprise single piece links, but in addition there are a number of tracks of which the complete linkage is made up of two or more dissimilar pieces. One class of such tracks is that consisting of a main link and a pair of side links to connect adjacent main links together. (Fig 3.5f). In this case the linkage can be regarded as a 1-2 linkage.

There are also examples of similar two piece tracks with a 2-3 linkage, (Fig 3.5g) 3-4 linkage (Fig 3.5h) 4-5 linkage (Fig 3.5i) and multishear linkages one of which has no less than a 10-11 linkage.

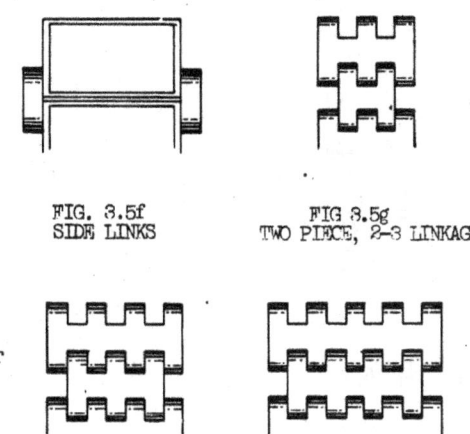

FIG. 3.5f SIDE LINKS

FIG 3.5g TWO PIECE, 2-3 LINKAGE

FIG 3.5h TWO PIECE, 3-4 LINKAGE

FIG 3.5i TWO PIECE, 4-5 LINKAGE

3.6 PIN RETENTION, SPLIT PIN WITH OR WITHOUT CASTELLATED NUT, S PIN

Numerous different methods have been employed for keeping the track pin in position and it cannot even now be said that there is any finally standardised practice.

Perhaps the simplest arrangement is to use a large split pin. One end of the track pin is formed with a circular head with a pair of flats which fit into a corresponding recess and prevent the pin from rotating whilst the other end of the track pin has a hole through it to receive the split pin. (Fig 3.6a).

In other arrangements the track pin has a similar head but is provided with a castellated nut in addition to the split pin (Fig 3.6b). This was standard in the Service for many years but the nuts were liable to come off especially owing to stones getting between the nut and the shoe. A nut and spring washer were substituted.

Certain tracks are provided with a washer and a split pin or S-shaped pin (Fig 3.6c). One practical advantage of it in the field is that if the correct spares are not available it is comparatively easy to improvise a substitute, for example from a piece of bent wire whereas in the case of more elaborate systems if the correct spare is not available the tank is immobilised.

FIG. 3.6a SPLIT PIN

FIG 3.6b CASTELLATED NUT

FIG. 3.6c S. PIN

3.7 FLOATING PINS. SOLDER AND LEAD PLUG

Various forms of pin retaining device have been used which engage the ends of the pin, so that it floats freely and does not come out if it should break. One of these was the solder or lead plug. This consisted of a cylindrical piece of solder or lead which fitted into the end of the pin hole. The latter was formed with a cannelure (in plain terms an annular groove) and the solder plug was hit with a hammer so as to spread it out into this cannelure. Naturally the solder had to be comparatively soft in order to spread out into the cannelure and as a result the rib so formed was comparatively easily sheared and the plugs were liable to get pushed out.

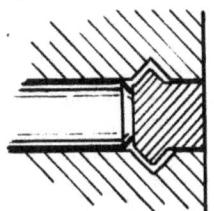

3.8 ANVIL AND SLEEVE

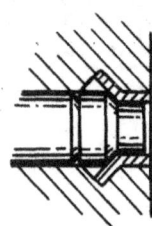

Accordingly the solder plug was superseded by the anvil and sleeve which can also be used with the existing cannelure. A stepped plug known as the anvil is inserted in a slotted sleeve, the slotted end of the sleeve being up against the step on the anvil. The two are placed against the pin and the sleeve is hammered so that the ends expand over the step of the anvil into the cannelure. This arrangement requires soft material for the sleeve which must also be of correct thickness to ensure a sound fit.

3.9 BENT BANANA

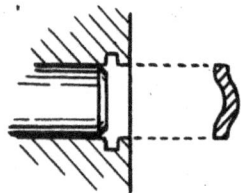

A device known as a bent banana is used in the heavy Churchill track. This is used as an alternative to the anvil and sleeve, being an easier method to produce, and again makes use of the cannelure in the pin holes. It consists of a suitably dimensioned, humped strip of soft steel, the ends of the strip being radiused to fit the cannelure. For insertion, the strip is placed in the pin hole up against the end of the pin, and, when hammered flat, the ends of the strip expand into the groove thus locking the pin in position.

3.10 WELDED PLATES

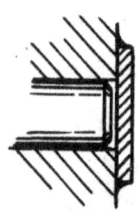

One method of retaining the pins is to weld a plate over each end. This, of course, means that the pins cannot be removed and replaced unless welding equipment is available. Such tracks are provided with a certain number of pins which are formed with slight steps but have no other retaining means. The track tension causes the lugs to be slightly staggered so as to engage these shoulders and thereby prevent the pins from coming out. By easing the tension the pins can be removed if necessary.

3.11 RIVETTED PIN END

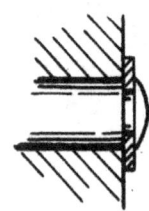

The commonest form of pin retention in current design is a plain rivetted end. This necessitates leaving the end of the pin in a soft condition during manufacture, a suitable process being adopted according to the method of case hardening used.

3.12 CIRCLIP

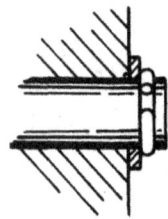

A satisfactory method of retaining pins $\frac{3}{4}$" diameter and over is by the use of circlips. This method requires a special countersunk washer between the circlip and the track shoe to prevent the circlip being pushed out by side pressure. This method can be used on both ends of a pin or on one end of a headed pin.

3.13 WEDGE AND FLAT

In other tracks the pin is formed with a flat and a bolt with a wedge shaped head fits into the link so that opposite faces of the wedge shaped head enter the flats formed in two neighbouring pins. A nut keeps the wedge bolt in position. This, of course, prevents the track pins from rotating relatively to the side links but in the case of the tracks concerned this is desirable since they employ a rubber bush between the pin and the main link and all pivotal movement must be in the rubber bush, any sliding pivotal movement in the side link being prevented.

In another case the track has a centre guide and a locking screw is inserted in a screwed hole just in front of the guide horn and engages a flat formed in the middle of the pin.

3.14 SKODA INCLINED GUIDE

In an arrangement patented by Skoda in 1934, each pin has a head at the end nearer the hull of the tank. There is nothing at the other end to prevent it from coming out, but on the hull is fixed an inclined guide or cam and if a pin starts to come out its head engages this cam as it passes it, and the pin gets pushed back into place.

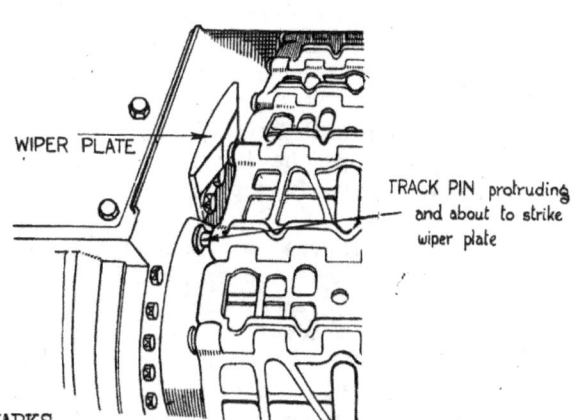

3.15 PIN RETENTION CONCLUDING REMARKS

It will be seen that methods of track pin retention fall into two main groups, (a) those in which retention is effected by the pin, i.e. by head, split pin etc. In this class, if the pin breaks, the broken portions can fall out.

(b) Those in which pin retention is effected by portions of the link, e.g. by the use of plugs, sleeves, wedges etc. In this class, if the pin breaks the pieces cannot fall out.

Both the above methods can employ a fully floating pin in which the pin retention arrangement does not restrict the rotation of the pin, with respect to the link. If the pin is to be held in on one or other end of the link, a very definite holding arrangement must be used.

A pin will always tend to float in the pin hole and the method of pin retention should normally allow for this.

CHAPTER 4.

HISTORICAL DEVELOPMENT OF TRACK LINKS.

4.1 HISTORICAL DEVELOPMENT

Chapter 3 has given an introduction to the characteristics which a track link may or must possess and some space will now be devoted to outlining the form actually adopted in various particular tracks. Before entering into details it may be useful to mention what appear perhaps to be the main milestones in the development of tank tracks.

The tanks of the 1914 - 18 war employed a built up construction, the link being formed of a number of parts joined by rivets, and this construction was followed for the Vickers Medium tanks.

In about 1927 a stamped type of link was substituted for the built up type, practically the whole link being made from a single forging. In all the Vickers Medium tracks the link had round the pin a phosphor bronze bush which could be renewed when it wore out.

Meanwhile (1925 onwards) for the small Carden Loyd tanks a track was developed having a link made relatively cheaply by casting in a single piece from relatively cheap material.

Efforts to increase the life of tracks included trials of various hinges incorporating rubber, but ultimately led in the direction of lubricated pins provided with seals to keep out mud and keep in lubricant.

About the same time, i.e. shortly before the present war, the Germans developed a luxury track for their half tracked vehicles in which the track pins were provided with seals and surrounded by needle roller bearings.

With the imminence of war, necessitating a colossal expansion of production, a policy was adopted for all tracks similar to that underlying the Carden Loyd track, i.e. to make the link as simply and cheaply as would meet requirements, without any luxuries such as mud-seals or machining, and try to design it so that different parts would wear out simultaneously.

The Americans have achieved considerable success with their rubber-bushed tracks in which the pin is surrounded by a rubber bush, and flexing occurs by shearing of the rubber without any sliding, but with this exception it appears that the simple dry pin type of track has been adopted by all countries for their wartime tanks.

With this introduction we will examine in rather more detail some of the main designs that have been employed.

4.2 EARLY DESIGNS

Early designs of track produced prior to the 1914 - 18 war show great diversity and in many cases great complication. In some cases they worked on the principle of a ball bearing having rollers interposed between fixed rails, corresponding with the fixed race, and the track, corresponding with the moving race. In the case of the Yuba tractor, the balls were entirely independent whereas in certain of Diplock's Pedrail designs the rollers were carried by a sort of additional track intermediate between the ordinary track and the fixed rails.

These complicated arrangements bear no very close resemblance to those adopted on modern tanks and will not be further discussed. Details can be obtained from the references already given in Section 1.3.

With regard to the form of the track links, these commonly consisted of blocks or feet of wood or some such material but were sometimes composed of a flat plate with one or more thin blades or spuds projecting from it to stick into the ground. The latter type of track is of interest from the practical point of view as it is still widely used on commercial tractors, and also from a theoretical point of view as it is believed to give a favourable adhesion factor due to the high loading on the part of the earth subjected to shear. This is discussed more fully in Chapter 23.

4.3 LAST WAR TANK TRACKS

Figure 4.3a. shows the type of track used in the tanks of the 1914 - 18 War. The surface resting on the ground was afforded by a sole plate of bullet-proof steel which was generally flat but was bent at one edge to form a slight rounded spud. Two different depths of spud were used.

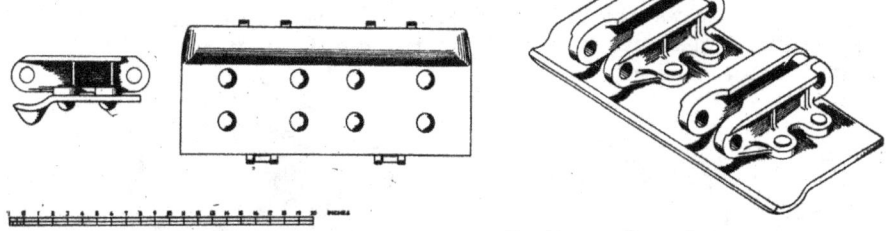

FIG. 4.3a. LINK FOR HEAVY MK.V.

Width 20.5 ins. Pitch 7.5 ins. Weight per linkage 82.15 lbs. Weight per foot 131.3 lbs.

The hinge was provided by rivetting the sole plates to the links of a pair of chains so that each track consisted of two chains, each link of one chain being joined to the corresponding link of the other chain by means of the sole plate. Each link consisted of a stamping having the lugs at one end closer together than at the other and joined by a boss so as to constitute a single male lug fitting between the female lugs of the next link and pivoted to them by a "1" diameter pin.

The upper surfaces of the links provided the wheel path for the wheels and certain of the latter were provided with flanges so that no guide horns were required on the track links.

A twin drive sprocket was used, each ring of which co-operated with one of the two chains, the sprocket teeth fitting between the bosses surrounding the pins. The drive to the sprocket was by causing the sprocket teeth on the part of the periphery not engaged by the track to mesh with the teeth of a driving pinion, so that the sprocket teeth had to be shaped to make this possible.

Similar tracks were fitted to the 1914 - 18 War Medium tanks.

4.4. POST 1918 EXPERIMENTAL TRACKS

As referred to in Section 1.6 there was considerable activity towards and after the end of the 1914 - 18 War in the design of various forms of laterally flexible track mainly intended for steering by curving the track.

FIG. 4.4a. EXPERIMENTAL TRACKS.

Figure 4.4a shows certain of these experimental designs.

Some further details of this work are given by Martel.(1) None of the designs were ripe for production when experimental work was curtailed and production started on the Vickers Medium tanks.

4.5 VICKERS MEDIUM TANKS. BUILT UP TRACKS

Figure 4.5a shows the original built up track link fitted to the Vickers Medium Tanks and Dragons from their introduction in 1922 and known as the No. 9. link.

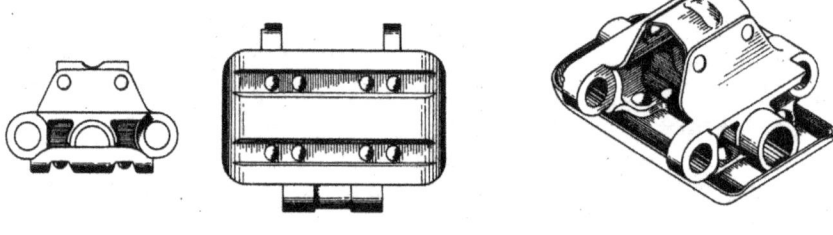

FIG. 4.5a. VICKERS BUILT UP LINK

Width 13.0 ins. Pitch 6.5 ins. Weight per linkage 19.0 lbs. Weight per foot 35.14 lbs.

In general construction the principle of this track is much the same as that of the 1914 - 18 War tracks in that it is built up from a chain having a sole plate secured to each link by rivetting. The sole plate has an under surface which is flat except for a slight dishing at the edges and a pair of shallow transverse grooves in which the heads of the rivets lie. The links of the chain are provided by a pair of stamped brackets, each of which has a flat upper surface for the wheel to run on, a projecting trunnion to be engaged by the sprocket, and an up-standing flange at its inner edge to act as a guide and keep the wheels on the track. A so-called bridge piece is rivetted between the two flanges to reinforce them. The lugs of the links are closer together at one end than the other and a distance piece is inserted between the narrower lugs which fit between the more widely separated lugs on the next link to form a 1-2 linkage. The inner lugs and distance piece are lined with a renewable phosphor bronze bush to take the wear. The pin has at one end a head with two flats on it to fit in a corresponding recess in one of the brackets, and confine rotation to the bushed lugs, and at the other end is provided with a castellated nut and split pin.

This link suffered from the weakness that the sole plate tended to wear through or break. In addition a trouble with all built up tracks is that the rivets are apt to work loose or come out. Accordingly means were sought for minimising the use of rivets by the introduction of the stamped type of track.

(1) Martel, Lieut Col G. le Q. "In the Wake of the Tank"

4.6 STAMPED TRACKS. VICKERS MEDIUM TANKS, MATILDA ETC.

Figure 4.6a. shows the stamped type of track link (known as the No. 3 link) for the Vickers Medium tanks. In general form this resembles the built-up type just described except that the sole plate and connecting brackets are combined in a single nickel chrome 60 ton steel stamping and only the bridge piece is separately made and secured by rivets.

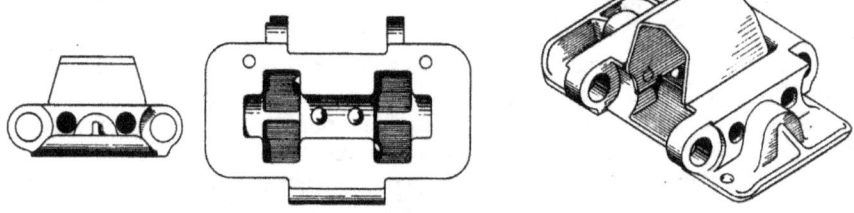

FIG. 4.6a. VICKERS STAMPED TRACK LINK.
Width 13.0 ins. Pitch 6.5 ins. Weight per linkage 20.0 lbs. Weight per foot 36.9 lbs.

In order to push up the wheel paths and trunnions on the upper part by stamping, and to avoid excessive weight, it is convenient to form pronounced recesses in the under surface of the link. Consequently the under surface of the link has in it a sort of double-cross shaped hollow which gives it a characteristic appearance.

In 1931 the Mechanical Warfare Board criticised the stamped track as discussed in the next section, but none the less it continued as the standard service track for many years and was slightly modified in a rather wider form for the Vickers Medium Mark III or 16-ton tank, and for the Experimental Heavy Tank known as the A.1.E.1., or Independent Tank. The same type was tried out for certain other experimental tanks and was also retained for Matilda (A. 12, Tank Infantry Mark II) as Design No. 50/2/1.

4.7 VIEWS OF THE MECHANICAL WARFARE BOARD 1930-31

In 1931 the Mechanical Warfare Board set out (1) what they regarded as the desiderata for future track designs and it seems worth while quoting these verbatim.

(i) The sole of the track must afford a good grip in a fore and aft direction, but must permit of lateral skid to ensure easy steering, and reduce stresses on the suspension.

(ii) The track must be light in order to reduce inertia stresses and so extend the life of sprockets, idlers, suspension etc.

(iii) The track must give a reasonably long life. This involves the employment of suitable materials and the exclusion of mud and grit from the joints.

(iv) The track must be economical to produce. This includes the use of materials, reasonable in price, and at the same time the assurance of easy manufacture and simple tools.

(v) The track should be as silent as possible. This appears to point to a short pitch in a metal track or to a rubber jointed track.

(1) 3rd Annual Report of the Mechanical Warfare Board, para 202

(vi) Joints to allow of easy removal and replacement of track shoes in the field.

"In addition to the above it would no doubt simplify matters, in regard to metal tracks with pin joints, if repairs in the field could be eliminated by producing a track, the various components of which would wear out simultaneously, so that when its useful life terminated it could be discarded in toto. Such a stage in design has not yet, however, been reached."

This is perhaps a convenient point also to mention the board's view, recorded in 1930, that spuds were quite unsuitable for roads especially of the tar macadam type, and their use was generally confined to the negotiation of difficult slopes in wet weather. This view persisted until about the beginning of the present war, for example in 1938 the Medium Mark III track modified for the A.17 tank by giving it a spud or bar tread was turned down on the ground that it damaged the roads and the extra adhesion was not wanted.

4.8 S. OF D.'S WELDED STAMPED DESIGN

In the same year, 1931, the Superintendent of Design put forward a scheme for a track link in the form of a hollow box built up from two stampings welded together. The investigation of this design took a leisurely peace-time course and seven years later (in 1938) it was decided not to proceed with it due to cracking of the weld and bad packing in gravel or loose soil. But the idea of using a box form to afford a smooth lower surface will appear again later.

4.9 CARDEN LOYD TRACKS

Returning now to 1925, the development of tracks for Carden Loyd Tankettes founded a dynasty in which a very large number of modern tracks can trace ancestry.

Figures 4.9a to f. show a number of stages in the development of the Carden Loyd tracks. The earliest of the tracks shown consists, as will be seen, of an ordinary conveyor chain having a 1-2 linkage of which the pins are slightly extended to fit into holes in a pair of angle brackets which are rivetted to a strip of metal constituting the sole plate.

At first the conveyor chain was tried alone as a track. Then about one link in four had a flat V or chevron shaped sole plate rivetted to it, and later the form shown in Fig. 4.9a. was tried. This small track had a width of $5\frac{1}{2}$" and a pitch of only $1\frac{3}{4}$".

As in the case of built up tracks for medium tanks, the rivets tended to shear and the next step consisted of forming the chain and sole plate in a single casting. The general form of the link was not much altered except that the sole plate was of the same length as the complete link, so as to give an overlapping effect, as seen in Figure 4.9b.

These two forms of link were for the early form of Carden Loyd One Man Tank Mark I. or 2 Man Tanks Marks II to IV. which employed twin rollers as road wheels and in which the central chain of the links constituted the guide to keep the wheels on the tracks. The Carden Loyd Tanks Marks V and VI used single rubber tyred wheels and a modified form of guide was required. The form of link shown at Figure 4.9c. therefore differs from the previous one in having a pair of upstanding guide horns between which the wheel runs.

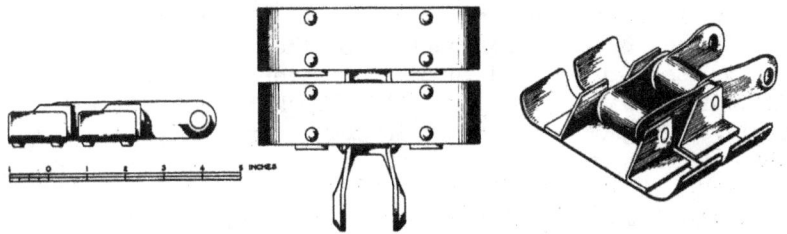

FIG. 4.9a. LINK FOR CARDEN LOYD TANK.
Width 5.75 ins. Pitch 1.75 ins. Weight per linkage 0.75 lbs. Weight per foot 5.14 lbs.

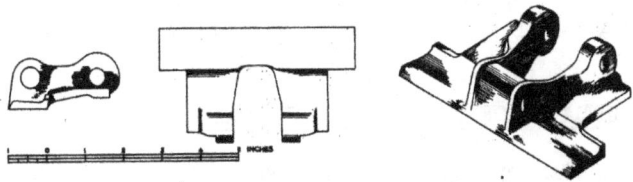

FIG. 4.9b. LINK FOR CARDEN LOYD TANK.
Width 5.0 ins. Pitch 1.75 ins. Weight per linkage 1.25 lbs. Weight per foot 8.57 lbs.

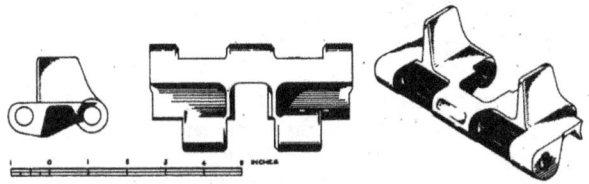

FIG. 4.9c. LINK FOR CARDEN LOYD TANK.
Width 5.25 ins. Pitch 1.75 ins. Weight per linkage 1.75 lbs. Weight per foot 12.0 lbs.

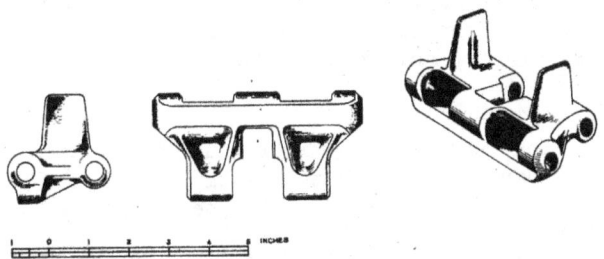

FIG. 4.9d. LINK FOR CARDEN LOYD TANK.
Width 5.25 ins. Pitch 1.75 ins. Weight per linkage 1.5 lbs. Weight per foot 10.28 lbs.

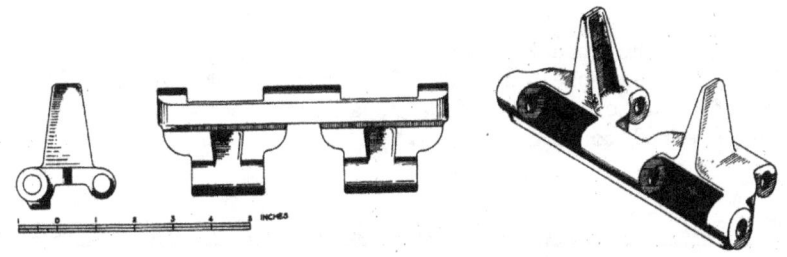

FIG. 4.9e. 7½" LINK FOR LIGHT TANKS.
Width 7.5 ins. Pitch 1.75 ins. Weight per linkage 2.0 lbs. Weight per foot 13.7 lbs.

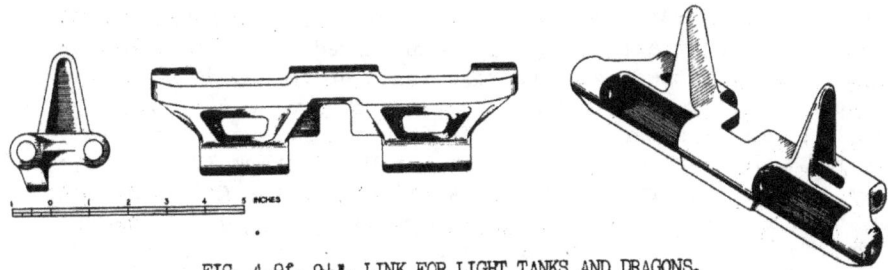

FIG. 4.9f. 9½". LINK FOR LIGHT TANKS AND DRAGONS.
Width 9.5 ins. Pitch 1.75 ins. Weight per linkage 3.25 lbs. Weight per foot 22.28 lbs.

In addition it will be seen that extra lugs are provided giving it a 2-3 linkage. Moreover, the under surface of the link shows a relatively pronounced bar or spud running transversely under the pin. Single sprocket drive was employed and the sprocket engaged the central pin lug, an adjacent gap being formed right through the link to receive the sprocket tooth.

Figure 4.9d. shows a further development in which the edges of the link are given a gradual taper from the female end to the male end. The under surface of the link shows a fairly pronounced spud under the female lugs and a number of ribs extending from it to the male lugs, with recesses between these ribs and a central gap extending right through the link for the sprocket tooth. This link was produced in some quantity in Malleable cast iron as design No. C.L.604.

4.10 DIRECT DESCENDANTS OF THE CARDEN LOYD TRACK

The original Carden Loyd track was some 5" to $5\frac{1}{2}$" wide and had a pitch of $1\frac{3}{4}$". When the Carden Loyd Mark VII became the Light Tank Mark I a similar track link with a width of $7\frac{1}{2}$" (Fig. 4.9e.) was adopted and this was further increased to $9\frac{1}{2}$" (Fig. 4.9f.) in 1932 (the pitch still being about $1\frac{3}{4}$") in order to take the additional weight of later Marks of Light Tank.

The Vickers two-ton tractor, when it became the Light Dragon Mk. I in 1931 was fitted with a skeleton type of track of manganese steel with a pitch of $3\frac{1}{2}$" and a width of $10\frac{1}{2}$". This is of some interest as being the direct ancestor of the German tracks, being almost identical with those of the Pz.Kpfw. I and II as referred to in Section 4.19. In 1932, however, this track was replaced on the Light Dragons by the $9\frac{1}{2}$" M.C.I. track used on the light tanks, since the performance of the latter was but little inferior, M.C.I. castings were more readily available, and standardisation was of course an advantage.

The form of link remained practically unchanged throughout later Marks of Light Tank, except that the guides were put further apart to accommodate the wider wheels introduced in 1935.

The same type of track was adopted for the Vickers chassis used for the Dragon Light Mark III and the M.G. carrier, later the universal carrier, which still employs the $9\frac{1}{2}$" track with a pitch of slightly under $1\frac{3}{4}$".

A number of other tracks show a distinct family likeness to the Carden Loyd, for example a number of British tracks of ribbed spudded form referred to in Section 4.18, and the German tracks of skeleton type referred to in Section 4.19.

4.11. VICKERS 6-TON TRACTOR, DRAGON MEDIUM MARK IV., AND TANK INFANTRY

MARK I. (A. 11)

Between about 1930 and 1935 Messrs. Vickers were developing their 6-ton tank and tractor which were purchased by various foreign countries. In 1934 these were provided with an improved type of track which is said to have been, "designed to give better road adhesion by means of a bar tread". In 1936 ten of these tractors were ordered and became known as the Dragon Medium Mark IV. Difficulty was experienced with very similar tracks fitted to the A.11E.1 (Pilot of Tank Infantry Mark I) owing to stones becoming wedged between the tracks and the sprockets due to the form of track which employed an internal tooth drive and the insufficient absorption of the suspension.

4.12 LUBRICATED MUD-SEALED TRACKS

From about 1930 onwards various trials made by the Mechanical Warfare Board led to the conclusion that, for reducing wear at the pin joints, the provision of seals to keep in lubricant and keep out mud was more promising than an attempt to find materials which would resist abrasive action.

In one scheme (1) put forward by Major Hordern (as he then was) rubber bushes of "silentbloc" type provided a seal without taking any of the load.

In another scheme for the service tracks of medium tanks patented by Hammond Foot (2), the pin was completely enclosed in three bushes of which the two outer ones were closed at their outer ends while mud seals were interposed between the opposed faces of the inner and outer bushes. This gave promising results as regards life but never reached the stage of production.

4.13. A.9, A.10 and EARLY VALENTINE TRACKS

In 1935 Messrs. Vickers produced a new form of malleable cast iron track which, as shown in Figure 4.13a., consisted of main links connected together by pairs of side links. The pins were welded in the side links and were provided with rubber mud seals.

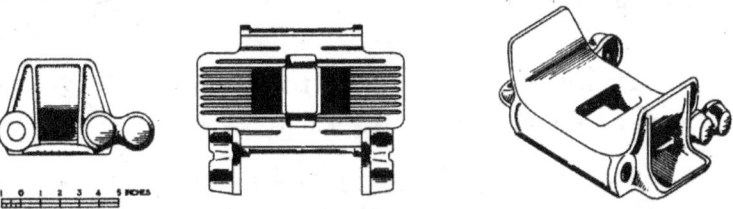

FIG. 4.13a. LINK FOR CRUISER MK I.

Width 10.5 ins. Pitch 6.25 ins. Weight per linkage 17.0 lbs. Weight per foot 32.3 lbs.

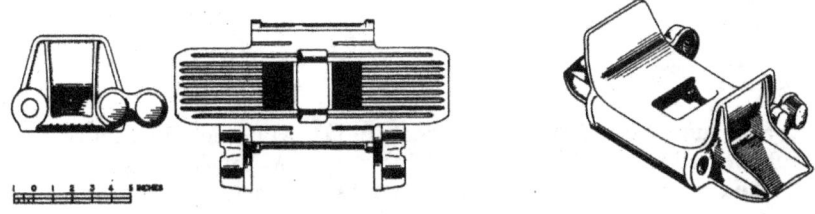

FIG. 4.13b. LINK FOR VALENTINE (ALL MARKS)

Width 14.0 ins. Pitch 6.25 ins. Weight per linkage 18.8 lbs. Weight per foot 36.0 lbs.

In accordance with prevailing ideas the under surface of this link was flat except for a central hole and a series of very narrow transverse grooves. On a few pilot tracks the results obtained from the point of view of life were good and in certain trials a life of 3,000 miles was obtained, but trouble was experienced from various causes notably gravel packing. It was suggested that tougher material should be used and the tension increased in the hope of avoiding jumping of the sprockets. Production tracks suffered frequent breakages. A similar track was developed for Valentine and is shown in Figure 4.13b.

(1) See British Patent No. 360168, & 1st Annual Report of Mechanical Warfare Board 1928-9 para. 126 (d)

(2) See British Patent No. 342725, & 2nd Annual Report of Mechanical Warfare Board 1930 para. 182 (ii).

4.14. A.13.E.1.

The tracks of the Russian B.T. and of the Christie Chassis on which A.13 was based, referred to in Section 1.11, were of an unusual design having a pitch of 10" and a width of $10\frac{1}{4}$". The shoes were flat cast steel plates connected by multiple shear hinges with renewable hardened bushes. Each alternate link carried at its centre a deep horn which served the dual purpose of keeping the wheels on the tracks and engaging with rollers on a special type of sprocket to take the drive. Considerable wear in the pin joints was attributed to the velocity of rub or rate of oscillation occasioned by a very small idler wheel and a track of unusually long pitch. Another reason for the abandonment of this track was the noise it made owing to its long pitch.

4.15. A.13.

Accordingly it was decided to provide the production model A.13 with a track of 4" pitch. Actually the track had a two piece link having pitches of $1\frac{3}{8}$" and $2\frac{5}{8}$" connected by a 5-6 linkage.

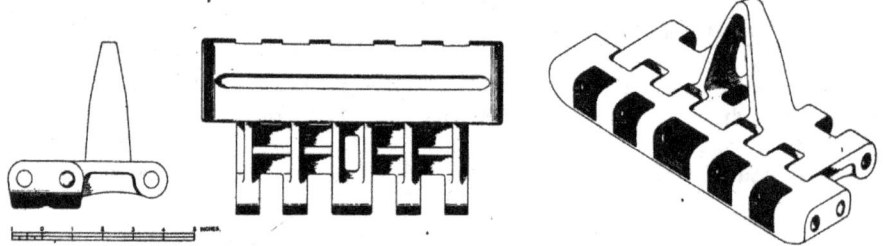

FIG. 4.15a. LINK FOR CRUISER MKS III AND IV.

Width 9.75 ins. Pitch 4.0 ins. Weight per linkage 9.6 lbs. Weight per foot 28.8 lbs.

As shown in Figure 4.15a. one piece provided the guide horn and was raised up so as not to come into contact with hard ground whilst the other afforded a wide flat supporting surface about 2" wide, that is to say, about half the pitch. A twin sprocket engaged the outermost female lugs.

4.16. BACK TO THE DRY PIN

The track just described, and practically all tank tracks introduced subsequently, are of the unlubricated or dry-pin type having no mud seals, and in view of the promising results obtained with sealed tracks as already referred to it seems desirable to give some reasons for their absence from current British, Allied and German tracks (with the exception of early tracks for Tetrarch and German half-tracked carriers.)

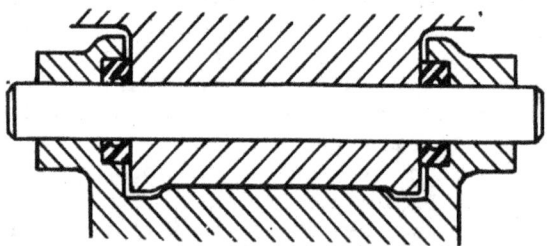

FIG. 4.16a. TETRARCH MUD SEALS.

Figure 4.16a. is a diagram of the arrangement of mud seals in the Tetrarch track. It will be seen that the space for the rubber seal is provided by cutting away the material of the outer lugs of a 1-2 linkage and it will be obvious that as a result of this the tendency to bending of the pin will be very much increased, indeed it might be said that the material is cut away just at the point where the pin most needs support. The matter is aggravated by the fact that only a 1-2 linkage is employed and in fact it seems hardly practicable to increase the number of lugs whilst retaining the seals.

In addition the provision of seals necessitates machining, and could not therefore be applied to a virtually unmachinable material such as high manganese steel, which has subsequently come increasingly into use for track links.

Hence, although for light duty the use of sealed pins may result in a more efficient track, it does not lend itself to arrangements having more than a 1-2 linkage, and this, coupled with the fact that it removes support for the pin at the edges of the lugs, just where it is most wanted, makes it difficult to produce a track with sealed pins having adequate strength for anything other than light tanks.

Be this as it may the sealed type of track is at the moment obsolete, and even the later forms of the side link type of track for A.9 and A.10 and Valentine, and those fitted to the Harry Hopkins which developed from the Tetrarch, have been of the dry pin unsealed type.

4.17 SINGLE SPUD BOX SECTION DESIGNS

In Feb. 1940 some trials were carried out at Bovington in connection with Cruiser Tanks A.9, A10 and A.13 to determine their performance as regards adhesion and steering. As described above none of the tracks had a pronounced spud and it was found that the grip they gave on muddy ground was quite inadequate. A great improvement was achieved by the addition of even quite a few detachable spuds or grousers and it was decided that a new design was required incorporating a fairly pronounced spud as part of the link. As noted in Section 4.7 it had for many years been fashionable to regard spuds as an attachment for use only on difficult slopes in wet weather. The fashion now changed completely and the Department of Tank Design set about designing for almost all tanks a form of track having a pronounced single spud cast integrally as part of the link. Actually these designs bore a close resemblance to the Carden Loyd type in being produced as a single casting with a pronounced spud directly under the pin at one end. This eliminates the tendency to rocking of the links that occurs with links supported at positions away from their ends. By a nice choice of spud dimensions in relation to pitch, damage to roads could be avoided while giving a good grip on soft ground. At the same time the designs resembled the welded stamped scheme of the S. of D. in that they consisted of a substantially closed box, although in the case of the D.T.D. designs they were produced by casting and not by stamping and welding. These designs of box section, single-spudded track aimed at presenting flat upper surfaces for the wheels to run on as well as uninterrupted under surfaces for engaging the ground without presenting a lot of recesses which could readily become filled with mud.

The links were formed with what were termed boat shaped sides, curving upwardly to help them to ride over the ground rather than digging in when skidded laterally for steering. It was also claimed that the spud section was shaped to a tooth form so as to enter and leave soft ground with a minimum of disturbance. To what extent this claim can be maintained is discussed in Chapter 23.

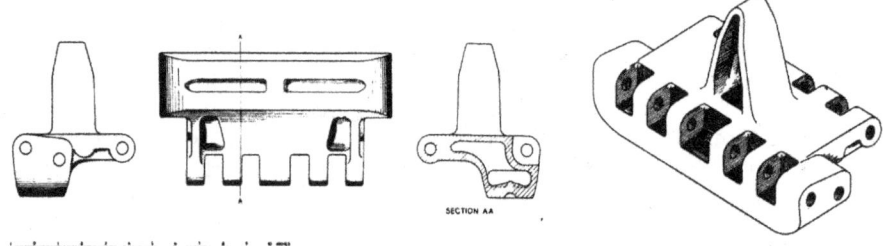

FIG. 4.17a. LINK MB 1173A FOR CRUISERS MKS III TO VI

Width 9.7 ins. Pitch 4.0 ins. Weight per linkage 11.3 lbs. Weight per foot 33.5 lbs

The designs generally adhered to the 5-6 linkage of the A.13 2-piece link, for example as shown in Figure 4.17a. on the box section spudded track MB. 1173A for Cruisers Mks. III to VI.

In order to use up existing stocks of stamped tracks for Matilda these were modified by welding on a pair of spuds. Design 50/2/3 consisted of the stamped track with a solid bar heel and a hollow box shaped spud whilst in a later design both the heel and the spud were solid.

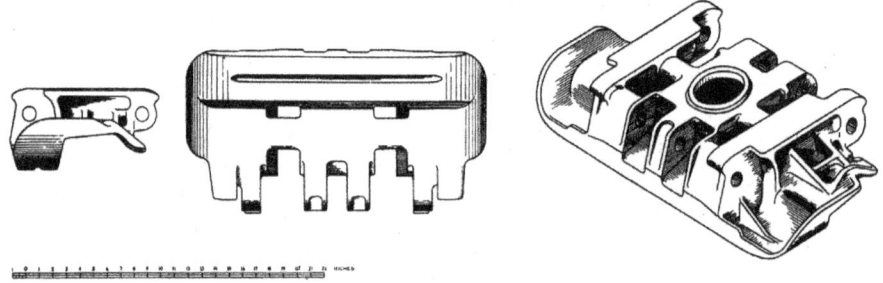

FIG. 4.17b. LINK TP.3665 FOR CHURCHILL.

Width 22.0 ins. Pitch 8.3 ins. Weight per linkage 58.0 lbs. Weight per foot 84.0 lbs.

The spuds were not under the pin and a tendency to rocking of the links occurred, and a box section design No. 1326/1 was tried. Churchill had box section tracks (MB.1354/1 and TP. 3665) of Ford 7A steel. (Fig. 4.17b)

4.18. SINGLE SPUD RIBBED DESIGNS

Later designs have not adopted the box section but have reverted to an under surface in which a number of ribs stand out from the underside of the flat wheel path as in the Carden Loyd designs. In the ribbed spudded designs for Covenanter and Crusader TD.507 in malleable cast iron and TD.1762 in manganese steel the 5-6 linkage was retained but in the ribbed spudded 14" designs TD.10560 for the Cromwell and TP.10813, 19006, 10701 and 19108 for Churchill, a 2-3 linkage is adopted.

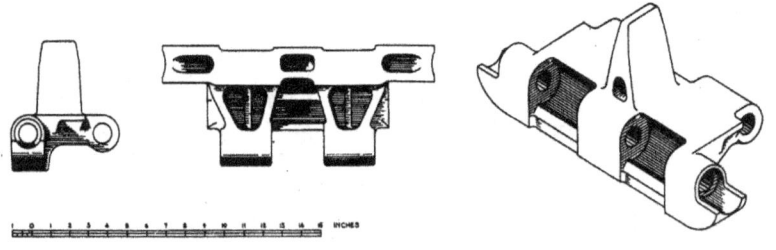

FIG. 4.18a. LINK TD.10560 FOR CROMWELL

width 14.0 ins. Pitch 3.9 ins. Weight per linkage 18.0 lbs. Weight per foot 53.5 lbs.

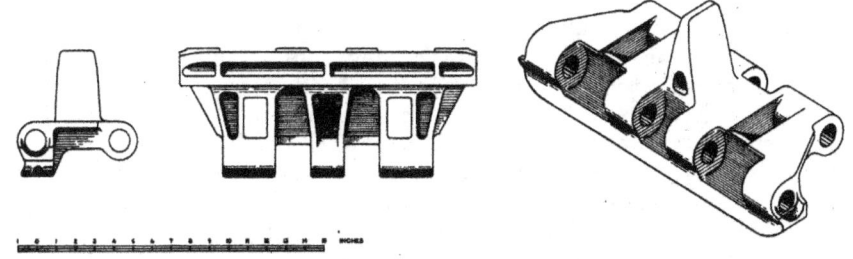

FIG. 4.18b. LINK TD.9250 FOR CROMWELL.

Width 15.5 ins. Pitch 4.4 ins. Weight per linkage 22.75 lbs. Weight per foot 62.2 lbs.

The wider 15½" Cromwell track TD.9250 (1) has a 3-4 linkage.

Opinions differ as to whether these changes were for the better. Numerous failures occured with the box section design No. MB.1173A when used on Covenanter and Crusader, but it is only fair to point out that these tanks weighed some 18 and 19½ tons respectively whereas the track was designed for Cruiser Mks. III and IV weighing 13½ to 16½ tons.

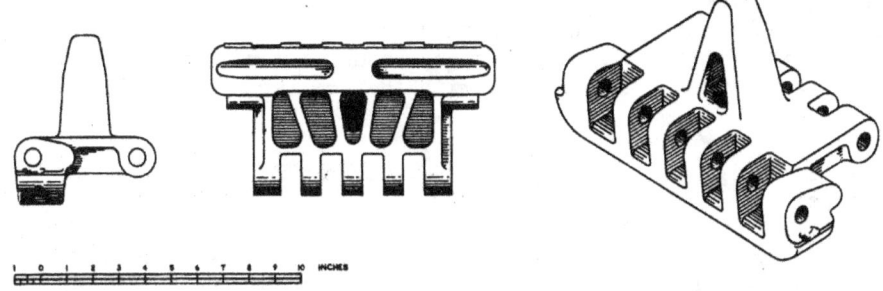

FIG. 4.18c. LINK TD.507 FOR CRUISER.

Width 10.7 ins. Pitch 4 ins. Weight per linkage 13.75 lbs. Weight per foot 41.25 lbs.

In its earliest form the ribbed link TD.507 for Cruisers was two inches wider than the box type link it was designed to replace (11.7" against 9.7") and weighed over 4 lbs. more (14.67 lbs.)against 10.4 lbs) making direct comparison of performance unfair. (To avoid the need for altering vehicles already in service it was reduced to 10.7" wide and 13.62 lbs.)

But it seems clear that at that time manufacturers regarded the ribbed link as the better production job. For example, a firm engaged in producing both types put forward to the track committee (2) figures for a week in 1941 showing that the average percentage of scrap on a weeks working was 19.3% in the case of the box section MB.1173A against 2.3% in the case of the ribbed TD.507, the former being largely blown castings resulting directly from the large box core. After quoting figures for percentage yield of good castings they went on:-

> "The foregoing figures do not cover the greater amount of coremaking involved in MB.1173A as against TD.507. The labour entailed and sand turnover with consequent mixing and baking are some four times that of the TD.507. The large box core also increases the work in cleaning the castings. The MB.1173A is wasteful in cyanide, and there is a carry over in the large cored section".

It was also considered a serious drawback that slight misalignment of cores causes thin sections which are not easily detected. Moreover if a box type link is bent it cannot be straightened, as is possible with a solid type, since this would tend to cave in the box.

(1) See The Development of the Cromwell. pp. 81-83
(2) Appendix to Report of 11th Meeting of Track Committee 20th June, 1941.

Moreover the M.C.I. link TD.507 was only regarded as an interim measure until such time as capacity could be developed for producing a link in high manganese steel. This material being more difficult to cast it was felt that when it could be introduced for Cruiser tracks (as it was in the ribbed design No. TD.1762) the difficulties associated with casting a box section would be accentuated.

On the other hand, on the score of mud-clearing, it would seem that the ribbed construction would involve some sacrifice in that the recesses between the ribs can pack with earth to which further earth can cling until the spud becomes ineffective, the resistance to steering is likely to be increased, as well as the tendency to pile up earth when steering, and the ability of the track to clear earth by the flexing between the links is reduced.

The box section track was however retained as the standard track for Matilda until that tank became obsolete and also for up to about 20% of the tracks made for Churchill tanks, but it is now (July 1944) being dropped, mainly because of its greater weight.

The tracks for Matilda and Churchill were made in Ford or B.T.S.3 track steels and, although the extra cores make production more difficult than with the ribbed design, troubles were not so great with these larger links as experienced with the smaller Cruiser links in M.C.I.

The box design is not thought to be suitable for casting in manganese steel.

Without expressing any final verdict enough has been said to indicate that arguments can be advanced on both sides of the question, and the same thing applies to the choice of the number of lugs.

Early in 1941 considerable trouble was experienced with failures of lugs, chiefly the end lugs of the Matilda box section links MB. 1325/1 having a 4-5 linkage, and the theory was that this was due to the bending moment about a vertical axis applied to parts of the track when steering. As soon as the outer lug failed the load would be transferred to the next one and so on. It was felt that the stress on each lug would be reduced by cutting down the number of lugs and making each one more massive. Tests were carried out at the Imperial College (1) which showed that the fracture could be reproduced by fatigue due to repeated application of an oblique load, but no direct comparison can be drawn since a link with a 2-3 linkage tested later was not of the same material.

On the other hand it seems clear that reducing the number of lugs increases the bending stresses in the pins (as discussed in Chapter 13) and increases vulnerability, since if one lug is shot away there is more chance of complete track failure. So here again arguments can be put forward on both sides of the question.

4.19. SKELETON DESIGNS. GERMAN TRACKS

From the ribbed spudded form of link it is a short step to the skeleton type, in which the ribs are retained without the webs between them so that there is a hole completely through the link.

It appears that German track design has been copied and developed from the skeleton link of the light Dragon Mark I shown at Figure 4.19a. which it will be seen is followed closely in the link of the Pz.Kpfw. II shown at Figure 4.19b.

(1) D.S.R. M. of S. File No. 287/Gen/517.

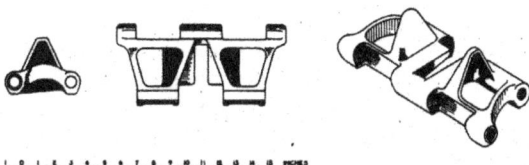

FIG. 4.19a. LINK FOR VICKERS LIGHT DRAGON MK I.

Width 10.5 ins. Pitch 3.5 ins. Weight per linkage 4.75 lbs. Weight per foot 16.29 lbs.

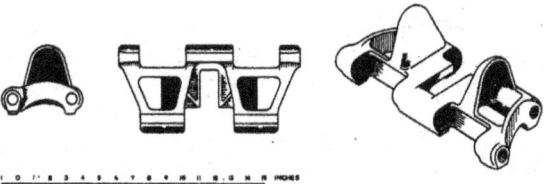

FIG. 4.9b. LINK FOR Pz.Kpfw II

Width 11 ins. Pitch 3.6 ins. Weight per linkage 8.4 lbs. Weight per foot 28.0 lbs.

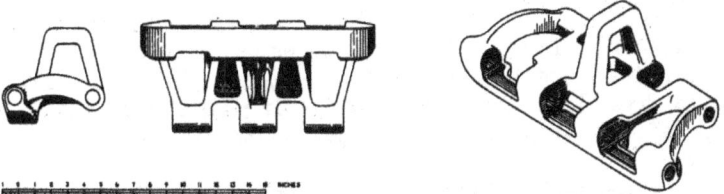

FIG. 4.19c 14" LINK FOR Pz.Kpfw III and IV

Width 14.25 ins. Pitch 4.75 ins. Weight per linkage 14.25 lbs. Weight per foot 36.0 lbs.

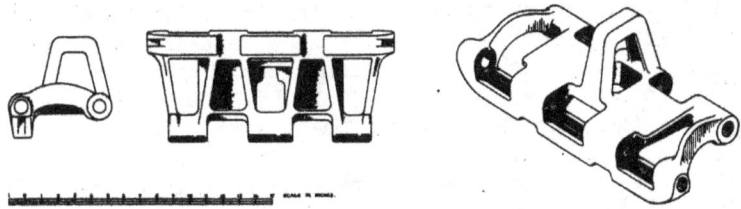

FIG. 4.19d. 15" LINK FOR Pz.Kpfw III and IV.

Width 15.0 ins. Pitch 4.75 ins. Weight per linkage 15.25 lbs. Weight per foot 38.5 lbs.

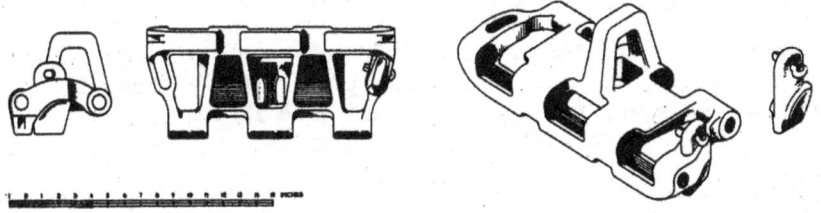

FIG. 4.19e. 15" LINK FOR Pz.Kpfw III and IV WITH SNOW PEGS.

Width 15.0 ins. Pitch 4.75 ins. Weight per linkage 18.0 lbs. Weight per foot 45.37 lbs.

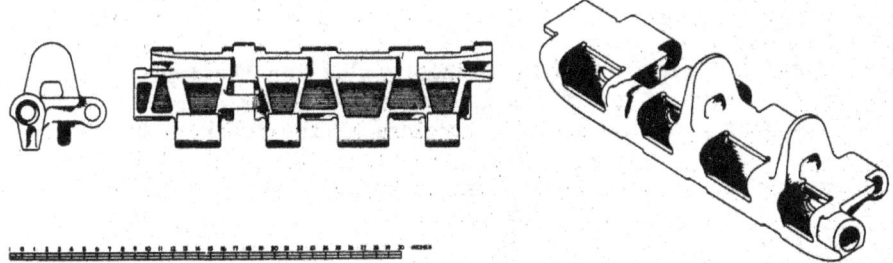

FIG. 4.19f. LINK FOR Pz.Kpfw VI (WIDE TRACK)

Width 28.5 ins. Pitch 5.12 ins. Weight per linkage 66.37 lbs. Weight per foot 155.0 lbs.

Table 4.19g. is a translated extract from a captured data table of the Wunsdorf Tank School indicating the type, width, pitch and height and number of guide horns on the track links fitted to the various early models of German Tanks. From the table it will be seen that Pz.Kpfw. III Models A. to D. and Pz.Kpfw. IV Models A. to C. used tracks of the same width and pitch but of different type number, that for the III having a guide horn 100 m/m high while that for the IV had a guide horn only 60 m/m. high.

Figures 4.19c, d, and e, show three types of link which are interchangeable between the Pz.Kpfw. III and IV. The narrow link shown at Figure 4.19c, appears to be type Kgs. 6111/380/120 which it will be seen from the table was fitted to Pz.Kpfw. III Models E, F, and G, and Pz.Kpfw. IV Models D, E, and F.

Pz.Kpfw. III Model H and later models carried a wider track shown in Figure 4.19d., which is also found on later models of the Pz.Kpfw. IV and is presumably type Kgs 61/400/120. For this track a wider sprocket was essential on both tanks. The overall track width was increased very little but the width of the wheel path was increased considerably. This was presumably to accommodate the wider tyres fitted on the road wheels of later models. Oddly enough, however, the adoption of the wider tyres, sprockets and tracks did not coincide with the increase of weight of the Pz.Kpfw. III and the change from 8-wheeled laminated spring to 6-wheeled torsion bar suspension, which were introduced on the Model E.

Possibly the 6-wheeled torsion bar suspension was tried with the existing narrow track on the E.F. and G. and was found inadequate. On the H wider tracks and on the J thicker torsion bars are used.

The introduction of the tracks shown in Figure 4.19e. with slots to receive teeth for improving grip on snow, appears to be a later development. These tracks are interchangeable with the earlier wide track on both the Pz.Kpfw. III and Pz.Kpfw. IV and we have an example of a tank with one track of each sort.

The Pz.Kpfw. VI has two types of track, a narrow one for road use and a wide battle track, of which the latter is shown in Figure 4.19f. This link is admittedly of less skeleton appearance than earlier tracks, but this may merely be due to the overlapping arrangement of the wheels which requires wheel paths at no less than six different portions of the width of the track.

It appears that the Germans favour the skeleton type of track partly on account of its self-cleaning properties. Thus, in the hand-book for the Pz.Kpfw. III Model C and also in that for the Models E, F and G the following passage occurs:-

"Gleiskette

Um eine möglichst grosse Griffigkeit zu erreichen, haben die Kettenglieder Greiferleisten, die zur Selbstreinigung unterbrochen ausgeführt sind. In die seitlichen Lücken der Kettenglieder greifen die Zähne der Triebräder ein."

(In order to achieve the best possible adhesion the track links have spuds and these are of interrupted form for self-cleaning. The teeth of the sprocket grip in the side openings of the track links.)(1).

(1) Gerätsbeschreibung und Bedienungsanweisung zum Fahrgestell.

Pz. Kpfw. III. Sd.Kfz. 141

Ausfuhrüng C. Chassis Nos. 60300 - 60315. 22/9/38.
also in same book for Ausführung E.F.G. 23/4/40.

TABLE 4.19g.

	Type No.	No. of Guide Horns	Width mm.	Pitch mm.	Ht. of Horn mm.	Width ins.	Pitch ins.	Ht. of Horn ins.
I A & B	Kgs 67	2	280	90	55	11.02	3.54	2.17
II ABC(F)	Kgs 67	2	300	90	60	11.81	3.54	2.36
D	Kgs 61	1	300	100	60	11.81	3.94	2.36
E	Kgs 49		300	175		11.81	6.39	-
F	Kgs 61	1	300	110		11.81	4.33	-
III A-D	Kgs 6109	1	380	120	100	14.96	4.72	3.94
EFG	Kgs 6111	1	380	120	80	14.96	4.72	3.15
H	Kgs 61	1	400	120	80	15.75	4.72	3.15
IV ABC	Kgs 6110	1	380	120	60	14.96	4.72	3.15
DEF	Kgs 6111	1	380	120	80	14.96	4.72	3.15

A note indicates that in every case the material is 12% Manganese cast steel 45.81 and the life 4-5000 km. and explains the meaning of the type indication such as Kgs.6111/380/120, viz :-

    K = track for tank.
    g = cast.
    s = floating pins
 6111 = characteristic number.
  380 = width mm.
  120 = pitch mm.

other types are:-

    Zgw = Track for half-track vehicle, cast roller bearings and
    Zpw = Track for half-track vehicle, pressed, roller bearings.

4.20. THE TRACKS OF THE GERMAN HALF-TRACKED CARRIER.

With the exception of a very few vehicles all German tank tracks have used plain dry pins. But the half-tracked carriers have been provided with a track of unusual form designed on what may be termed luxury lines. These vehicles are referred to in an article by Kühner (1) in 1938 dealing with factors that affect rolling resistance, and it seems possible that the track was developed with these desiderata in mind.

The pin joints are provided with needle roller bearings sealed by rubber seals and generously lubricated from a reservoir formed within the hollow guide horn. The latter serves to take the drive from the sprocket which is provided with a number of rollers.

(1) Kühner K. Fahrwiderstand und Leistungsbedarf geländegängiger. Kraftfahrzeuge. V.D.I. Zeitschrift. 19 Feb. 1938.

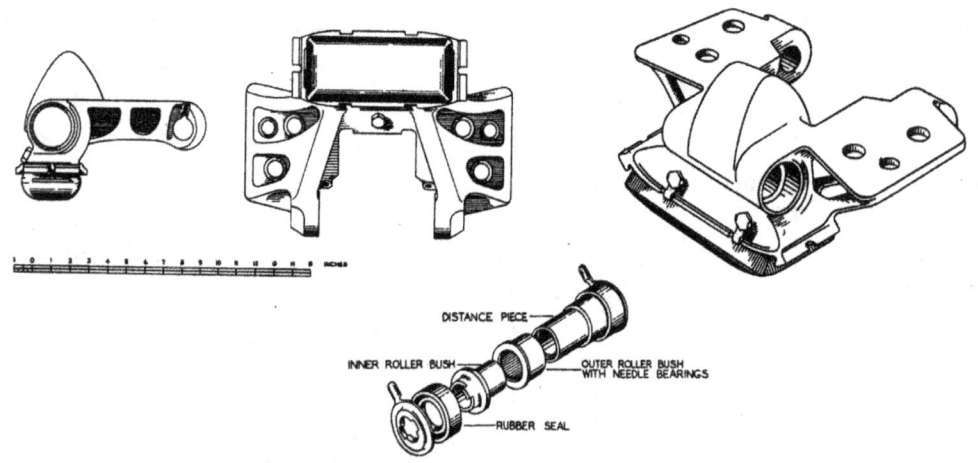

FIG. 4.20a. LINK FOR GERMAN HALF TRACKED CARRIER.

The form of link, which has rubber sole pads detachable for renewal, is indicated in Figure 4.20a.

4.21. RUBBER AND RUBBER JOINTED TRACKS.

From the end of the 1914-18 war numerous attempts were made to evolve a satisfactory track using rubber, of one of the forms set out in Section 2.1.

Many designs of continuously flexible endless band type were developed by Kégresse and whilst they gave satisfactory results for light half-tracked vehicles it never appears to have been found possible to get a material which would stand up to service on a medium or heavy tank.

At the present time a continuously flexible track having steel cables and cross pieces embedded in an endless rubber belt, is used by the Americans, but only in connection with relatively light half-tracked vehicles. (1)

From 1928 to 1934 the Mechanical Warfare Board carried out various experiments (2) on a number of designs of rubber jointed tracks.

These included various designs put forward by Messrs. Roadless Traction Ltd. and a scheme by Major Hordern (as he then was) using a pin of cruciform section in a square hole with four rubber cylinders interposed.

The general conclusion reached by the Board was that rubber takes up too much room to be accommodated in a track which is not unduly heavy. If an attempt is made to cut down the size of the rubber it becomes overstressed and fails by fatigue.

The main advantages which it had been hoped to achieve by the use of rubber were absence of wear and quiet smooth running, but experimental work with mud seals on ordinary tracks showed better promise of giving a long life, and the advent of the Carden Loyd tracks indicated that smooth

(1) Mayne R & Delzell H.W. The Square-wheel tractor goes to Town.
S.A.E. Jnl. March 1942.
U.S. War Dept. Technical Manuals. T.M. 9-1710C. Chassis and body for half-track vehicles. and T.M. 9-707. Basic Half-Track Vehicles.

(2) Annual Reports of Mechanical Warfare Board, 1929, para. 126, 1930 paras. 181 and 185, 1931 paras 202-205, 1932 para 135, 1933 para 137, 1934, para 111.

4.22

relatively quiet running could be achieved with a pin jointed track of short pitch, so interest in rubber jointed tracks subsided in Great Britain.

In America, however, the use of rubber was pursued.

4.22. AMERICAN TRACKS

The great bulk of tracks adopted for both light and medium tanks in America have been of a type unlike those used in any other country. Initially they made extensive use of rubber but partly owing to the shortage of that material its use in later tracks has been reduced or even eliminated.

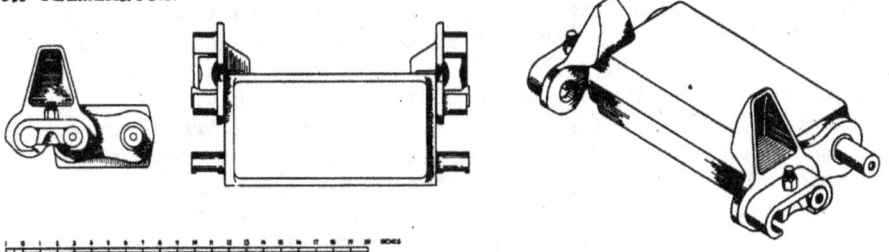

FIG. 4.22a. AMERICAN RUBBER BLOCK LINK (SHERMAN).
Width 16.0 ins. Pitch 6.0 ins. Weight per linkage 26.6 lbs. Weight per foot 53.2 lbs.

In the rubber block tracks shown in Figure 4.22a. the surface engaging the ground and the wheel path are both of rubber being afforded by a single rubber block and in addition the pin joint incorporates rubber bushes. The rubber bush is formed from a number of rubber rings or "doughnuts" which are squashed radially so as to fit between a steel tube and the track pin. Two such steel tubes are assembled together to form a frame which is embedded in the rubber block.

The original rubber block tracks when first used in the Middle East were regarded with some suspicion but put up an astonishingly good performance as regards life. But as regards adhesion the flat uninterrupted under-surface gives a poor performance especially on wet ground. To improve adhesion under these conditions detachable grousers are provided for attachment to the tracks but as has already been noted the regular use of such devices, although corresponding with views held in this country some years before the war, is not now considered desirable.

The general view held by the U.S. War Dept. is that the ideal medium tank track would be one with a steel underside and a rubber wheel path, but in carrying this aim into effect some difficulty has been experienced in getting the rubber to stick sufficiently firmly to the steel, and partly as a result links with a steel wheel path are widely used.

The problem of embodying an adequate spud as an integral part of a track interchangeable with that shown in Figure 4.22a. is not an easy one, since the side link arrangement makes it impossible to put a spud under every pin (in order to prevent snaking or rocking of the track link on hard ground) unless two spuds are provided on each link. A link with two continuous spuds tends to become clogged up with mud more readily than one with only a single spud and to prevent this the Americans have gone for two different forms of spud both of which aim at minimising clogging while supporting the link throughout its length when resting on a hard flat surface. The chevron type of spud has a central portion near one end of the link from which it curves to the other end finishing in two short end portions along that end, while the interrupted parallel spud comprises a heel and toe arrangement having a spud extending across the central portion of one end of the link and a pair of short spuds extending across the two outer portions of the other end of the link.

The construction of the link varies in the different types of track although in most cases the arrangement of the rubber bush is substantially the same. Usually the steel bottom plate and steel or rubber wheel paths are built up round the standard frame consisting of the two rubber bushes in their tubes. (1).

In addition to the tracks referred to above which are all fundamentally similar, and of which those for medium tanks are interchangeable, there have more recently appeared a number of totally different American tracks. For example, the 76 mm. Gun Motor Carriage T.70 (2) (which embodies a torsion bar suspension of five fairly large wheels per side and compensated sprocket and idler), employs a single-spudded track link with a 2-3 linkage and centre guide horns. In these particulars the track is much closer to current British practice, but the pin arrangement follows more closely that of the American medium tanks. Thus in each of the two male lugs there is a rubber bushing squashed between the surface of the pin hole and a concentric tube having a key on its inner surface to engage a longitudinal keyway in the track pin. At its centre the track pin is also formed with a flat to be engaged by a grub screw which projects through the centre female lug and serves not only to prevent the pin from coming out but also to prevent it from turning in the female lugs. A twin sprocket drives on the ends of the pins.

Again the track for the light tank T.9.E.1 or Locust (3) goes a stage further towards what may be termed British practice in that it employs a single spudded track with dry pin jointed hinges having no rubber bushings. It embodies a 2-3 linkage with the spuds on the two male lugs whilst the outer female lugs are somewhat prolonged in the form of cylindrical bosses to take the drive from the twin sprocket. Since the suspension embodies single road wheels each track link has a pair of guide horns.

Reference has already been made to the endless rubber band tracks fitted to the American Half-Track vehicles. These consist of a number of cables embedded in the rubber band and each secured to steel cross members and guide plates of which the former take the drive from the sprocket while the latter, overlapping like fish scales, keep the road wheels on the track. (4)

The track fitted to Landing Vehicle, Tracked, Mark I and II, (5) (also) known as the Roebling Alligator), is of quite unusual design more nearly resembling a commercial tractor track than that of a tank. It is built up of two chains each having links of generally U section of which alternate links fit inside and the remaining links outside their neighbours. Corresponding inside links of the two chains are interconnected by what are termed chain cross plates, whilst corresponding outside links are interconnected by plates provided with grousers. As well as fulfilling the function of spuds these grousers serve as paddles when the vehicle is travelling in the water and accordingly they are of considerable depth and are bent to approximately W shape.

(1) Some further information concerning the different types of American track was given by W.S.5. War Office under their reference WS5/4190H dated Feb. 11th 1944.
See also War Dept. Technical Manuals T.M.

(2) War Dept. Technical Manual TM 9-755.

(3) War Dept. Technical Manuals TM 9-724 & TM 9-1724B

(4) War Dept. Technical Manual TM 9-710.

(5) War Dept. Technical Manual TM 9-775.

TABLE 4.24a.

TANK	TRACK	TYPE	HINGE	WIDTH (Inches)	PITCH (Inches)	LENGTH ON GROUND (Inches)	WEIGHTS OF LINKAGE (lbs.)	WEIGHTS PER FT. (lbs.)	WEIGHTS OF TK. (lbs.)	MEAN GROUND PRESSURE (lbs./sq.in)	NO. OF ROAD WHEELS	DIA. OF ROAD WHEELS (Inches)	P.C.D. OF SPROCKET (Inches)	DIA. OF IDLER (Inches)	REVERSE BEND
Heavy Mk.V Narrow		Built up	2x1-2	20.5	7.5	No Sinkage 55	82.5	131.3	63,000	28.7 No Sinkage	6+19	8.4	30.0	27.0	–
Heavy Mk.V Wide		Built up	2x1-2	26.5	7.5	No Sinkage 55	92.1	147.4	64,000	22.2 No Sinkage	6+19	8.4	30.0	27.0	–
Vickers Med.		Built up	1-2	13.0	6.5	108.0	19.0	35.1	24,000	6¼ @ 3"	24	9.0	27.2	22.0	–
"	88124G	Stamped	1-2	13.0	6.5	108.0	20.0	36.9	24,000	–	24	9.0	27.2	22.0	12⁰
Carden Loyd	–	Webbed Spudded	2-3	5.25	1.75	–	1.5	10.28	–	–	8	–	–	–	–
"	–	"	2-3	7.5	1.75	–	2.0	13.71	–	–	8	–	–	–	–
Carrier	T.L.2948	"	2-3	9.5	1.72	56.0	3.56	24.85	9,630	8.96	6	20.0	19.6	18.4	45⁰
Lt. Dragon	–	Skeleton Spudded	2-3	10.5	3.5	–	–	–	–	–	–	–	–	–	25⁰
Tetrarch	C.L.24123	Sealed Pin	1-2	9.5	3.09	108.0	6.0	23.25	17,020	8.3	8	28.5	–	–	40⁰
Cruiser Mk.I	15752 T	Side Link - Cast	1-2	10.5	4.45+1.8	123.5	18.8	32.3	29,000	10.3	8	19.5 & 23.5	28.0	24.0	40⁰ – 45⁰
Cruiser Mk.III	Shoe DDM 30268 Link DDM 3103	Two piece	5-6	9.7	4.0	136.0	9.6	28.8	44,130	15.1	8	31.6	25.8	20.0	–
Cruiser Mk.V & VI	MB 1173A	Spudded Box Section	4-5	9.7	4.0	125.0	11.3	33.5	43,130	15.15	Mk.V 8 Mk.VI 10	31.6	25.8	20.0	15⁰
"	TD 1782	Webbed Spudded	5-6	10.7	4.02	125.0	13.0	36.8	43,130	15.15	"	31.6	25.8	20.0	30⁰ – 35⁰
Cromwell	TD 10560	"	2-3	14.0	3.9	147.0	18.0	53.5	62,720	15.1	10	31.6	25.8	19.5	40⁰-45⁰
"	TD 9250	"	3-4	15.5	4.4	147.0	22.75	62.2	62,720	15.1	10	31.6	25.8	19.5	"

Tank	Model	Track Type	Col3	Col4	Col5	Col6	Col7	Col8	Col9	Col10	Col11	Col12	Col13
Matilda	50/2/1	Stamped	1-2	14.0	6.5	130.0	21.2	39.0	59,360	16.3	20 + 2	9.5	26.0	17.75	12°
"	MB 1326/1	Box Section Spudded	3-4	14.0	6.35	130.0	28.0	52.9	59,360	16.3	20 + 2	9.5	26.0	17.75	20°-24°
"	TD 3522	Webbed Spudded	2-3	14.0	6.41	130.0	26.7	50.0	59,360	16.3	20 + 2	9.5	26.0	17.75	15°
Valentine	20267 T	Side Link Cast	–	14.0	.45+1.8	122.0	18.8	38.2	38,300	11.1	12	19.5 & 24.0	28.0	24.0	35°-40°
"	22846 T	Webbed Spudded	2-3	14.0	4.36	122.0	15.25	42.0	38,300	11.1	12	19.5&24.0	28.0	24.0	15°-18°
Churchill	TP 3865	Box Section Spudded	3-4	22.0	8.3	149.5	58.0	84.0	87,360	12.6	16 + 6	10.0	30.0	26.5	20°-22°
"	TP 10813	Webbed Spudded	2-3	22.0	7.96	149.5	54.6	82.0	87,360	14.5	16 + 6	10.0	30.0	26.5	25°
Stuart	–	Rubber Bushed Rubber Block	1-2	11.6	15.5	113.0	19.57	42.8	28,000	10.65	8	20.0	25.0	30.0	–
Sherman	–	"	1-2	16.0	6.0	147.0	26.6	53.2	69,440	13.9	12	20.0	25.0	21.5	20°
"	–	Rubber Bushed Chevron Steel	1-2	16.0	6.0	147.0	47.3	94.6	70,780	13.9	12	20.0	25.0	21.5	12°
T.70	–	Rubber Bushed Steel	2-3	14.37	5.09	–	–	–	–	–	10	–	–	–	–
K.V. I	–	Webbed Spudded	4-5	28.0	6.25	173.0	56.0	107.2	37,500	11.4	12	–	38.5	20.0	45°
T.34	–	2 Piece, Horn Dve	4-5	21.375	6.75+6.75	145.0	62.2(2 Links)	55.45	105,280	10.9	10	32.0	25.0	–	35°-40°
Pz.Kpfw.I	67/286/90	Skeleton	2-3	10.25	3.69	101.0	–	–	62,720	10.2	10	20.0	24.0	22.0	–
Pz.Kpfw.II	67/300/90	"	2-3	11.1	3.8	94.0	8.4	28.0	11,980	–	10	22.0	25.0	25.0	35°
Pz.Kpfw.III	6111/350/120	" Spudded	3-4	14.25	4.75	126.0	14.25	36.0	21,280	15.37	12 Twin	20.5	30.75	31.0	35°
"	61/4000/120	"	3-4	15.0	4.75	126.0	15.25	38.5	49,280	11.0	"	20.5	32.0	31.0	–
Pz.Kpfw.V	–	"	4-5	26.0	6.0	154.0	–	–	100,800	–	16	33.5	32.7	24.0	25°
Pz.Kpfw.VI	–	"	4-5	28.5	5.12	150.0	66.37	155.0	125,440	14.7	16	31.5	32.7	27.0	25°

4.23. RUSSIAN TANK TRACKS

In general the width of Russian tracks is greater than those of other countries, partly, no doubt, in order to improve their ability to negotiate snow. On the 28 ton T.34, three different forms of track have been used, which, like the original Christie track, are driven by a roller type of sprocket which engages a driving and guiding horn on each alternate link. One form of track has a relatively flat under surface with a multiple shear hinge comprising no less than an 8-9 linkage. The part of the link having the guide horn on it has 9 lugs at each end whilst the companion part has 8 at each end.

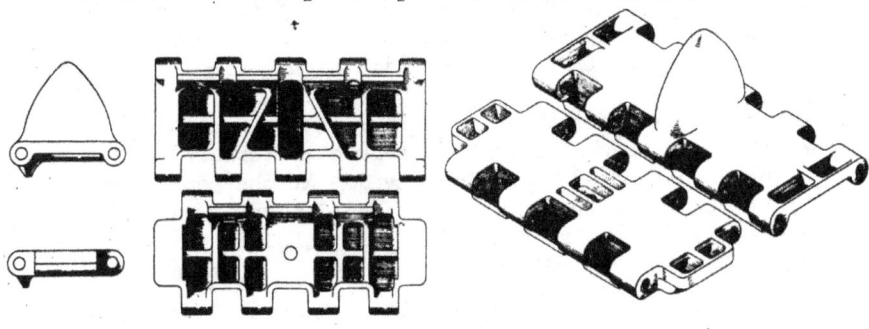

FIG. 4.23a. LINKS FOR RUSSIAN T.34.

Width 21.0 ins. Pitch 6.75 ins. Weight per linkage 37.0 lbs. Weight per foot 65.78 lbs. (with horn)
Width 21.0 ins. Pitch 6.75 ins. Weight per linkage 28.0 lbs. Weight per foot 49.78 lbs. (without horn)

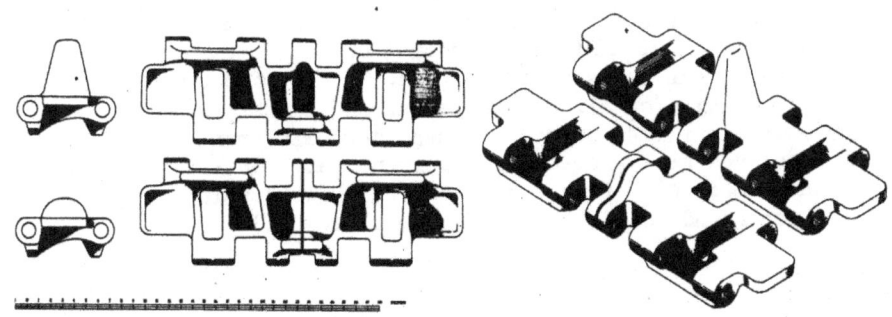

FIG. 4.23b. LINKS FOR RUSSIAN K.V.1.

Width 28.0 ins. Pitch 6.25 ins. Weight per linkage 56.0 lbs. Weight per foot 107.2 lbs. (with horn)
Width 28.0 ins. Pitch 6.25 ins. Weight per linkage 55.5 lbs. Weight per foot 106.65 lbs (split link)

An alternative form of track (Fig. 4.23a.) for the T.34 has a webbed under surface but in other respects is very similar to that already described except for the use of only a 4-5 linkage, the part of the link with a guiding and driving horn having 5 lugs at each end. The heavy K.V.I. also employs a two part link presenting a webbed under surface. In this case the drive is by a conventional twin drive sprocket, the teeth of which pass through holes spaced apart in the width of the links (Fig. 4.23b.)

4.24. TRACK DATA

Reference has been made to some of the main types of modern tracks but it will be realised that no attempt has been made to refer to the countless detailed differences that have arisen during development and a great number of tracks have had to be omitted altogether.

Table 4.24a. gives approximate data of a number of British and foreign tracks. This has been kindly checked by D.T.D. but as such information rapidly becomes out of date it should be verified before being relied on as anything more than a general guide for comparative purposes (1)

(1) For further data of current British and U.S. Tank Tracks see D.T.D. collection of Tank Track Data sheets, also Handbooks of individual tanks.

5.1

CHAPTER 5

MATERIALS AND MANUFACTURE.

5.1. INTRODUCTORY.

The conditions of use of a track demand a material having a rather unusual combination of properties. It must possess toughness to resist impacts, strength to resist steady loads, resistance to fatigue to stand up to fluctuating loads, and the ability to resist wear under abrasive conditions, which may or may not be synonymous with high surface hardness.

Having decided what is wanted it is to some extent for the metallurgist rather than the track designer to suggest materials and processes by which these properties can be achieved. At the same time it is clearly desirable that the track designer should have a reasonable knowledge of the materials and their manufacture, to help him to avoid putting forward designs which are difficult or impossible to manufacture, and to appreciate the problems of manufacturers.

It is assumed that the reader has some knowledge of the properties and manufacture of iron and steel, and foundry and forge practice, and for those who have not there is a wide choice of books available.(1) Also in Sections 5.8 to 5.11 we shall describe in detail the stages by which the metal is prepared and the links cast in a modern mechanised foundry producing manganese steel track links.

For the rest we shall now refer briefly to the chief materials now in use, followed by a short historical account of some other materials that have been made or used in the past. It is of course impossible to include details of all developments, and the story may perhaps have been over-simplified in some places where different developments and alternatives were proceeding simultaneously, whilst in addition no mention is made of various materials which were tried experimentally but not found to give promising results. (2)

5.2. MANGANESE STEEL.

Probably the foremost material in use to-day for tracks is manganese steel, (3) details of which are given in Table 5.2a. For medium and heavy tracks it is used almost exclusively in Great Britain and Germany and to some extent in Russia and elsewhere. In the natural condition as cast it is extremely brittle, but it can be rendered tough and resistant to impacts by heating and quenching. The resulting material, austenitic in structure, is non-magnetic and tough and has the property of work-hardening. This is a valuable property in a track since whereas an ordinary case-hardened surface can be worn away to the soft metal beneath, a work-hardened surface continually renews itself by hardening of a fresh layer of metal as each layer of the surface is worn away.

(1) e.g. Encyclopaedia Britannica, Articles on Iron and Steel, Blast furnace etc. etc. Steeds, W. Engineering Materials, Machine Tools and Processes. Rolf, R.T., Steels for the User. Barr and Honeyman, Steels.
(2) See M.W.B. and Mech. Board reports, Records of Track Committee Meetings, and D.T.D. reports.
(3) The manganese steel referred to here, sometimes known as high manganese steel or Hadfields austenitic manganese steel, contains about 11 to 15% of manganese and is not to be confused with a considerable range of manganese steels or carbon-manganese steels containing something under 2% of manganese. (e.g. S.A.E. Standard Steels 1330 to 1350).

TABLE 5.2a MANGANESE STEEL.

ANALYSIS.		MECHANICAL PROPERTIES. (1)	
Carbon	1.00 – 1.40%	Ultimate Tensile	60 tons/sq.in.
Silicon	1.00%	Yield	21 tons/sq.in.
Manganese	11.00 –14.00%	Elongation	70%
Sulphur	0.06%	Brinell (2)	240 max.
Phosphorus	0.12%		200 average.

The ratio of manganese to carbon should be about 11 to 1.

METAL FOR CASTING.

In a basic arc furnace mild steel scrap (mixed with some lime and iron ore) is melted down under an oxidising slag which removes the phosphorus, carbon, manganese and silicon and leaves a bath of dead mild steel. The oxidising slag is raked off with the impurities it has collected. A reducing slag (lime, anthracite etc.) is put on and a little silicon is added, to remove oxides and give a small silicon content. The manganese can now be added without fear of its being promptly oxidised, and this is done by adding ferro-manganese. In some cases a second arc furnace is used to hold a supply of molten metal for continuous mechanised casting.

<u>Alternatively</u> steel scrap and pig iron are melted in cupolas and reduced to low carbon steel in a converter. Ferro-manganese is melted in a small cupola and mixed with the low carbon steel in the ladle.

The material as cast has a brittle structure of austenite with considerable carbide in patches and in an intergranular network.

HEAT TREATMENT.

To take the carbide into solution and produce a uniform austenitic structure the castings are heated to 1000 – 1050°C and quenched in cold water. The resulting material is tough and resistant to impacts and capable of a high degree of work-hardening (to about 600 – 800 V.P.N.)   (3)

PRECAUTION.

After heat treatment the links must not be heated much above about 400°C or they will revert to the brittle condition. It is therefore difficult or impossible to remove cooling stresses by reheating after quenching and these stresses are liable to be aggravated by the fact that manganese steel has a heat conductivity about one sixth and a coefficient of thermal expansion about $1\frac{1}{2}$ times the corresponding figures for pure iron. Hence in the design of a manganese steel track link it is particularly important to avoid heavy or unequal sections and aim at a uniform rate of cooling when quenching.

SPECIFICATION. A.F.V. 1025

---

(1) These properties need to be accepted with due allowance for work hardening. For example the extension of a tensile test piece is distributed along its length since work hardening takes place at any point where necking starts to occur.

(2) It will be recollected that for softish materials the Brinell Hardness number does not differ much from the V.P.N. or Vickers Pyramid Hardness Number; for example:-

| Brinell | 95 | 248 | 269 | 302 | 352 | 401 | 461 | 514 | 555 | 601 | 653 | 712 | 780 |
| V.P.N. | 95 | 248 | 270 | 305 | 363 | 420 | 494 | 567 | 633 | 717 | 820 | 960 | 1150 |

See Metals Handbook p.127.

(3) Appendix to Record of 14th Meeting of Track Committee 8/8/41.

TABLE 5.3a. MALLEABLE CAST IRON.

ANALYSIS.		MECHANICAL PROPERTIES ANNEALED.		
Carbon	3.00 - 3.50%	Ultimate Tensile	22-27 tons/sq.in.	
Silicon	0.45 - .70%	Yield	13-16 tons/sq.in.	
Manganese	0.15 - 0.25%	Elongation on 2"	5%	
Sulphur	0.15 - 0.25%	V.P.N. of	$\tfrac{5}{8}$"	1" section
Phosphorus	0.08%	core	180-220	220-280
		near surface	140-180	140-180
		MECHANICAL PROPERTIES OIL HARDENED.		
		Ultimate Tensile	35-40 tons/sq.in.	
		Yield	25-30 tons/sq.in.	
		Elongation on 2"	1-2%	
		V.P.N. of	$\tfrac{5}{8}$"	1" section
		core	280-340	350-380
		near surface	180-220	180-220

METAL FOR CASTING.
 Returns, scrap and pig iron are melted in a cupola. The composition must be such as to give a pure white fracture, i.e. with the carbon in the form of cementite and pearlite rather than free graphite. The metal as cast is therefore very hard and brittle (V.P.N. 420, elongation: nil.

ANNEALING. WHITEHEART.
 The castings are packed into iron boxes surrounded by iron ore and the boxes are piled up in a furnace and heated up to 950-1000°C over a period of 40-50 hours, held at that temperature for 115 hours, and cooled over a period of 30 hours at a rate not exceeding 8-10°/hour. This throws the carbon out of combination and decarburises the metal nearer to the surfaces, resulting in a core of high carbon steel (ferrite and pearlite with some nodules of graphite) merging to surfaces and thin sections practically free of carbon, (pure ferrite).

ANNEALING. BLACKHEART.
 The process is similar to whiteheart but the castings are surrounded by a neutral material, such as sand, cinders or mill scale, instead of an oxidising agent, and a lower temperature is used (850-900°C). In this case the carbon is not eliminated to the same extent but the carbide is broken down into nodules of graphite which give the material a blackish fracture from which the name Blackheart arises.

SPECIFICATIONS. A.F.V. 1023 and B.S.S. 309.

5.3 MALLEABLE CAST IRON.

Malleable Cast Iron was until recently used almost exclusively in this country for the tracks of light vehicles such as carriers and light tanks as well as early cruiser tanks, and there must be many millions of links of this material in existence. Whiteheart cast iron as cast is extremely hard and brittle and would not be suitable for tracks. To render the castings malleable they are subjected to a heat treatment consisting of heating and slow cooling, lasting for several days.

There are two kinds of malleable cast iron known respectively as Whiteheart and Blackheart. In the whiteheart treatment, which is the more widespread in this country, the castings are annealed in an oxidising agent such as iron ore, the effect of which is to eliminate the carbon at the surface and progressively into the body of the metal, whereas in the blackheart process, used widely in America and by a few big firms in this country, a neutral material and a lower temperature are used, and the carbon, instead of being eliminated, is broken down into nodules of graphite which gives the metal the characteristic blackish fracture from which the name blackheart arises.

Malleable cast iron, details of which are given in Table 5.3a., is a relatively weak and soft material and efforts were made to improve its wear resistance by surface hardening, first by so-called cyanide-hardening, which consisted of heating in a bath of salts including sodium cyanide to introduce carbon and nitrogen into the surface and then reheating and quenching in oil, and at a later date by so-called oil-hardening which consisted of the heating and oil-quenching alone. Details of this are given in Table 5.3b.

The terms "oil-hardening and cyanide hardening" may be found somewhat confusing since both processes as commonly practised employ a bath of molten cyanide followed by quenching in oil, (see Table 5.3b). The basic distinction between the processes is that in the cyanide hardening the cyanide salt is relied upon to introduce carbon and nitrogen into the surface of the metal and form a hard skin, whereas in the oil hardening process the cyanide simply acts as a vehicle for heat and other suitable salts or even air can be used equally well. For foundries already provided with pots for cyanide hardening these form a convenient means of heating, but others are unwilling to purchase costly and highly poisonous salts where air will do equally well, and some foundries accordingly heat the links in air in a continuous furnace, the specification (A.F.V.1023) being worded to permit this.

The chief merit of malleable cast iron is that it is easy to produce since cast iron has a lower melting point than steel and flows easily for casting, so that there has in the past been vastly more capacity available for producing iron-castings than for producing steel-castings. But the material is at best only suitable for quite light vehicles and even in this application it is now being replaced by carbon steels or even manganese steel.

TABLE 5.3b. CYANIDE AND OIL HARDENING (OF WHITEHEART M.C.I.)

OIL-HARDENING.

The annealed castings are heated to a temperature of 820°C in a pot of molten salts containing 20-25% of sodium cyanide, and quenched in oil. If a complete charge is put into the bath at once it may take perhaps 45 minutes to recover its temperature but if the links are put in and taken out a few at a time about ten minutes may suffice to bring them up to temperature. The salt bath has little or no effect on the composition of the metal and serves merely as a vehicle for heat, and other salts than cyanides (which are extremely poisonous) such as chlorides and/or soda ash, can be used, or the links can be heated in an ordinary air furnace.

CYANIDE HARDENING. 1st STAGE. CARBURISING.

The annealed castings are preheated and then immersed in a pot of molten salts containing 50% of sodium cyanide at a temperature of 950°C. This introduces carbon and nitrogen into the surface, resulting in a hard skin.

CYANIDE HARDENING. 2nd STAGE. HEATING AND OIL QUENCHING.

The second stage of the cyanide-hardening process was identical with the oil-hardening process described above.

5.4 CARBON STEELS. B.T.S. 3F.

Certain Carbon steels are widely used for tracks in America and have recently come increasingly into the picture in this country both as an improvement on malleable cast iron for light tracks and as an emergency substitute for manganese steel. The particular material standardised in this country is known as British Track Steel No. 3F, of which details are given in Table 5.4a. As is well known, a carbon steel can be rendered very hard by heating and quenching, but in this state it lacks ductility. The toughness and ductility can be restored by tempering, that is re-heating to a lower temperature.

TABLE 5.4a. BRITISH TRACK STEEL NO. 3F. (B.T.S. 3F).

ANALYSIS		MECHANICAL PROPERTIES	
Carbon	0.40 - 0.47%	Ultimate Tensile	55 tons/sq. in.
Silicon	0.15 - 0.50%	Yield	45 tons/sq. in.
Manganese	0.85 - 1.05%	Elongation on 2"	10%
Sulphur	0.06%	Brinell	269-302 (pref. 269-285)
Phosphorus	0.06%	Izod	10 ft. lbs.
METAL FOR CASTING.			
Any preferred process may be used, for example molten pig iron is mixed with molten mild steel from a converter, or alternatively a cold charge can be melted in an electric furnace.			
HEAT TREATMENT.			
The castings are normalised at 900 - 940°C, air-cooled, reheated to 820°C, quenched in water at 40°C, and tempered at 550°C.			

5.5. HISTORICAL AND GENERAL. POST-1918.

Having referred to what are perhaps the most important three track materials we will discuss a number of other materials in roughly chronological order.

The tracks of the 1914-1918 tanks were built up from stampings and bullet-proof steel plates, rivetted together, and similar materials and construction were used for the built-up tracks of the Vickers medium tanks. The stamped track for the Vickers medium tanks was made by drop stamping from nickel chrome steel, and was very satisfactory from the point of view of strength and of wear of the sole plate. In fact the strength and life of the track would have been satisfactory but for the rapid wear of the pins and the phospher-bronze bushes in which they worked.

When the Mechanical Warfare Board was set up in 1928 a sub-committee was formed to investigate this problem and the general question of track materials.

Experiments were initiated both with homogeneous and surface hardened materials. The former included manganese steel (discussed above), "Vibrac" (a nickel chrome molybdenum steel), and nickel-chrome steel (of which the service tracks were made) whilst the latter included materials hardened by chromium plating and by nitriding.

Various experiments were made over a period of years, but no very striking results appear to have been obtained. In general, the conclusion reached was that the best way of minimising wear at the pin joints was by the provision of seals to keep in lubricant and keep out mud rather than by the choice of materials to resist abrasive action.[1]

---

[1] *Mechanical Warfare Board 2nd Annual Report 1930, para. 182*

In the meantime the Carden Loyd type of track had been developed in the form of a single-piece casting and cast tracks were adopted for light tanks and dragons either of whiteheart or blackheart malleable cast iron or of manganese steel. Malleable cast iron, whether blackheart or whiteheart, (see Table 5.3a) being relatively soft, suffered from excessive wear and gave a comparatively short life. In 1935 Cyanide hardening (see Table 5.3b) was adopted for whiteheart malleable cast iron and this greatly increased the life of the tracks.(1) Trials concluded in 1938 indicated that blackheart malleable cast iron is not suitable for cyanide hardened tracks, and at the same time the double hardening process, including a 50% cyanide bath, was standardised for whiteheart links.

Hence shortly before the war the situation was that Medium tanks were fitted with the stamped track made from 60 ton Nickel Chrome Steel, light vehicles used tracks of malleable cast iron, and the difficulties associated with seals had never really been overcome. In addition, ever since the introduction of the Vickers Utility tractor and Light Dragon Mk.1. (see Section 4.19) Messrs. Vickers Armstrong had been producing a small quantity of track in Manganese Steel.

5.6. THE REARMAMENT EXPANSION.

With the rearmament expansion the problem arose of producing track in vast quantities. The stamped track was practically ruled out by lack of forging and machining capacity as it required three sets of dies used in succession, followed by various machining operations and a rivetting operation, and it was decided that cast designs with cored pinholes must be used and machining eliminated or reduced to an absolute minimum.

Manganese steel was only being produced in very small quantities.

Accordingly it was necessary to fall back on malleable cast iron. The high carbon content of cast iron gives it a considerably lower melting point than steel and partly for this reason a large number of foundries existed that were capable of producing M.C.I. although the available capacity for steel casting was very limited. As a result track production was chiefly in M.C.I. although the material left much to be desired at all events for any but the lightest vehicles.

In 1939 attention was directed to a material known as Ford No. 7A (see Table 5.6a) something between a steel and a cast iron, developed by Messrs. Ford for continuous mechanised casting. This material, being cheap and easy to cast, gave satisfactory results with carrier tracks and by the outbreak of war was in production on a substantial scale.

5.7 WARTIME PRODUCTION.

Hence at the beginning of the War the choice lay between malleable cast iron, Ford No. 7A and a small quantity of manganese steel.

While the production of manganese steel was increased to perhaps double what it had been and was adopted for Infantry Tank Mk.1. and late in 1940 for Valentine, it was still at that time only on quite a small scale. Production of track links in M.C.I. was rapidly expanded and early cruiser and Valentine tracks were of this material, while other links for example for carriers and later for Matilda, were produced in Ford No. 7A.

With the advent of the Churchill programme a big expansion in a material better than M.C.I. was sought, and it was decided to lay out a number of new foundries for continuous mechanised casting in Ford No. 7A.

---

(1) But trials made in 1941 suggested that untreated tracks would have as good a life as treated tracks.
10th Meeting of Track Committee, 6 June 1941.

TABLE 5.6a. FORD NO. 7A.

ANALYSIS		MECHANICAL PROPERTIES.	
Carbon	1.05 - 1.20%	Ultimate Tensile	40-53 tons/sq.in.
Silicon	0.90 - 1.10%	Yield	28-35 " "
Manganese	0.40 - 0.60%	Elongation on 2"	8% min. (usually 16-20).
Sulphur	0.08%		
Phosphorus	0.06%	Brinell	187-220

METAL FOR CASTING.

Liquid pig iron from a cupola is mixed with cold steel scrap in an electric furnace. A very small percentage of ferro-titanium is used as a grain-refiner.

As cast the structure consists mainly of pearlite in a light intergranular carbide network.

HEAT TREATMENT: 1st STAGE. NORMALISING.

To homogenise the structure and break up the intergranular carbide network the castings are normalised by heating to 1700 - 1750°F for $1\frac{1}{2}$ to 2 hours and allowed to cool to about 750°F.

HEAT TREATMENT: 2nd STAGE. SPHEROIDISING.

To spheroidise the carbon they are then soaked for at least 3 hours at 1450 to 1500°F followed by a slow cool to 1100°F at a rate not exceeding 100°F per hour. It has later been decided that the cooling rate should not exceed 50°F per hour, thus involving a total heat-treatment period of well over 12 hours. The resulting structure comprises spheroidised pearlite sometimes accompanied by some fine temper graphite.

Meanwhile experience was being gained with these materials and it was generally agreed that M.C.I. was only suitable for tracks of quite light vehicles. Ford No. 7A, as might be expected from its high carbon content, showed satisfactory wear-resisting properties but a very poor resistance to impact whether due to enemy attack or rocky ground.

In the latter part of 1940 in the newly formed D.T.D. considerable apprehension was felt at the prospect of fighting Churchill on tracks of Ford No. 7A, and as the results obtained with manganese steel had been much more satisfactory the question arose of employing this material for continuous casting. This of course involves maintaining a continuous supply of molten metal which is available for pouring at all times, rather than periodically preparing a complete charge and pouring it. It was not known whether this would be practicable with manganese steel and the English Steel Corporation made the experiment of holding a batch of metal molten for six hours in a melting arc furnace before pouring. As a result it was decided to change over to manganese steel certain of the foundries planned to produce Ford 7A while others would proceed with No. 7A to minimise interruption of the supply.

Little if any consideration appears at that time to have been given to other materials, for example carbon steels of more normal carbon content than Ford No. 7A, and by the middle of 1941 it was generally agreed that manganese steel was the preferred material for all tank tracks.

The wisdom of this view was questioned at the time, and, although probably fully justified by subsequent experience, the decision to change over to manganese steel does seem to have been made with little opportunity for a clear-cut scientific comparison between the relative advantages, both in performance and production, of this and other materials.

As regards its comparison with Ford No.7A it may well be that the disappointing results obtained with the Matilda link in the latter material were partly due to the design of the link and partly to the fact that the annealing time was not sufficient for so large a link, but taking everything into consideration it does seem that its poor resistance to impact was a fatal drawback in a track material.

But it was pointed out that No.7A was not the only alternative to manganese steel and indeed two other materials, a .40% carbon steel known as Ford No.4 (see table 5.7a) and a carbon manganese vanadium steel known as "Hylastic" (see table 5.7b) were being used in America for tracks. Little appears to have been known of these materials in Great Britain and no trials had been made of them in this country, although Canadian trials indicated that Ford No.4. did not suffer the impact weakness of No.7A. As compared with manganese steel it was pointed out that they would be easier to cast and would not mean the provision of a big tonnage of imported manganese and in many cases relining of furnaces and acquisition of new foundry technique.

It was however decided (in the middle of 1941) to go all out for manganese steel, retaining some production of Ford 7A for a time and M.C.I. for light carrier tracks.

Consideration was then given to the possibility of changing over from Ford No.7A to Ford No.4. There was some difference of opinion as to whether this would be wise. The protagonists of No.7A maintained that No.4., with its lower carbon content and higher melting point, would have poor resistance to wear and would be hard on furnace linings and result in reduced production. Against this it was argued that a reduced production of a more reliable material might be a step in the right direction, while trials were put in hand to determine whether the wear resistance would be satisfactory. Moreover although melting output might be reduced the substitution of an ordinary quench for prolonged annealing should increase heat treatment output in the long run.

On the whole it does seem that the main reason for the composition of Ford No.7A was not so much the properties of the resulting metal as the purely accidental circumstances of the plant available at Dagenham. Here it was made by diluting molten pig iron with cold steel scrap in an electric furnace. The output was limited by the capacity of the latter and hence to get a maximum output it was desirable to use as much molten pig and as little cold steel as possible. This meant accepting the highest percentage of carbon and silicon consistent with getting the required properties by heat treatment, and the latter had necessarily to be somewhat prolonged. Failure to realise this resulted in the anomalous position that one American Foundry (Messrs. Campbell, Wynant and Cannon) who were not subject to the same limitations and normally produced Ford No.4., were asked to produce Ford No.7A. They accordingly went to some trouble and reduced their output in order to produce a material inferior to their normal product.

At this particular foundry a compromise known as "Ford No.7A modified" or Ford No 7B (see Table 5.7f) was suggested, having a percentage of carbon between those of Ford Nos. 4 and 7A, and this enabled the output to be doubled by simplifying the heat treatment.

TABLE 5.7a. FORD NO.4 CAST STEEL (later known as British Track Steel No. 3)

ANALYSIS		MECHANICAL PROPERTIES	
Carbon	0.38 - 0.45%	Ultimate Tensile	60 tons/sq. in.
Silicon	0.15 - 0.40%	Yield	54 " "
Manganese	0.70 - 0.90%	Elongation on 2"	8%
Phosphorus	0.05%	Brinell	269 - 302.
Sulphur	0.06%		
Copper (Optional)	0.50 - 0.60%		

METAL FOR CASTING.

Molten pig iron is mixed with molten mild steel from a converter. **Alternatively** a cold charge can be melted in an electric furnace.

HEAT TREATMENT

The castings are normalised at 1650°F to 1750°F, reheated to 1500°F, waterquenched, and tempered at 1050° - 1100°F.

Table 5.7b. "HYLASTIC" STEEL.

ANALYSIS		MECHANICAL PROPERTIES
Carbon	0.30%	
Silicon	0.40%	
Manganese	1.60%	
Sulphur		
Phosphorus		
Vanadium	0.10%	

TABLE 5.7c. BRITISH TRACK STEEL NO.1. (B.T.S.1)

ANALYSIS		MECHANICAL PROPERTIES	
Carbon	0.25 - 0.35%	Ultimate tensile	47 tons sq./in.
Silicon	0.25 - 0.45%	Yield	40 " "
Manganese	1.35 - 1.55%	Elongation	16%
Sulphur	0.06%	Brinell	228 - 255
Phosphorus	0.06%	Izod	30 ft. lbs.
Molybdenum	0.20 - 0.30%		
Copper (optional)	0.50 - 0.60%		

HEAT TREATMENT   Water - quenched.

But apart from the circumstances of its original production at Dagenham, No. 7A appears to have no special advantages over No. 4 and has sunk into abeyance, while the use of No. 4 has been extended in America and recognised in this country under the name British Track Steel No. 3, as referred to later.

Towards the end of 1941 the supply situation for track links became somewhat critical as our capacity was quite inadequate to meet requirements. The U.S.A. were prepared to supply the deficit under lease-lend but could only offer a small proportion in manganese steel and it was therefore necessary to accept some other material for the balance. In addition we had been trying other materials in case the supply situation for manganese were to deteriorate.

Messrs. American Steel Foundries, said to have the largest steel casting capacity in the U.S.A., were making tracks for American tanks from a carbon-manganese-vanadium steel sold under the trade name "Hylastic" and suggested producing British tracks in a similar material (which was christened British Track Steel No.1, or B.T.S.1 — see Table 5.7c) using molybdenum in place of vanadium in view of the supply situation. In addition tracks could be produced in Ford No.4 steel.

These materials were accordingly approved for tracks produced in U.S.A. and a quantity of track in each material was ordered towards the end of 1941. As will be seen from Tables 5.7a and 5.7c B.T.S.1 contained rather less carbon than Ford No.4, but contained some molybdenum.

Early in 1942 it became apparent that the requirements for light tracks which were being made in M.C.I. and Ford 7A would tend to give place to heavier tracks for which these materials were unsuited, and it was suggested that the change in melting practice which a change to manganese steel would involve could be avoided by going over to B.T.S.1. instead. Accordingly extra quenching equipment was ordered for several of these foundries.

There was some difference of opinion as to whether high or low carbon gave the best combination of toughness and hardness, the British generally favouring fairly low carbon to facilitate satisfactory water-quenching, while the Americans favoured a somewhat higher range to facilitate continuous casting from holding furnaces.

In 1942 one of the American foundries (Messrs. Campbell, Wynant & Cannon) who were making Crusader, Matilda and Valentine links nominally from B.T.S.1. and carrier links from Ford No. 4, departed from the specification and raised the carbon percentage of the B.T.S. material to the same as that of the Ford material, namely .35 – .45%, to facilitate holding and to enable both steels to be poured from the same furnace. As was to be expected this high carbon percentage had resulted in cracking when water-quenching and they had changed over to air-hardening.

A number of the British foundries who were awaiting their water-quenching equipment adopted a similar measure as a stopgap and this air-hardened material (containing .35 – .45% carbon) was embodied in a second specification as B.T.S.2 (see Table 5.7d).

There has been some confusion between B.T.S.1 and B.T.S.2.

It had been suggested to Messrs. Campbell, Wynant & Cannon that as their air hardening sometimes produced uneven results they might try a controlled quenching in water followed immediately by tempering, and similar suggestions were made later to British firms.

This formed the basis of what Messrs. Vauxhall embodied in their specification for B.T.S.2 (see Table 5.7e), namely something between

TABLE 5.7d. BRITISH TRACK STEEL NO. 2 (B.T.S.2)

(Original Form)

ANALYSIS.		MECHANICAL PROPERTIES.	
Carbon	0.35 - 0.40%	Ultimate Tensile	37 - 45 tons/sq.in.
Silicon	0.50%	Yield	33 - 45 " "
Manganese	1.35 - 1.70%	Elongation on 2"	10%
Sulphur	0.06%	Brinell	217 - 241
Phosphorus	0.06%	Izod	15 ft. lbs.
Molybdenum	0.20 - 0.30%		
Copper (optional)	0.50%		

HEAT TREATMENT. Air hardened.

TABLE 5.7e. BRITISH TRACK STEEL NO.2 (B.T.S.2)
Latest Vauxhall Specification.

ANALYSIS.		MECHANICAL PROPERTIES.	
Carbon	0.40 - 0.50%	Ultimate Tensile	52 - 60 tons/sq.in.
Manganese	1.20 - 1.60%	Yield	40 - 52 " "
Molybdenum	0.10 - 0.30%	Elongation	11%
Sulphur	0.06% max.	Izod	11 ft. lbs.
Phosphorus	0.06% max.	Brinell	241 - 285.
Silicon	0.25 - 0.50%		

Steel must be fully fine grained not coarser than McQuaid-Ehn No.5 - by aluminium (or equivalent) addition.

HEAT TREATMENT.

Castings to be uniformly and thoroughly normalised at 900-940°C - at least 1 hour at temperature - followed by air cooling. Reheat to 820 - 860°C, maintain at least 45 mins. and quench in water 60-100°C (or time controlled cold water). Temper at 650-670°C; after soaking through maintain at temperature at least 45 mins. and air cool.

TABLE 5.7f. FORD NO. 7A (MODIFIED) OR FORD NO. 7B.

ANALYSIS.		MECHANICAL PROPERTIES.	
Carbon	0.83%	Ultimate Tensile	50 tons/sq.in.
Silicon	0.97%	Yield	33 " "
Manganese	0.56%	Elongation	21.5%
Sulphur	0.05%	Brinell	228
Phosphorus	0.04%		
Copper	0.58%		
Chromium	0.03%		
Titanium	trace		

METAL FOR CASTING

As for Ford No. 4 with suitable additions.

HEAT TREATMENT

As for Ford No.7A but requiring only half the annealing time.

the original B.T.S.1 and B.T.S.2, i.e. a water-quenched carbon manganese molybdenum steel containing .40 - .50% carbon, which it is sometimes felt should more properly be termed B.T.S.1. The matter is now of minor importance in view of the tendency to replace this material by B.T.S.3, which appears to have equally good properties while requiring no molybdenum.

Meanwhile the Americans had produced a substantial tonnage of links in Ford No. 4, which met with considerable success, and as a result of this, coupled with a shortage of molybdenum, certain British foundries changed over from B.T.S.1 to a steel similar to Ford No. 4 which became known as B.T.S.3 (see Table 5.7g).

TABLE 5.7g. BRITISH TRACK STEEL NO. 3 (B.T.S.3)
(Vauxhall Specification)

ANALYSIS		MECHANICAL PROPERTIES	
Carbon	0.43 - 0.56%	Ultimate Tensile	48 (45-53) tons/sq.in.
Silicon	0.15 - 0.50%	Yield	34 (28-40) " "
Manganese	0.65 - 0.95%	Elongation	16 (9-21) %
Sulphur	0.06%	Brinell	227 (205-255)
Phosphorus	0.06%	Izod	14 (9 - 23)

METAL FOR CASTING.

Any preferred process may be used, for example as described for Ford No. 4.

HEAT TREATMENT.

The castings are normalised at 900 to 940°C, air-cooled, reheated to 820°C, water-quenched and tempered at 630°C.

As compared with 12% Manganese steel, B.T.S.3. has the advantage of saving imported manganese, avoiding the need for providing melting furnaces with basic linings, and being easier to cast. It is therefore regarded as a useful substitute for manganese steel although not quite equal to it in performance.

There has also been some thrust and parry over the composition of B.T.S.3. Possibly from fear of poor wearing qualities with a lower percentage of carbon, the original Vauxhall specification for B.T.S.3, specified a carbon content of .43 - .56%, which was appreciably higher than that of the original Ford No. 4, developed at Detroit, for which the limits were .38 - .45%. The Ford Motor Co. at Dagenham doubted the advisability of departing without good reason from the analysis established by long experience, but suggested that the analysis ought to be suited to the shape of the particular casting, taking into account its effect on the access of the quenching water to various parts of it. Accordingly for the Churchill box section link a special composition was suggested by Messrs. Ford and embodied in Messrs. Vauxhall's final specification known as B.T.S.3F. In this the carbon limits are .40 - .47% (see Table 5.4a). Production of this link in this material ceased in 1944 since when all heavy tracks and even some carrier links have been produced in manganese steel.

5.8 German Track Materials.

As indicated in Sections 4.10 and 4.19 early German tracks appear to have followed closely, both in form and material, the manganese steel skeleton track of the Light Dragon Mk.1 or Vickers 2 ton tractor. Until recently all German tank tracks have been of manganese steel, but the latest captured tracks of the Royal Tiger are of a carbon steel. Whether this material is preferred or is the result of shortage of supplies it is at present impossible to say.

5.9 AN EXAMPLE OF THE MANUFACTURE OF MANGANESE STEEL TRACK LINKS. PREPARING THE MOULDS.

We will now describe as an example the procedure employed in one particular foundry manufacturing manganese steel track links for Cromwell and Comet tanks.

The foundry in question is completely mechanised and makes use of a number of conveyors of which the chief circuits are those for the moulding boxes, the moulding sand and the cores. The general layout is indicated in Figure 5.9a.

The core sand is fed by conveyors to core blowers, which blow the sand into the appropriately shaped cavities in the core boxes. Usually one or more wires are inserted in the core box to remain in the core as a strengthening skeleton, but it simplifies matters if this can be avoided, although in this case it is more than ever important that the cores should be supported and prevented from sagging until they have been baked. Thus each core is carried to and through the oven on a support resembling half a core box. After blowing the core, one half of the core box is removed, the support substituted, the core inverted and the other half of the core box removed. The cores on their supports then travel along on a conveyor that takes them to a tall vertical oven in which they rise to the hot upper part and then gradually descend, and emerge at the bottom hardened by the baking.

The moulding sand on arrival is dried so that its moisture content can be controlled by adding to it a known quantity of water (about 3 per cent.) It is mixed with "Full-bond", a synthetic clay, and milled for about five minutes to increase its bond strength to a figure of about 7 to 8 lbs. per square inch (as measured in a compression test).

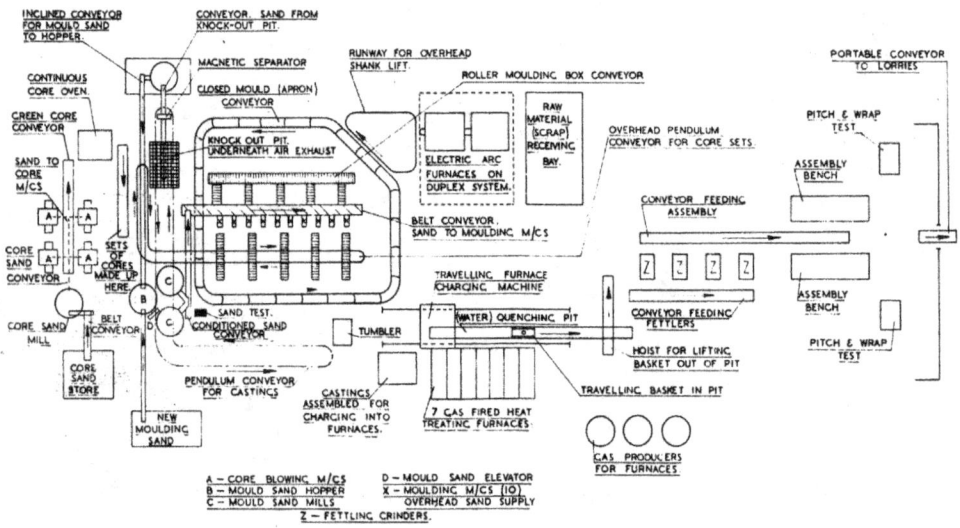

FIG. 5.9a.
FOUNDRY LAYOUT.

5.9

The prepared moulding sand is fed by a belt conveyor to a line of moulding machines. These are supplied with empty moulding boxes by roller conveyors and operate in pairs. Each machine uses a plate pattern representing the upper or lower halves of two links, the complete mould being prepared by two neighbouring machines, one doing the top halves and the other doing the bottom halves. (Figure 5.9b & c). The moulding box is placed on the pattern plate on the moulding machine, filled with sand from a hopper and jolted and rammed by the machine. The machine then withdraws the pattern, while vibrating it to make it come away easily, and the mould is placed on one of a series of roller conveyors for filled moulds. An overhead pendulum conveyor crosses these roller conveyors and brings sets of cores which are placed in position in the appropriate half of the mould. The two halves of the mould are then assembled and clamped together on the main apron conveyor which carries the completed mould round to the point where pouring occurs. (Fig. 5.9d.) shows the assembly of the two halves of the mould for another type of link, with the cores in position).

FIG. 5.9b.
MOULDING MACHINE WITH PLATE
PATTERN FOR UPPER HALVES OF TWO LINKS.

FIG. 5.9c.
MOULDING MACHINE WITH PLATE

FIG. 5.9d. CLOSING THE MOULD ON THE MAIN APRON CONVEYOR.

5.10 <u>MELTING THE METAL.</u>

The metal is melted in a pair of electric arc furnaces working on the duplex or tandem system. A load of some 4 tons of mild steel scrap is loaded into a charging bucket the bottom of which consists of hinged petals held closed by means of a rope. The top of the first arc furnace is lifted and swung aside and the charging bucket is lowered into the furnace by a crane. (see Figure 5.10a). After a minute or so the rope burns, the petals unfold and the charge is deposited in the furnace.

FIG. 5.10a.
CHARGING THE MELTING ARC FURNACE.

FIG. 5.10b.
POURING A CHARGE FROM THE MELTING FURNACE
TO THE HOLDING FURNACE.

The top is then swung and lowered into position, the electrodes descend and with a loud crackling the arc starts up. With a current of 15,000 amperes at 155 volts the charge takes about three quarters of an hour to melt. During this period an oxidising slag is maintained by the addition of about 1 cwt. of iron ore which oxidizes impurities such as phosphorus, carbon, manganese and silicon and results in a bath of dead mild steel. This oxidizing slag and the impurities it collects are then raked off and the bath is "killed" by an addition of silicon which removes oxides in the form of SiO_2 and gives the steel a small content of about .7 per cent silicon. A reducing slag is now put on by shovelling in lime, fluorspar, and anthracite, when free calcium carbide is formed thus ensuring a reducing atmosphere to keep the metal free from oxides and prevent alloys subsequently added from being oxidised. The stage is now set for the addition of manganese, and $14\frac{1}{2}$ cwt. of ferro-manganese (containing about 78% manganese and 6.7% carbon) is shovelled in. Under the reducing conditions prevailing in the furnace the composition remains unchanged and after a short period for refining the metal is ready for use. The slagging off, the charging of ferro-manganese and the refining together occupy perhaps half an hour during which time a lower voltage tapping is employed giving perhaps 2,000 to 3,000 amperes at 98 volts which suffices to keep the charge molten. The total period for preparing a charge of molten metal is therefore about $1\frac{1}{4}$ hours.

The use of the conveyor system of casting makes it impossible to wait $1\frac{1}{4}$ hours, or even half an hour, for supplies of molten metal, and a continuous supply must be provided so that ladles can be recharged every few minutes. Accordingly, a second arc furnace is provided the function of which is simply to hold a supply of molten metal and keep it hot. This furnace has a capacity of 9 tons, about double that of the melting furnace, and it only takes a steady load of some 250 to 300 kilowatts to maintain the temperature of the steel. As soon as a charge of molten metal is ready in the melting furnace it is poured through a trough known as a launder, into the holding furnace (as shown in Figure 5.10b.).

FIG. 5.11a.
POURING THE MOULDS.

5.11. CASTING THE MANGANESE STEEL LINKS.

The ladles for pouring the moulds are suspended from trolleys which run on an endless rail or overhead girder so that they can be brought to the outlet from the holding furnace and filled up, and then moved round alongside the apron conveyor carrying the closed moulds, into which the metal is poured (as shown in Figure 5.11a.).

The moulds are carried a short distance on the apron conveyor to allow the casting to solidify and when they come alongside a knock-out pit the sand is knocked out and falls through a grating on to a conveyor by which it is returned for re-use after passing a magnetic separator. The moulding box is put on to a roller conveyor for return to the moulding machine and the casting is hooked on to a pendulum conveyor. The pendulum conveyor takes the casting on a longish journey to give it an opportunity of cooling and finally brings it to a point (Figure 5.11b.) at which it is removed from the conveyor and rough dressed. This consists of knocking with a hammer to separate the two links which are made in a single casting, from each other, and from the runner.

FIG. 5.11b.
ROUGH DRESSING.

5.12. HEAT TREATMENT OF MANGANESE STEEL LINKS.

The castings are then assembled on a table so that they can be picked up by a charging machine and deposited in gas fired, heat-treating furnaces. The table has on it a number of longitudinal girders and the track links are arranged to bridge across the spaces between the girders. The charging machine has a pair of long arms which can be extended into the space between the girders and then lifted so as to pick up the track links. These arms are then retracted and the charging machine is traversed along so as to come in front of a vacant furnace, (see Figure 5.12a.) the arms are advanced into the furnace and lowered.

FIG. 5.12a.
HEAT TREATMENT FURNACES AND CHARGING MACHINE.

FIG. 5.12b.
REMOVING LINKS FROM HEAT TREATMENT FURNACE

The furnace has in it,, low walls of brickwork corresponding exactly with the girders on the assembly table, so that the tracks bridge across these walls and can be left on them by lowering and withdrawing the arms of the charging machine (See Figure 5.12b.) and can subsequently be removed in a similar manner. The heat treatment cycle lasts altogether about $2\frac{1}{2}$ hours, of which one hour is spent in heating the links up to 1,050°C, and the remaining $1\frac{1}{2}$ hours ensures thorough "soaking" (heating right through) to give an opportunity for the carbides to enter into solid solution resulting in an austenitic structure. In order to maintain this structure the links are quenched in water, the temperature of which should not be allowed to rise above about 40°C.

For this purpose a quenching pit or trough of water about 10 ft. deep extends along the fronts of the heat treating furnaces between them and the charging machine, and at the bottom of the pit in the water is a travelling trolley which can be moved along by means of a cable so as to be brought in front of any particular furnace. The trolley carries a large square basket about as high as the water is deep to catch the links when they are dropped into the water. When the heat treatment is complete in a particular furnace the trolley and the charging machine are projected into the furnace, raised, and withdrawn carrying the links, and a ram on the charging machine scrapes off all the links so that they drop into the water and sink down into the bottom of the basket. The trolley is then moved along to the end of the pit where it comes under a hoist by which the basket is lifted out of the water to enable the links to be removed. The links are then drifted, which consists of knocking them with a hammer to remove the scale from the pin holes, which latter are then tested for diameter with go and not-go gauges to a tolerance of three thousandths of an inch. They are then subjected to rumbling, grinding and further rumbling, the rumbling consisting of placing the links together in a rotating drum so that they knock against one another and remove sharp corners and edges. The links are then assembled into wraps consisting of twelve links each and subjected to a wrap test (see section 14.14.) for which the tolerance on the complete wrap is a length of .2 inches.

Each wrap is then curled round into a rose or cheese and the pins are rivetted (cold) by pneumatic rivetting hammers.

In addition to the tests referred to, and inspection at various other points, the links are subjected daily to a test for line in which a wrap is hung up by one end and the lengths of the two sides must not differ by more than one quarter of an inch. In addition a bend test is done on a sample of each batch of steel, the sample consisting of a bar $\frac{1}{2}"$ x $\frac{3}{4}"$ which must be capable of bending 150° round a 1" diameter bar without cracking.

5.13. SOME OTHER MATERIALS AND PROCESSES.

The above is typical of the sort of procedure employed in casting tracks although obviously different foundries differ in more or less important details too numerous to describe. For example in one track foundry manganese steel is prepared by melting steel scrap and pig iron in a cupola, reducing this to low carbon steel in a converter, melting ferro-manganese in another (small) cupola, and mixing the two in a ladle. In this case the heat treatment is carried out in rotary gas-fired furnaces.

PART II

CHAPTER 11

THEORETICAL AND CONTROVERSIAL SUBJECTS

11.1. INTRODUCTORY - INCOMPLETENESS OF EXISTING THEORY

In the preceding chapters an attempt has been made to outline the history of tracks and the present practice regarding their design and manufacture without including matters which are purely theoretical and likely to be controversial.

In the chapters which follow an attempt is made to lay a theoretical basis for a number of aspects of track design as such theory appears hitherto to have been either completely lacking or not readily accessible. In normal times such an undertaking would occupy a long period and one would hesitate to put forward conclusions based upon theory without having first checked them to a greater or less extent by experiment. Under present conditions it seems desirable not to delay the issue of the present book in this way for the reasons given in the introduction, but it is thought worth repeating that the following chapters are put forward with the full realisation that as further work is done and further information collected and conclusions based on calculation are compared with actual experience, considerable modification may be necessary.

11.2. REQUIREMENTS FOR MODERN TRACKS.

Chapters 2 and 3 have indicated in outline the functions a track has to perform and the possible shapes of the various parts of the link necessary for performing these functions.

Before examining in detail the design features of these various parts it will be desirable to discuss the requirements which a modern track is expected to fulfil.

It is suggested that a modern tank track should fulfil the following requirements.

1. Ease of manufacture.
2. Sufficient strength to avoid fracture and ensure reliability and satisfactory functioning.
3. Long life.
4. Obstacle crossing performance to the standard specified.
5. Adequate support and adhesion under the widest possible range of conditions.
6. Low rolling resistance.
7. Comparative silence.
8. Detail points, ease of replacement by crew, invulnerability, mud and wire clearing.

It is not suggested that the above requirements are necessarily in order of importance.

11.3. EASE OF MANUFACTURE

It is a moot point to what extent ease of manufacture should be allowed to interfere with the choice of the best design from the point of view of performance. Obviously the goal to aim at is a combination of ease of manufacture with technical excellence but in many cases some compromise may be unavoidable.

11.4.

There is no doubt that at the beginning of the present war track links manufactured by stamping were regarded as superior to M.C.I. links. To what extent subsequent improvements and the change of material have developed the cast link until it is equal to or better than the stamped link it is difficult to say since development of the stamped link has not been continued.

Other examples could no doubt be cited in which an alternative, probably second best from the point of view of performance, has been adopted, and rightly so, in the interests of obtaining adequate quantity production. The test of the design is not the performance of a few pilot links but the performance of hundreds of thousands of production links, and an adequate pilot followed by 100% sound castings may be preferable to a superlative pilot followed by a high proportion of faulty castings. Faulty material and faulty castings can to some extent be eliminated by careful inspection, testing and supervision of manufacture to secure uniformity, but in addition the design of the link will have a considerable bearing on the extent to which it is possible to produce 100% sound castings, and it may be well worth while to accept some sacrifice in other directions in order to avoid a greater sacrifice due to faulty links being supplied with consequent loss of reliability.

For example, the shape of a cast link must be carefully designed for ease of casting so as to prevent uneven cooling and the stresses resulting from it, and also to ensure the flow of sound metal to fill every part of the cavity in the mould.

Two points in the carrier link may be mentioned. The material of the lugs was thinner in the middle than at the edges and this thin section was a source of trouble. Subsequent links have lugs of equal thickness all along. Secondly the part-cylindrical recesses between the lugs terminated in a sharp edge and cracks tended to start in this edge. In later links a rib runs along this edge giving a certain thickness of material with a rounded edge which has cured the trouble. Manufacturers could no doubt cite many similar cases where a change of design, whether great or small, has added to ease of manufacture and reliability.

11.4. STRENGTH AND RELIABILITY

The design of track links as regards strength is rendered difficult firstly because the loads to which they are liable to be subjected are extremely difficult to predict, and secondly because even if the load were known, the distribution of stresses in such a complicated shape would be almost impossible to assess accurately.

The first and most obvious type of loading is pure tension. This has in the past been assessed on a basis depending on the tractive effort of which the engine is capable, with a safety factor of something like 7 to 10. In Chapter 12 an attempt is made to indicate how a somewhat closer estimate can be arrived at of what the track tension is likely to be.

It is not easy to say what bending stresses a track pin is likely to have to sustain but Messrs. Rolls Royce have investigated this on a theoretical basis and the matter is discussed in Chapter 13.

As regards lug stresses produced by a given tension opinions differ as to the correct basis to adopt. This question is also discussed in Chapter 13.

Other loads than pure tension include sideways bending, twisting and transverse bending due to uneven ground. All these must be considered in the design.

Last but by no means least considerable fatigue loading may be introduced by hammering and vibration, due either to passage over rocky ground or to the inherent properties of the track itself.

In particular as discussed at the end of Chapter 15 a high alternating tension may be produced by the fact that the sprocket tends to move the track in a series of jerks and not smoothly at a uniform speed.

11.5. LONG LIFE.

The life needed by different parts of a track is largely a question of keeping in step with each other and with other components. If the track can just about be relied on to last for the normal period between major overhauls dictated by other components of the vehicle, and if then the various wearing parts of the track are all more or less worn out, the track can be replaced by a new one without shedding a tear, and there would be relatively little advantage in a slight addition to its life. As a pair of tracks may weigh anything up to 5 or 6 tons it is obviously desirable to make them last as long as possible, but the urgent and essential problem is to ensure that they do not wear out before the tank would in any case require major overhaul for other reasons. At the present time life mileages are of the order of 2000 miles although naturally this figure is liable to wide variation.

Reference has already been made to the attempts made to increase track life by making certain parts replaceable (involving heavy maintenance) and by sealing the pins to keep out mud and keep in lubricant, and the fact that they have now fallen into the background. Consequently the quest for long life has mainly been a search for materials which would suffer the minimum of wear.

The limit of life of a few early designs was set by wear of the spuds or sole plate which wore down after a certain amount of road running. It is however a comparatively simple matter to thicken up these parts and consequently the limit of life of modern tracks is set by pin hole wear resulting in such increase of pitch that the track will not satisfactorily mesh with the sprocket, as discussed in Chapter 14. In addition to choice and treatment of materials it seems possible that there may be scope for reducing pin hole wear by design of lugs so as to distribute the pressure as uniformly as possible.

11.6. OBSTACLE CROSSING PERFORMANCE.

The obstacle crossing performance must be up to the standard specified, which is not necessarily the highest possible standard. In fact the step climbing performance of most modern tanks falls considerably short of that of the last war heavy tanks.

But whatever the figure specified the track must be up to it. As mentioned in Section 2.10 this involves (among other things) the length of the tank and the height and therefore the diameter of the sprocket and idler which are linked up with the general design of the machine and also have a bearing on track wear and allied problems. Then again the obstacle crossing performance will affect and be affected by track tension as discussed in Section 12.17, the connection depending on whether there are any wheels between the front road wheel and the front sprocket or idler.

11.7. ADEQUATE SUPPORT & ADHESION UNDER THE WIDEST POSSIBLE RANGE OF CONDITIONS.

Modern tank tracks must be universal in application. This means not only that a track must be capable of functioning on roads and soft ground without alteration or the fitting of spuds or grousers but also that the same track must be of use in all parts of the world and in all climates hot and cold.

The present war illustrates how the same tank may have to operate in conditions including the Russian winter, tropical heat, desert sand and European mud.

In some cases it may be possible to adapt a track or even provide alternative tracks for different conditions (e.g. the Pz.Kpfw.III and IV. track is made to take wedges for snow, while the Pz.Kpfw. VI. has a wide and a narrow track) but problems of supplies and spares are enormously eased if this can be avoided altogether.

Suitability for both roads and soft ground involves a compromise for as indicated in Chapter 13 the best arrangement for soft ground is believed to be a thin sharp spud which digs into the ground easily and does not take the weight off the neighbouring flat surface. Such an arrangement is used on commercial tractors but on a tank would be unsuitable for road use as on roads it would make steering difficult and do too much damage. Accordingly a compromise is adopted somewhere between the sharp spudded shoe and the flat shoe, namely a shoe with a spud of considerable thickness, say perhaps a third of the pitch of the track.

These questions are intimately bound up with the properties of the soil upon which the tank is operating. In view of what has been said it is useless to base design on a detailed study of the individual properties of one specific type of soil. On the other hand it is of the greatest importance to study the properties of typical classes of soil in order to have some idea how one track will compare with another on average soils of various types and under various different weather conditions. The question of support is obviously bound up with an examination of actual ground pressure, and whilst the mean ground pressure of the whole area of track in contact with the ground may not be entirely useless as a starting point for certain considerations of design, it is clearly not good enough for any detailed examination of the supporting power of various types and states of ground for various designs of track and suspension. This matter is examined in greater detail in Chapter 25.

The question of adhesion also clearly involves a knowledge of soil properties and in particular their resistance to failure in shear. Some factors governing the choice of depth, width and distribution of spuds are discussed in Chapter 23.

11.8. LOW ROLLING RESISTANCE

The question of rolling resistance, more particularly on soft ground, is one that appears never to have been really investigated. It is hardly necessary to emphasize the extreme importance of this question since it must be clear that on soft ground a large part of the power developed by the engine is devoted simply to squashing down the ground which may absorb hundreds of horse power. Clearly if the power wasted in this way could be reduced, the speed and range of the tank would immediately be increased without any alteration to the engine or transmission, or alternatively it would be possible to obtain the same speed and range with a smaller engine, more compact transmission and less fuel.

The factors which affect rolling resistance on hard ground, such as tyre losses, joint friction, hammering and scrub are discussed in Chapter 15, while the loss due to squashing of the soil is examined in Chapter 25.

11.9. SILENCE

From a tactical point of view silence is clearly desirable and it is obviously useless to silence the engine to a high degree if the noise made by the tracks on roads represents a major proportion of the total noise. Existing knowledge does not enable us to make any quantitative estimate of the influence of various factors on the noise but it is possible to calculate such things as the velocity with which, subject to given assumptions, the spud of a given track will strike the surface of a road when travelling at a given speed, and so obtain some idea of the probable trend of the influence that various factors are likely to exert. These questions are examined in Chapter 15 in connection with the rolling resistance due to hammering.

11.10. DETAIL POINTS.

(a) Ease of replacement of links or whole track.

In the normal life of a track half a dozen or more links may have to be removed to adjust the length as the pitch increases due to wear. In addition links may get damaged by enemy action or natural causes and hence it is essential that the job of removing or replacing links or changing a track should be within the capacity of the crew with the tools available.

(b) Invulnerability.

The standard of vulnerability tolerated is liable to vary and it is generally accepted that the tracks of a tank cannot be expected to withstand the same attack as its armour. On the other hand the more they can resist the better and resistance to 20 mm. attack is generally expected to-day.

(c) Mud clearing.

In sticky ground mud may pack between the track and sprocket or idler and break the track or some part of the suspension such as the idler supports. In general this is said to be less likely to happen with a centre guide horn (1) which allows the mud to be squeezed or pushed off the sides of the wheelpaths. The increased tension produced will depend on factors such as the softness of the suspension as discussed in Chapter 12.

(d) Wire clearing.

Certain tracks have in the past been provided with special wire guards to prevent wire from getting tangled in the hinges, but in recent designs the link has a smoothly tapered side and the hinge is designed to avoid any crevices in which wire would readily get caught.

---

(1) *But it is stated that the Russians find Valentine performs well in mud.*

CHAPTER 12.

TRACK TENSION, AND TRACK SLACK.

12,1. INTRODUCTORY

An examination of track tension is a suitable prelude to any discussion of the strength of tracks since the simple chain tension is the most obvious load on a track link and a certain amount of information regarding it can be fairly simply established.

Fundamentally there is no reason why a track need necessarily have any tension in it at all, and in fact in rigid girder tracks applied to trailers there is often no tension at all, (1) but normally various factors produce tension which differs at different times and at different parts of the track. Perhaps the most obvious of these factors is tractive effort, which can only be transmitted by producing tension in certain parts of a driven track. There is a prevalent but quite incorrect idea that the maximum tension in a track is equal to the maximum tractive effort transmitted by the track. Actually, of course, the tractive effort is equal to the difference between the tension on the taut and slack sides of the sprocket, so that the maximum tension is equal to the tractive effort added to a sort of basic minimum tension which exists throughout the track and is independent of the tractive effort, whether the latter is limited by stalling of the engine or by slipping of the track.

Just as the tension in a belt depends on the length of the belt in relation to the size and compressibility of the person wearing it, so this basic minimum tension depends on the length of the track in relation to the perimeter of the contour it has to encompass as it passes round the sprocket, idler and road wheels and perhaps over obstacles or uneven ground, and how much this perimeter shortens as the tension rises.

An ordinary pin-jointed track is of course incapable of stretching more than a very small amount (2) so that if this contour were completely rigid any increase in its perimeter, as when crossing an obstacle or due to mud packing, could only occur by producing a very high tension and breaking the track. Actually as the perimeter increases at one point the resulting tension can cause it to shorten at another point. The tension produced in any particular circumstances consequently depends on how easily the demand for an extra length of track at one part can be met by a length of track made available from another part.

We shall use the term "slack" (for want of a better) to mean any extra length of track that can be made available in one way or another. Clearly track tension and track slack are interdependent, the tension being governed by the laws of supply and demand for track slack.

There are a number of factors which may take up slack and tend to increase tension, or give out slack and tend to decrease tension, either as a result of change of tension or as a result of external causes such as passage over uneven ground.

---

(1) *And a recent form of Rigid Girder track works in compression, See Roadless News, July – August 1944.*

(2) *In the case of a rubber bushed track the stretch may be appreciable, for example 4" on a complete track or nearly 1% for 10,000 lbs. tension.*

12.2

In the first place with most tank tracks certain parts of the top run of the track hang freely between various supports such as return wheels or sprockets and idlers or the tops of road wheels, and this of itself takes up any available slack and produces a certain amount of tension in the track. So before the track begins to perform any function at all it has in it a certain initial tension dependent on the distance between the points of support, the amount the track sags between these points, and the weight of the track per unit length. In these freely suspended spans of track the length of track determines the depth of sag and the depth of sag determines the tension, and conversely the tension determines the amount of slack that can be taken up or made available.

Round the front and rear road wheels the tension will tend to lift the road wheels and as the tank sinks on its springs this will release a certain length of track. Normal movement of suspension when travelling along will alternately demand and release a length of track and if no slack is available rebound will be restricted.

Passage over an obstacle will produce track tension which will depend on the available slack and would theoretically be infinite if there were no slack available. Mud packing or jamming of stones or gravel round the sprocket will demand an extra length of track and the slack that can be made available by the top run or by the suspension will determine the tension produced.

12.2. RELATION OF TENSION TO SHAPE OF A FLEXIBLE BAND FOR VARIOUS FORMS OF LOADING.

The amount of sag and slack in the top run can be varied by the track adjusting mechanism and actually in the instructions for adjustment for most tanks the correct setting is given not in terms of a particular tension in pounds but in terms of a certain depth of sag, which can, of course be far more readily measured. For example, in the case of the Cromwell series the instruction is that the track should just touch the middle three wheels but not the first and fifth wheels. Mathematically it is a relatively simple matter to work out the tension and the length of track corresponding to a given depth of sag. Similarly the relation between tension and slack can be worked out for various other forms of loading such, for example, as that due to crossing an obstacle. As a first step it is convenient to consider in general how the shape assumed by a flexible band such as a chain or track is related to the tension in it for a number of different forms of the loading applied to it.

12.3. TWO STRAIGHT LINES: POINT LOADING

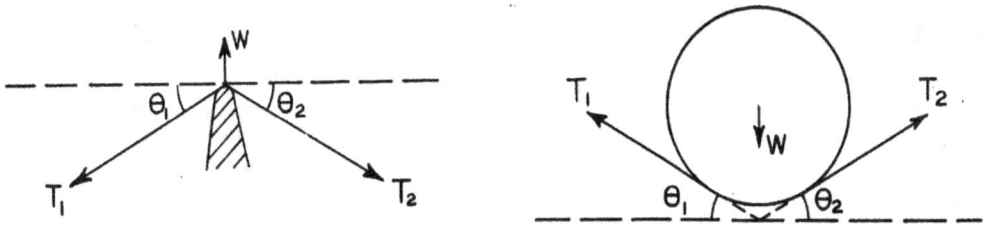

FIG. 12.3a   FIG. 12.3b

Where a given total load is applied to the band at a point or within a certain region the parts of the band outside that region are a pair of straight lines whose inclinations determine the relation between load and tension.

If the load W is vertical and the two parts of the band have tensions T_1 and T_2 and inclinations θ_1 and θ_2 we can resolve the forces horizontally and vertically and get

$$T_1 \cos \theta_1 = T_2 \cos \theta_2 \quad \ldots \ldots \ldots \ldots (i)$$
$$W = T_1 \sin \theta_1 + T_2 \sin \theta_2 \quad \ldots \ldots \ldots (ii)$$

This applies to a length of track passing round a wheel, for example a road wheel suspended and prevented by the track from sinking into a trench. Where the wheel is free to rotate or for any other reason $T_1 = T_2 = T$ the first equation shows that $\theta_1 = \theta_2 = \theta$ and hence

$$W = 2 T \sin \theta$$

12.4. CIRCULAR ARC: RADIAL LOADING UNIFORM ALONG CURVE E.G. CENTRIFUGAL FORCE

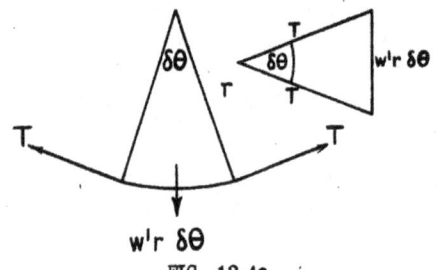

FIG. 12.4a.

If the total loading is w^1 per unit length directed at right angles to the length of the band the relation between loading and tension is, from a triangle of forces:-

$$2T \cdot \frac{\delta\theta}{2} = w^1 r \delta\theta \text{ or } T = w^1 r \quad \ldots \ldots (i)$$

where r is the radius of curvature. This is true of a small element of the band whether the loading is uniform or not. If the loading is uniform (i.e. w^1 is a constant) then r is also a constant and the form taken by the band is a circular arc. One example of this form of loading is a track acted on by ground pressure of constant bearing capacity as discussed in Section 25.4.

Another instance is the centrifugal action of, for example, a track passing round a sprocket. In this case we must write $\frac{wv^2}{gr}$ in place of w^1 for the load per unit length, and

$$T = \frac{wv^2 r}{gr} = \frac{wv^2}{g} \quad \ldots \ldots \ldots \ldots \ldots \ldots \ldots (ii)$$

where w is the weight per unit length and v the linear velocity relative to the centre of rotation (the velocity of the latter being constant).

It is of interest to note that the tension due to centrifugal force does not depend on the radius or on the angle through which the track is turned. This may at first seem surprising, but it will be realised that if the bend is sharp, the centrifugal force will be large, but the tension occasioned by it will be proportionally smaller, whereas if the track is only slightly curved, the centrifugal force will be small, but it will enjoy a great mechanical advantage as regards producing tension in the track.

Table 4.24a. shows the weights per foot of various tracks which it will be seen vary from 25 lbs. per foot for a carrier to 156 lbs. for the Tiger. Thus, in the case of the Tiger, travelling at 15 m.p.h. the tension due to centrifugal force would be 2350 lbs. In the case of the Cromwell, $15\frac{1}{2}$" track, T.D. 9250 weighing 62.2 lbs. per ft. travelling at 40 m.p.h. the centrifugal tension would be about 6700 lbs. This does not necessarily mean that if the track is unduly slack it will tend to swing outwardly at any point where it takes a curve as when going round the idler or sprocket.

12.5.

Since $\frac{wv^2}{g}$ is constant throughout the track each part will be held in by neighbouring parts.

12.5. PARABOLA: VERTICAL LOADING UNIFORM ALONG HORIZONTAL

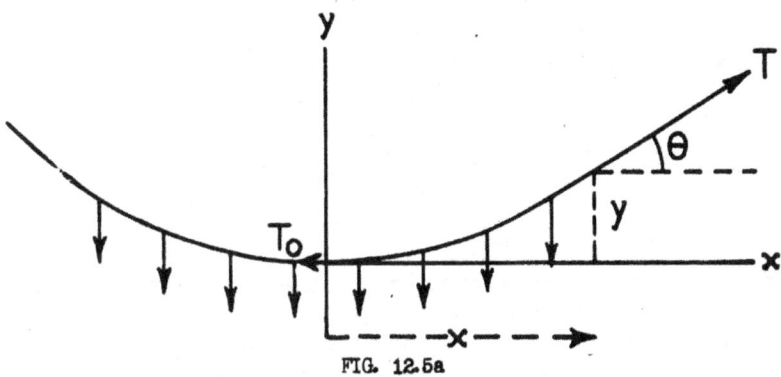

FIG. 12.5a

This case would arise in the case of a suspension bridge if the weight of the bridge suspended were uniform along the horizontal. It also forms a convenient approximation to the catenary (discussed in the next section) when the band is tightly stretched and is therefore itself practically horizontal.

Resolving horizontally and vertically:-

$$\left. \begin{array}{l} T \cos \theta = T_0 \\ T \sin \theta = wx \end{array} \right\} \therefore T^2 (\cos^2\theta + \sin^2\theta) = T^2 = T_0^2 + w^2 x^2 \quad \ldots \ldots (i)$$

Taking moments about the point (x,y) :-

$$T_0 y = \frac{wx^2}{2} \quad \ldots \ldots \ldots \ldots \ldots \ldots \ldots \ldots \ldots \ldots (ii)$$

which is the equation of a parabola.

If s is the length of the curve from the origin to the point (x,y)

$$\frac{ds}{dx} = \sqrt{1+\left(\frac{dy}{dx}\right)^2} = \sqrt{1+\frac{w^2 x^2}{T_0^2}}$$

$$\therefore \quad (1) \quad s = \int \sqrt{1+\left(\frac{wx}{T_0}\right)^2} \, dx$$

$$s = \frac{x}{2}\sqrt{\left(\frac{wx}{T_0}\right)^2 + 1} + \frac{T_0}{2w} \sinh^{-1} \frac{wx}{T_0} \quad \ldots \ldots \ldots (iii)$$

---

(1) For the integration of this type of expression see for example:-
Caunt, G.W. "Introduction to Infinitesimal Calculus" p. 258.

12.6. CATENARY: VERTICAL LOADING UNIFORM ALONG THE CURVE. LEVEL SPAN.

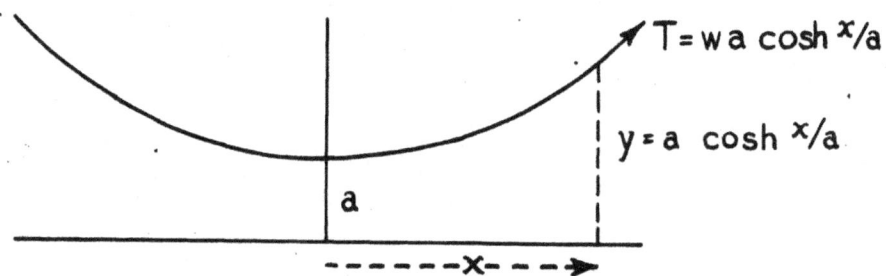

FIG. 12.6a

Finally we come to the case of a band subjected to vertical loading uniformly distributed along its own length, for example a uniform band hanging freely under the action of its own weight. The curve taken up is known as the catenary and its equation is of the form $y = a \cosh x/a$. [Those whose hyperbolic functions are rusty may like to be reminded that $\cosh x = \tfrac{1}{2}(e^x + e^{-x})$ while $\sinh x = \tfrac{1}{2}(e^x - e^{-x})$]

If a length S hangs between two points at the same level a distance l apart and the sag in the middle is h it can be shown (1) or is obvious that

$$\frac{h}{a} = \cosh \frac{l}{2a} - 1 \quad \ldots \ldots \ldots (i)$$

$$\frac{S}{2a} = \sinh \frac{l}{2a} \quad \ldots \ldots \ldots (ii)$$

$$T = wy = wa \cosh \frac{l}{2a} = \frac{wS}{2} \coth \frac{l}{2a} \quad \ldots \ldots (iii)$$

It will be seen that these equations involve an inconvenient constant a and it is believed that it is not possible to express the slack and the tension in terms of the sag in a simple mathematical form from which this constant is eliminated. (2). It is however, a simple matter to tabulate values of $\frac{l}{2a}$ and $\frac{S}{2a}$ ($= \sinh \frac{l}{2a}$) and by dividing one by the other to obtain corresponding values of $\frac{S}{l}$, that is to say, the length of the chain divided by the length of the straight line joining its ends. Values of $\frac{h}{a}(= \cosh \frac{l}{2a} - 1)$ can similarly be tabulated and divided by the corresponding values of $\frac{l}{a}$ giving values of $\frac{h}{l}$ that is to say, the depth of sag divided by the span of the chain. The values of $\frac{h}{l}$ can then be plotted against values of $\frac{S}{l}$ (or more conveniently $\frac{S-l}{l}$).

Similarly the values of $\frac{2T}{wl} = \left(\frac{\cosh l/2a}{l/2a}\right)$ can be tabulated and plotted against the values of $\frac{S}{l} - 1$

---

(1) See Caunt G.W. "Introduction to Infinitesimal Calculus" pp.191, 204 and 392 or
Lamb H, "Infinitesimal Calculus" pp.250 and 290.

(2) Since this was written J.Commdr. Knox has pointed out that :-
$$\frac{T}{w} = \frac{4.h^2 + S^2}{8.h}$$

This has been done in Figure 12.6b. which comprises two curves, one indicating the relative slack and the other indicating the relative tension corresponding to given relative depths of sag.

From these curves it is possible for any particular tank to ascertain what is the tension in the top run of the track and how much slack is available between any two return rollers for a given amount of sag in the span between them, for example when the amount of sag corresponds with the instructions given for track tension adjustment.

A point worth noting is that

$$T = wy \quad \ldots \ldots \ldots \ldots \ldots (i)$$

Hence the difference in tension between any two points of a span of chain is equal to their difference in level multiplied by the weight of the chain per unit length.

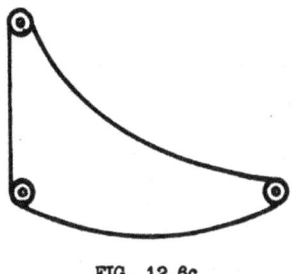

FIG. 12.6c.

Actually this is obvious without mathematics from consideration of a length of chain passing round smooth pulleys at the corners of a triangle - having a vertical side and a horizontal side, Figure 12.6c. The difference in tension between the top corner and one bottom corner must be the same as that between the top corner and the other bottom corner.

For example if a track weighs 5 lbs. per inch and one point is 10 inches higher than another the tension at the upper point will always be 50 lbs. greater than at the lower point regardless of the slope of the track or what the tensions actually are (of course assuming the track hangs freely between the two points.)

In practice the difference of level is hardly ever more than say 40 inches corresponding to a difference of tension of 200 lbs. which means that we can generally neglect differences in tension between different parts of a span of track.

12.7. TENSION AND SLACK IN INCLINED SPAN OF CATENARY.

We have assumed above that the two ends of the span of track considered are at the same level. We must now consider the case in which they are not.

Although the equation of the catenary is a simple one it is apparently impossible to express mathematically the relation between tension and slack in a chain hanging between two points at different levels. It is however possible, by tabulating values of various hyperbolic functions, to plot a curve relating the relative tension to the relative slack in a chain, for each of a number of inclinations of the line joining its ends.

The manner in which this has been done is outlined in 12.7.1. and the results are shown in the curves of Figure 12.7a. Logarithmic paper is used to cover a big range of values with a reasonably open scale.

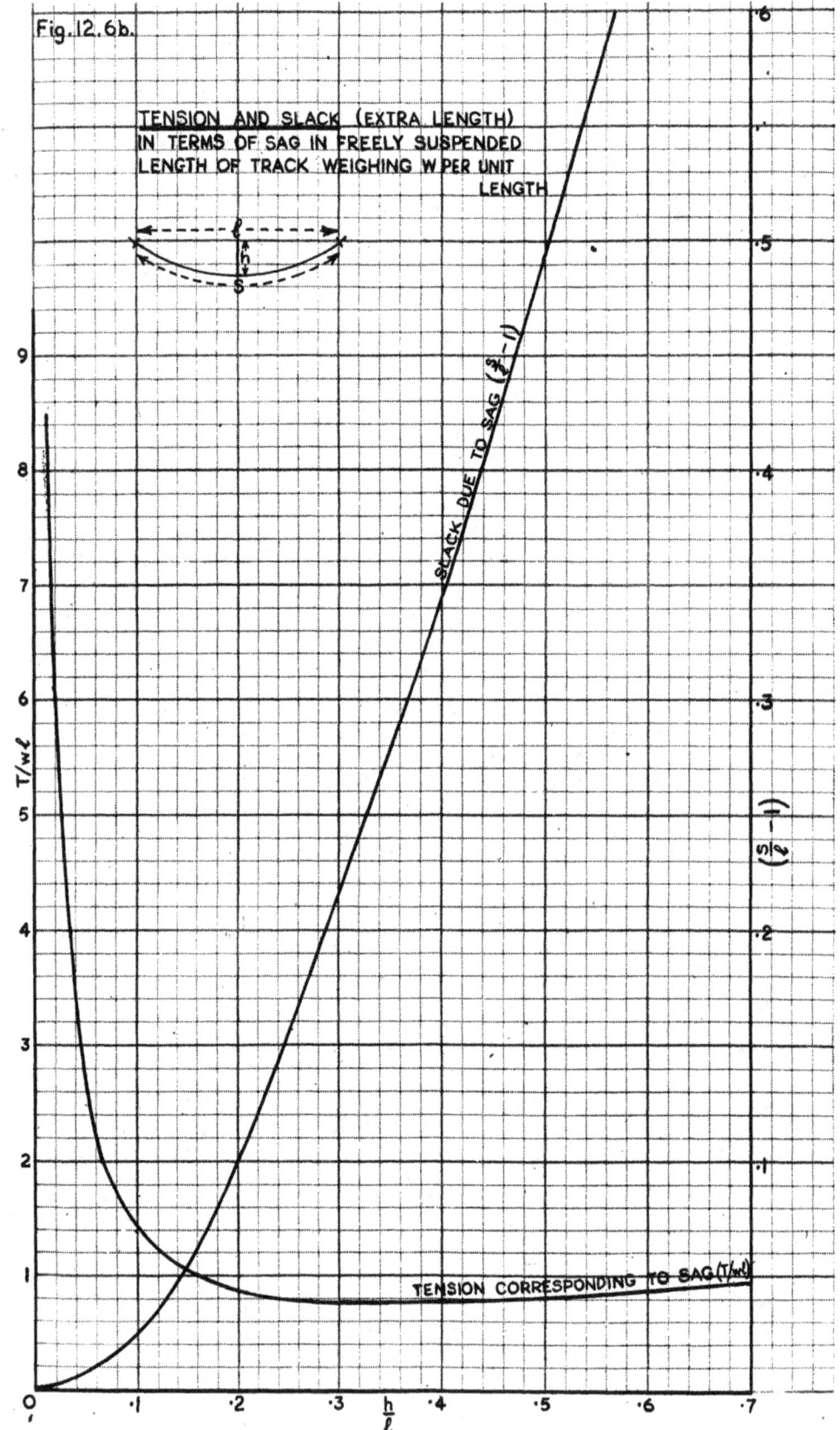

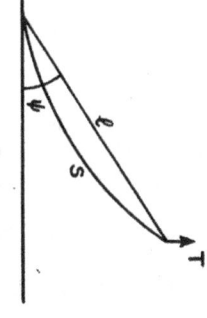

RELATION BETWEEN 'T' AND SLACK S−ℓ IN A PIECE OF CHAIN OF LENGTH 'S' AND WEIGHT 'W' PER UNIT LENGTH WHEN THE STRAIGHT LINE JOINING ITS ENDS IS OF LENGTH 'ℓ' AND IS INCLINED AT AN ANGLE ψ

Fig. 12.7a.

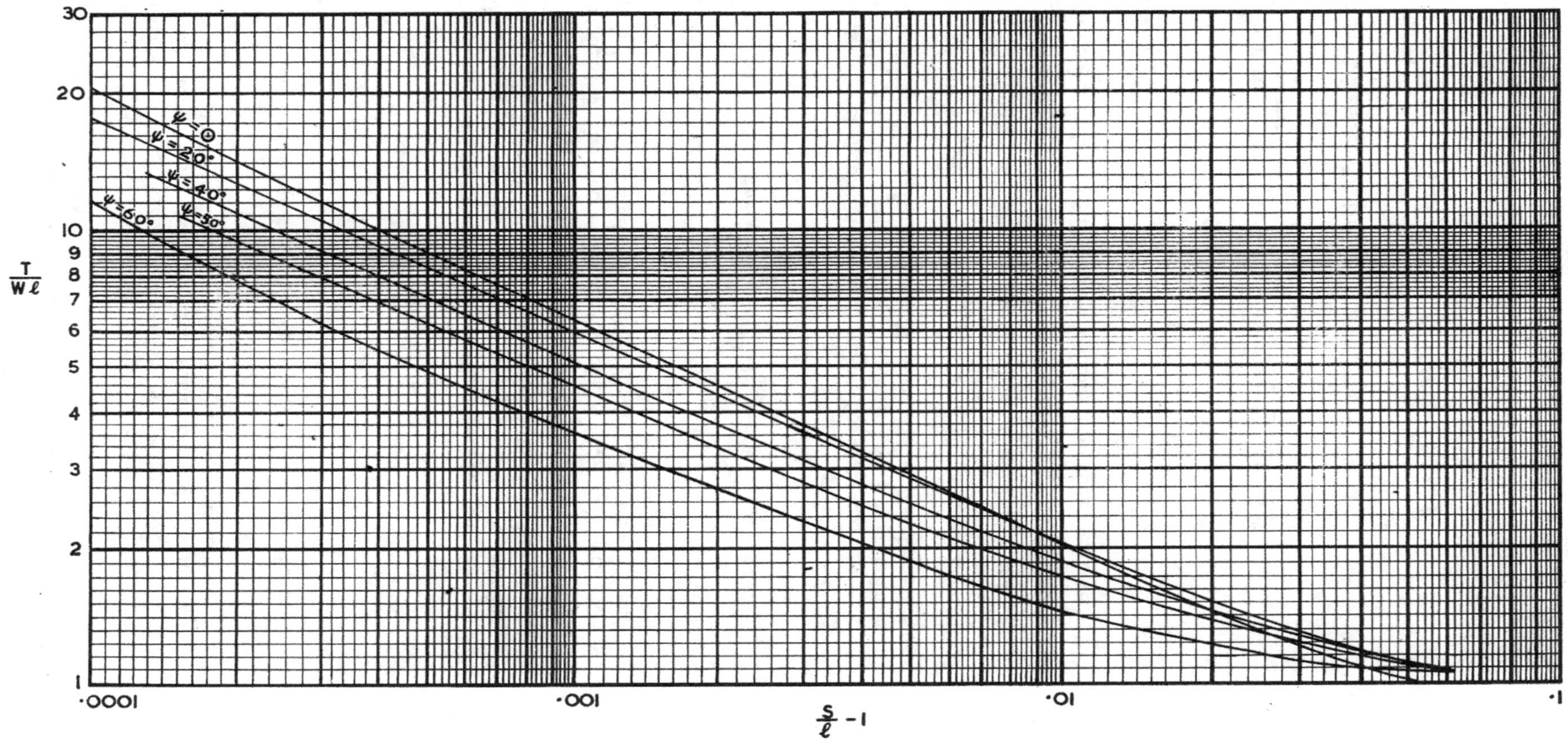

APPENDIX I

THE CATENARY (INCLINED SPAN)

In theory the mathematics of the catenary are quite simple, but in the practical case of a chain hanging between two points which are not at the same level there is no mathematical solution and any general relationships can only be expressed rather laboriously by tabulating figures and plotting curves.

If x and y are the co-ordinates of a catenary it can be shown that

$$y/a = \cosh x/a = T/wa \quad \ldots \ldots \ldots (i)$$

$$s/a = \sinh x/a \quad \ldots \ldots \ldots (ii)$$

where a is a constant for the catenary equal to the tension at the lowest point divided by w the weight per unit length, T is the tension at any point, and s is the length of chain from the lowest point to any other point.

If the line joining the two ends of the chain (x_1, y_1) and (x_2, y_2) is of length l and inclination ψ then $(y_2 - y_1) = l \sin \psi$ and $(x_2 - x_1) = l \cos \psi$

It is shown in Appendix 2. that

$$\left(\frac{s_2 - s_1}{a}\right)^2 = 2 \cosh(l/a \cos \psi) - 2 + (l/a)^2 \sin^2 \psi \quad 12.7.2. \ldots (i)$$

In other words if we choose a certain value for ψ (the inclination of the line joining the ends of the chain) we can tabulate values of $\frac{s_2 - s_1}{a}$, corresponding to various values of l/a and by dividing one by the other get values of $\frac{s_2 - s_1}{l}$ i.e. the actual length of chain divided by the length of the straight line joining its ends.

Now with regard to tension, we may choose the tension either at the upper or at the lower end. Suppose we choose the upper end we have

$$\frac{T_2}{wa} = \cosh \frac{x_2}{a}$$

So we need to find $\frac{x_2}{a}$ in terms of l/a or $\frac{s_2 - s_1}{a}$ or $\frac{s_2 - s_1}{l}$.

It is shown in Appendix 3. that

$$\coth\left(\frac{x_2 + x_1}{2a}\right) = \frac{s_2 - s_1}{l \sin \psi} \quad \ldots \ldots \ldots (12.7.3. (i))$$

Hence we can tabulate values of $\frac{x_2 + x_1}{2a}$, from which, knowing that $\frac{x_2 - x_1}{2a} = \frac{l}{2a} \cos \psi$ we can tabulate $\frac{x_2}{a}$ and hence $\cosh \frac{x_2}{a} = \frac{T_2}{wa}$
Dividing the last by l/a gives us $\frac{T_2}{wl}$

This has been done for values of $\psi = 0°$, $20°$, $40°$, $50°$, and $60°$, and the results are plotted at Figure 12.7a. To get a satisfactory range of values logarithmic paper is used.

APPENDIX 2.

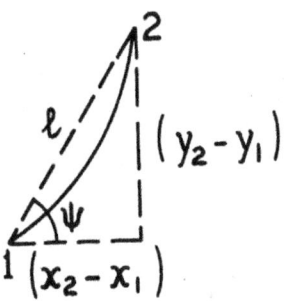

FIG. 12.7.2a

$$\cosh(l/a \cos\psi) = \cosh\frac{x_2 - x_1}{a}$$

$$= \cosh\frac{x_2}{a} \cosh\frac{x_1}{a} - \sinh\frac{x_2}{a} \sinh\frac{x_1}{a}$$

$$= \frac{y_2 y_1}{a^2} - \frac{s_2 s_1}{a^2} \quad \text{Since} \quad y/a = \cosh\frac{x}{a} \text{ and } \quad s/a = \sinh x/a$$

$$\therefore 2a^2 \cosh(l/a \cos\psi) = 2y_2 y_1 - 2s_2 s_1$$

Now since $\sinh^2 x - \cosh^2 x + 1 = 0$

$$s^2 - y^2 + a^2 = 0$$

and we can add this to the right hand side of the above equation without making any difference

$$\therefore 2a^2 \cosh(l/a \cos\psi)$$

$$= 2y_2 y_1 - 2s_2 s_1 + s_1^2 - y_1^2 + a^2 + s_2^2 - y_2^2 + a^2$$

$$= (s_2^2 - 2s_2 s_1 + s_1^2) - (y_2^2 - 2y_2 y_1 + y_1^2) + 2a^2$$

$$\therefore (s_2 - s_1)^2 = 2a^2 \cosh(l/a \cos\psi) + (l \sin\psi)^2 - 2a^2$$

(since $y_2 - y_1 = l \sin\psi$)

$$\therefore \left(\frac{s_2 - s_1}{a}\right)^2 = 2(\cosh(l/a \cos\psi) - 1) + (l/a)^2 \sin^2\psi \quad \ldots \ldots (i)$$

APPENDIX 3.

If $\dfrac{x_2}{a} = 2A$ and $\dfrac{x_1}{a} = 2B$

$$\dfrac{s_2-s_1}{l\,\sin\psi} = \dfrac{\sinh 2A - \sinh 2B}{\cosh 2A - \cosh 2B}$$

$$= \dfrac{\sinh[(A+B)+(A-B)] - \sinh[(A+B)-(A-B)]}{\cosh[(A+B)+(A-B)] - \cosh[(A+B)-(A-B)]}$$

$$= \dfrac{\sinh(A+B)\cosh(A-B) + \cosh(A+B)\sinh(A-B) - \sinh(A+B)\cosh(A-B) + \cosh(A+B)\sinh(A-B)}{\cosh(A+B)\cosh(A-B) + \sinh(A+B)\sinh(A-B) - \cosh(A+B)\cosh(A-B) + \sinh(A+B)\sinh(A-B)}$$

$$= \dfrac{2\cosh(A+B)\sinh(A-B)}{2\sinh(A+B)\sinh(A-B)}$$

$$= \coth(A+B) = \coth\left(\dfrac{x_2+x_1}{2a}\right)$$

For computation this may be put in logarithmic form thus

$$\dfrac{x_2+x_1}{2a} = \coth^{-1}\left(\dfrac{s_2-s_1}{l\,\sin\psi}\right) = \tfrac{1}{2}\log_e\left(\dfrac{s_2-s_1 + l\,\sin\psi}{s_2-s_1 - l\,\sin\psi}\right) \quad \ldots \ldots \text{(1)}$$

$$= \tfrac{1}{2}\log_e\left(\dfrac{\dfrac{s_2-s_1}{a} + \dfrac{l}{a}\sin\psi}{\dfrac{s_2-s_1}{a} - \dfrac{l}{a}\sin\psi}\right)$$

---

(1) See for example Plummer H.C. *Four figure tables with mathematical formulae.* p.59

12.8. TENSION AND SLACK IN TERMS OF SAG IN A SPAN OF THE TRACK.

As a particular example one may take the Cromwell track arrangement, and, given the instructions for track tension adjustment, estimate what will be the actual tension and what will be the amount of slack.

The instructions for track adjustment specify that the top run of track should just make contact with the three centre road wheels. The horizontal distance between the idler and the second road wheel or between the sprocket and the fourth road wheel is approximately 68" (which we shall regard as half the span) whilst the level of the top of each of these is approximately 4" above that of the road wheels. The 14" track (T.D.3945) (1) weighs 16 lbs. per linkage and has a pitch of some 4" so that its weight per inch length is 4 lbs. Hence in Figure 12.6b. we have $\frac{h}{l} = \frac{4}{2 \times 68}$ = approximately .03. Then, from the graph, $\frac{T}{wl}$ = approximately 4.5 whence $T = 4.5 \times 4 \times 2 \times 68 = 2448$ lbs. Hence the tension in the track is over a ton.

Using Figure 12.6b it is also possible to estimate how much slack there is in each span of the track. Thus, from the curve of slack if $\frac{h}{l} = .03$, $\frac{s}{l} - 1$ = approximately .001 whence $s - l = 2 \times 68 \times .002 = .27$". In addition there will be some slight slack between the second, third and fourth wheels. In this case the tension must be the same as before but the span in this case (designated l_2) is 40".

Hence $\frac{T}{wl_2} = \frac{2448}{4 \times 40} = 15.3$ Hence from the curve of tension $\frac{h}{l}$ = approximately .01 and from the curve of slack $\frac{s_2}{l_2} - 1$ = approximately .0002. Thus $s_2 - l_2$ = approximately $40 \times .0002 = .008$".

Accordingly the total slack in the top run of the track = $(s_1 - l_1) + 2(s_2 - l_2) = .27 + 2 \times .008$ = approximately .3".

A warning is perhaps desirable that the figure obtained in this way is the difference between the actual length of track in the various spans and the horizontal length of these spans. In this particular case this does indicate the amount of slack that will become available if the top run is brought up to the straight line from sprocket to idler, but in some cases this might not be so where some spans are not horizontal.

12.9. TENSION AND SLACK IN INCLINED SPANS. THE CROMWELL

It is also worth seeing whether there is any appreciable slack in the inclined spans of track at the front and rear, which we can do with the aid of Figure 12.7a.

For the front span $l = 34"$ & $\psi = 28°$ whence, taking the tension already calculated namely 2448 lbs., $\frac{T}{wl} = \frac{2448}{4 \times 34} = 18$.
This is slightly outside the range of Figure 12.7a. but from the latter it can be estimated that $s/l - 1$ = about .00009 and thus $s - l = 34 \times .00009 = .003$" approximately.

For the rear inclined span $l = 32"$ and $\psi = 21°$

Whence $\frac{T}{wl} = \frac{2448}{4 \times 32} = 19.25$, $\frac{s}{l} - 1 = .00009$, and $s - l = 32 \times .0009 = .003$ approximately.

---

(1) *The later 14" track T.D.10560 is somewhat heavier.*

12.10

Hence the combined slack in these two inclined spans amounts to only some six thousandths of an inch, and can be neglected.

12.10. TENSION AND SLACK IN TERMS OF SAG. Pz.Kpfw.III

To take another example the tension and slack in the track of the German Pz.Kpfw.III can be worked out in exactly the same way. In this case the instructions are that the sag between two return rollers, (which are 1270 mm. or 50" apart) should be 40 mm. Hence $h = 40$ mm., $l = 1270$ mm., $h/l = .0315$ and hence from the curves of Figure 12.6b $T/wl =$ approximately 4.5. The weight of the track is 14.5/16 lbs. per linkage and the pitch $4\frac{3}{4}$" so that the tension $= 4.5 \times \frac{229}{16} \times \frac{4}{19} \times 50 =$ 678 lbs. i.e. the tension is of the order of one third of a ton.

In a similar manner the slack in this span of 50" can be shown to be approximately 0.1" whilst that in each of three neighbouring spans of some 40" would be .052. Hence the total slack in the top run of the track would be approximately a quarter of an inch.

12.11. TRACK TENSION. ITS DISTRIBUTION ROUND THE TRACK.

In the above sections consideration has been given to the track tension which exists when the vehicle is at rest on flat ground with the track performing no function at all beyond that of a carpet resting on the ground with the wheels standing on it. If the track is called upon to perform any function beyond that of a carpet, and in particular when it is relied upon to drive the vehicle forward, other tensions will necessarily be set up in it.

In this connection it will be seen that there is a difference between front sprocket drive and rear sprocket drive. In the case of rear sprocket drive the suspended spans of the top run of track will take up any slack and maintain a tension on the slacker side of the sprocket. Accordingly, if T_0 is the tension corresponding to the spans of the top run of track and T_D the tension corresponding to the tractive effort then the tension on the slacker side of the sprocket will be T_0 and that on the driving side will be $T_0 + T_D$. On the other hand with front sprocket drive there is only a short inclined span of track on the slack side of the sprocket to maintain the tension and the tendency will be for the tension there to become negligible. The tension on the driving side of the sprocket will then be little more than T_D.

Thus, the tension at every point in a track with rear sprocket drive tends to be greater than that at the corresponding point of a track with front sprocket drive by an amount equal to the track tension when at rest. This, as indicated in previous sections, may be anything from a few hundred pounds to a ton or more.

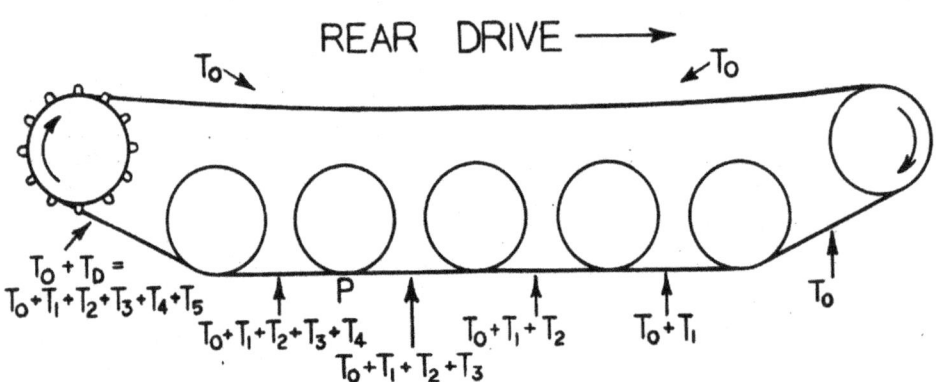

FIG. 12.11a

12.12.

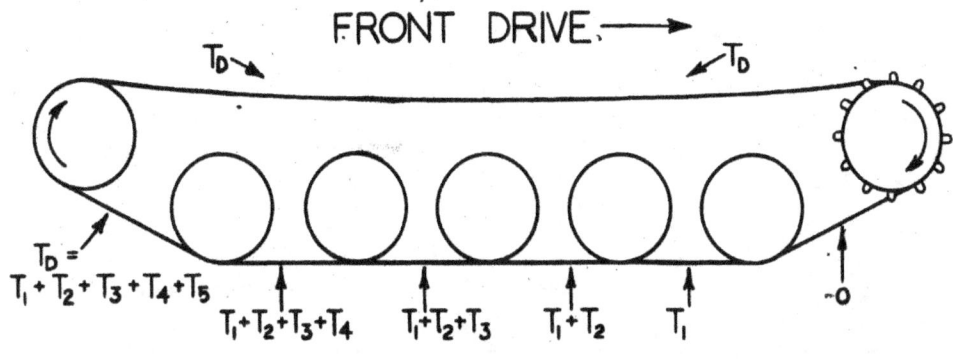

FIG. 12.11b

Figure 12.11a. indicates diagramatically the distribution of tension round the track of a rear sprocket drive arrangement with five road wheels whilst Figure 12.11b. is a corresponding diagram for a front sprocket drive arrangement. In each case the tensions T_1, T_2 etc. are those corresponding to the adhesion of the portion of the track under the first, second, third, etc. road wheels. It is clear that the sum of these tensions must in each case make up the total tractive effort i.e. $T_1 + T_2 + T_3 + T_4 + T_5 = T_D$.

Just how the tension is distributed it is more difficult to say. In the ordinary way, at all events in the case of the front sprocket drive arrangement at low speed, the track is laid on the ground comparatively loosely and there will be nothing to produce any tension in a particular portion of it until a tension is applied to the end of that portion. Starting at the rear end it is clear that in the case of the front drive arrangement there will be a tension T_D. This will be opposed by the force due to adhesion under the rearmost wheel. If this adhesion is insufficient to provide the whole tractive effort slight slip will occur and the remainder of the tension i.e. $T_D - T_5$ will be communicated to the part of the track between the fourth and fifth wheels. This tension will tend to be balanced by the adhesion under the fourth wheel and if this is insufficient the balance will be transmitted to the part of the track between the third and fourth wheels and so on. Thus, if the track is just about to slip it is safe to say that the tension in it will fall by a series of steps from its maximum value T_D corresponding to the total tractive effort, (each step being of magnitude μW, where W is the weight on each wheel) until in front of the front road wheel the tension is zero.

On the other hand when the resistance to movement is slight and the tractive effort required to propel the tank is very much less than the maximum possible adhesion it is quite possible that the whole of the track on the ground will be slack except for the parts under the rearmost road wheel and extending from it round the idler to the front sprocket. As indicated above the track is laid in a relatively slack condition and unless the rearmost parts of the length of it on the ground move rearwardly there appears to be no way in which the track can be tensioned.

The same remarks apply to the rear sprocket drive arrangement but in this case there is at every point an additional tension T_0 corresponding to the tension maintained by the weight of the top run of the track hanging freely by its ends. Any tension due to centrifugal force at speed, or due to negotiating obstacles, will be added to the tension due to static forces at each point.

12.12. EFFECT OF SUSPENSION MOVEMENT ON TRACK TENSION

In the above sections no account has been taken of the movement of the suspension, but it is clear that since the sprocket and idler (and return wheels if any) move up and down with the hull, the length of track necessary to pass round them and under the road wheels (which do not move up and down) will be continually varying.

For the moment it will be sufficiently accurate to assume that as a road wheel moves up relatively to the hull each portion of track extending from it remains parallel to its previous direction as indicated in Figure 12.12a. If $(90° - \theta)$ is the angle between this direction and the direction in which the wheel moves, then the amount by which the track shifts parallel to its own direction will be $d \sin \theta$ where d is the distance moved by the wheel. Where the wheel moves substantially vertically it is only necessary to consider the sloping run of the track leading to the front road wheel and from the rear road wheel.

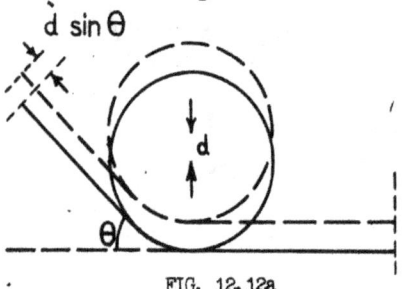

FIG. 12.12a

If we consider a Cruiser tank on which the wheels move vertically, the angle of attack being 28° ($\sin\theta = .47$) and the angle of departure 21° ($\sin\theta = .36$) then a downward bounce of the whole tank of 1" will free a length of $.47 + .36 =$ approximately .8" of track.

What is perhaps equally important is that an upward movement of the tank will take up slack to a corresponding extent and if, as calculated in Section 12.8, the available slack is only approximately .3" it will be clear that the front and rear wheels cannot rebound simultaneously more than about $\frac{.3}{.8}$ or $\frac{3}{8}$ of an inch. Hence as regards the suspension the track serves as a rebound bumper for the front and rear wheels as far as bounce is concerned but imposes no restriction on pitching movement.

12.13. UPWARD FORCE ON FRONT AND REAR ROAD WHEELS DUE TO TRACK TENSION

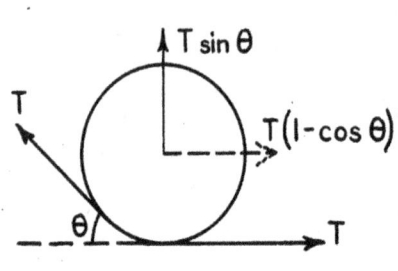

FIG. 12.13a

As will be seen from Figure 12.13a. the effect of track tension in a portion of track wrapped round part of a road wheel will be to exert a lateral force on it. In the case of the first wheel there will actually be a rearward force as well as an upward force but confining our attention to the upward force it will be clear that this must be equal to the vertical component of the tension in the inclined run of track i.e. $T \sin\theta$ where θ is the angle of attack. In fact the spring pressing the wheel downwards is balanced by the upward force exerted on the track by the ground plus the upward force resulting from track tension. Hence if the track tension exceeds a certain figure it will be sufficient alone to balance the force due to the spring and will lift the road wheel off the ground. Using the figures for angle of attack and departure given above (which are those for Cromwell) the track tension necessary to lift the front road wheel off the ground if the the spring exerts a force of 3 tons would be $\frac{3}{.47} = 6.4$ tons whilst that necessary to lift the rear road wheel off the ground would be $\frac{3}{.36} = 8.3$ tons.

In actual fact of course these wheels would not normally be lifted off the ground except in extreme cases or if the absorption of the suspension were small.

For example, if the normal load W on each of five wheels per side is (neglecting bump stops) doubled for the full deflection of say 9", then if two of the wheels take no load the remaining three will each have to take $W \times \frac{5}{3}$ lbs.

Hence, the tank as a whole will sink on its suspension a distance $9 \times \frac{2}{3} = 6$ inches.

The spring load on the front and rear wheels will increase correspondingly to $W \times \frac{5}{3}$ so that the figures given above for T would be increased from 6.4 and 8.3 to 10.6 and 13.9 tons respectively.

The front and rear wheels would not lift off the ground till these tensions had been reached and an amount of track had been absorbed corresponding to a sinkage of 6". Assuming that the geometry were not affected (which would not be accurately true) this length would be $6 \times .8" = 4.8"$ of track.

From these calculations and those of preceding sections it will be clear that the suspension has an important effect and perhaps a controlling effect on the amount of slack available in the track and also on the tension in the track. A very slight upward movement or rebound of the hull as a whole can absorb the whole of the slack normally available in the top run whilst any tension in the track will have the effect of taking some weight off the front and/or rear road wheel and causing the hull to sink down on the remaining wheels. If the tension is produced in the form of tractive effort it will tend to lift the rear road wheel and not the front road wheel and in these circumstances the tank may rock back as the rear wheel is relieved of some of its normal load (accentuating the normal effect of acceleration). In these circumstances the tendency may be for the front of the hull to rise so that little or no slack will be produced in the track as a whole by this rearward pitching action. If, however, the tension in the track as a whole increases the whole tank will tend to crouch down and the front and/or rear road wheel can even be lifted off the ground; and this will tend to act as a sort of safety valve to prevent the tension rising to a dangerously high value.

12.14. SPRUNG IDLER OR SPROCKET AND COMPENSATED IDLER OR SPROCKET ARRANGEMENTS.

In the preceding two sections it has been assumed that the tank has the conventional arrangement of raised sprocket and idler, and also that the movement of the wheels does not affect the top run of the track.

In arrangements which do not adopt the conventional sprocket and idler the situation will be different. Thus a number of U.S. light tanks (and some old British light tanks) have a trailing idler which rests on the ground and is sprung to support part of the weight of the tank. In this case clearly the up and down movement of the suspension will not affect the periphery of the rear part of the track contour.

In other cases, such as Tetrarch and Harry Hopkins, there is no separate sprocket or idler, apart from the four road wheels. Consequently the up and down movement of the suspension will not affect the periphery of the track contour either at the front or at the rear. (It so happens that in this case the idler or front road wheel has a spring tensioning arrangement to allow for slack taken up and made available when steering by curving the track. This has the slight objection of causing bunching of the track when braking hard).

The same thing will apply to a lesser degree to any arrangement with a very low sprocket or idler giving a very small angle of attack or departure (as on the Pilot A.11.E.1. in its original form).

A similar situation arises in the case of tanks having a so-called compensated sprocket or idler, or both, as in the case of the American 76 mm. Gun Motor Carriage T.70.(1).

---

(1) 76 mm. Gun Motor Carriage T.70
U.S. War Dept. Technical Manual T.M. 9-755, Page 250.

In this vehicle the front sprocket is mounted on a swinging final drive coupled to the suspension arm of the front road wheel so that as the latter rises relatively to the hull the front sprocket is thrust forward to take up the slack which would otherwise be made available in the track. The rear idler is similarly coupled to the rear road wheel. The purpose of such compensation is to improve suspension characteristics as discussed by Olley (1).

If complete compensation is provided it is clear that when the tank goes over an obstacle it will not be possible for additional slack to be made available by deflection of the suspension, and hence unless the design is carefully watched there may be a possibility of excessive tension being produced in the track.

12.15. RELATION BETWEEN TRACTIVE EFFORT AND ADHESION ON THE LEVEL AND ON A SLOPE.

The question of adhesion is discussed in greater detail in Chapter 23, but it will be convenient at this point without entering into the mechanism of adhesion, to consider how the maximum possible tractive effort will depend upon the adhesion factor. The adhesion factor for a particular track on a particular sample of ground is analogous to the coefficient of friction, and is the maximum tractive effort divided by the total normal force between the track and the ground, the limit being set by track slip. With a steel spudded track the adhesion factor under the best dry cross country conditions may be as high as .7 while on macadam it might be .5 and on concrete .4. Under wet conditions all these figures would be more or less reduced.

It is worth emphasizing that the limit of tractive effort corresponding to a given adhesion factor when the tank is on level ground and the load is applied by making it tow something, is different from the corresponding tractive effort when the tank is going up a hill and the load is applied partly or wholly by the weight of the tank itself. This is because on level ground the normal force is equal to the whole weight of the tank whereas on a slope it is only equal to the component of the weight at right angles to the slope.

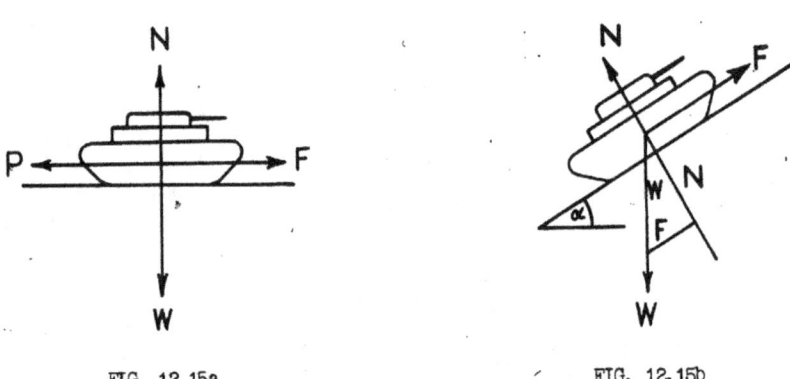

FIG. 12.15a   FIG. 12.15b

Figure 12.15a. is a diagram of a tank of weight W, proceeding on the level against a drawbar pull P which is increased until slip occurs. If N is the normal pressure, F the frictional force and μ the adhesion factor or coefficient of friction, then when slip occurs.

$$\frac{F}{W} = \frac{\mu N}{W} = \mu \quad \dots \dots \dots \dots \dots \dots \dots \dots \dots (i)$$

Figure 12.15b. is a similar diagram of the tank ascending a hill which gets steeper until it reaches an angle α at which slip occurs.

---

(1) Olley, Maurice. Technical Report No.1 British Ministry of Supply Mission. Appendix H. Compensated Track Suspension, December 18, 1942.

In this case

$$\frac{F}{N} = \tan \alpha = \mu$$

$$\frac{F}{W} = \sin \alpha = \frac{\mu}{\sqrt{\mu^2 + 1}} \quad \ldots \ldots \ldots \ldots \ldots \ldots (ii)$$

Thus for example if $\mu = .7$

$$\frac{\mu}{\sqrt{\mu^2 + 1}} + \frac{.7}{\sqrt{1.49}} = .573$$

So that the limiting value of tractive effort for a 30 ton tank (15 tons per track) would be :-

    on the level   - 15 x .7   = 10.5 tons per track.
    on the limiting slope - 15 x .573   = 8.6 tons per track.

In other words, if the tank is caused to tow a load on level ground and the load is increased until the tracks slip, the tractive effort may be as high as 10.5 tons per track, but if, on ground of the same adhesion factor, the tank is driven up a hill and the slope increases until slip occurs the tractive effort would not exceed some $8\frac{1}{2}$ tons per track.

One circumstance in which the tractive effort is increased on the level until slip occurs is when steering, but in this case the tractive effort involved is always less than that required to produce slip in a longitudinal direction. The actual values of tractive effort required have been calculated by Merritt (1) and more comprehensively by Steeds, (2) and by Wilcox and Hartree (3) but in general it may be said that a typical value of the tractive effort required to produce steering would be of the order of three-quarters that required to produce longitudinal slip. The direct track tension produced by steering is of course, associated with sideways thrust which may be equally important, if not more important.

12.16. TRACK TENSION DUE TO A HUMP.

The above sections have assumed that the tank is standing or running on smooth level ground. Figure 12.16a. is a diagram of a length of track passing over a hump under such tension that the adjacent road wheels are lifted off the ground. Before examining the relationship between the tension and other conditions, it is necessary to consider how a length of track could come to be in such a position.

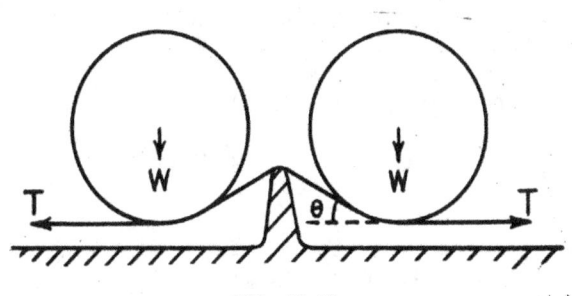

FIG. 12.16.a

If the track were quite slack the front wheel would approach the obstacle as indicated in Figure 12.16b. and the track on the opposite side of the obstacle would be spread out so as to be relatively slack. The wheel would then mount the obstacle as indicated in Figure 12.16c. and as it passed over it as indicated in Figure 12.16d. would come down again on the ground without imposing any undue tension on the track.

---

(1) Merritt H.E. *The design of High Speed Track Vehicles. Proc. I.A.E. 1939*
(2) Steeds W. *Theoretical Aspects of Tank Steering. S.T.T. Paper.*
(3) Ministry of Supply. *Tank Steering Technical Reports Nos. I and II.*

In other words, looking upon a track as a roll of carpet, sufficient carpet would be unrolled to fit easily over the obstacle, provided, of course, that there were plenty of carpet available. It will be realised that the length of track extending between the wheels shown in Figure 12.16d. is considerably more than the distance between the wheels and consequently the condition shown in Figure 12.16d. can only arise if there is sufficient slack available in the track. If on the other hand all the slack is taken up the position will be more like that indicated in Figure 12.16a.

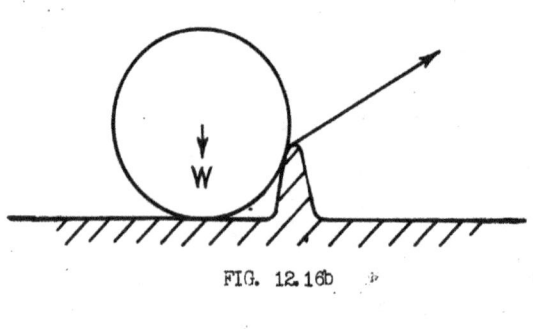

FIG. 12.16b

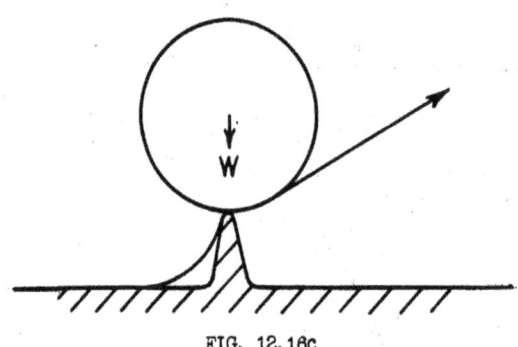

FIG. 12.16c

Consider now the condition indicated in Figure 12.16a. If the inclination of each portion of the track passing over the obstacle is θ then the

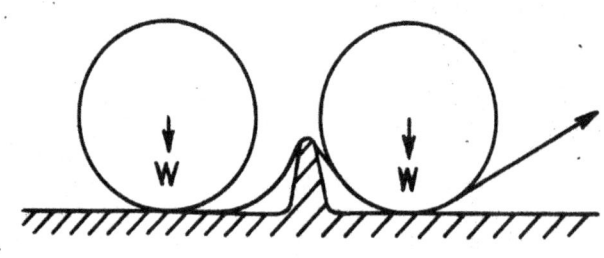

FIG. 12.16d

total length of the track from the bottom of one wheel to the bottom of the other is $2a + 2l = 2r\theta + 2(l - r\sin\theta)\sec\theta$ where the total distance between the wheel centres is $2l$. Hence $a/l = \sec\theta - 1 - r/l\,(\tan\theta - \theta)$.

If the weight on each wheel is W and the tension in the track is T then $\frac{T}{W} = \operatorname{cosec}\theta$. Figure 12.16e shows values of T plotted against values of a/l. In normal cases (except for overlapping wheels like those of the Pz.Kpfw.VI) the values of r/l will lie somewhere between 0 and 1 (corresponding to very small wheels and wheels so big that they touch) and accordingly curves have been plotted for these two limiting values in Figure 12.16e. For these curves scales are marked not only of a/l and $\frac{T}{W}$ but also for values of the actual slack if the wheels are spaced 40" apart, and the actual track tension if the weight carried by each wheel is 3 tons.

From these curves it will be seen that in these circumstances if an inch of slack is available the tension due to passing over an obstacle of this sort may be over 12 tons. If in certain circumstances only about one third of an inch of slack were available the tension might amount to 20 or 30 tons. For crossing an obstacle of this sort the amount of slack provided in the top run of the track by the normal adjustment would not prevent the tension from rising to considerable values, but the absorption of the suspension would provide enough slack to do so. It must of course be born in mind that in some cases the whole weight of the tank would be taken, through the track, by an obstacle of this sort. In such a case the track tension would be considerable in spite of the slack made available by the suspension.

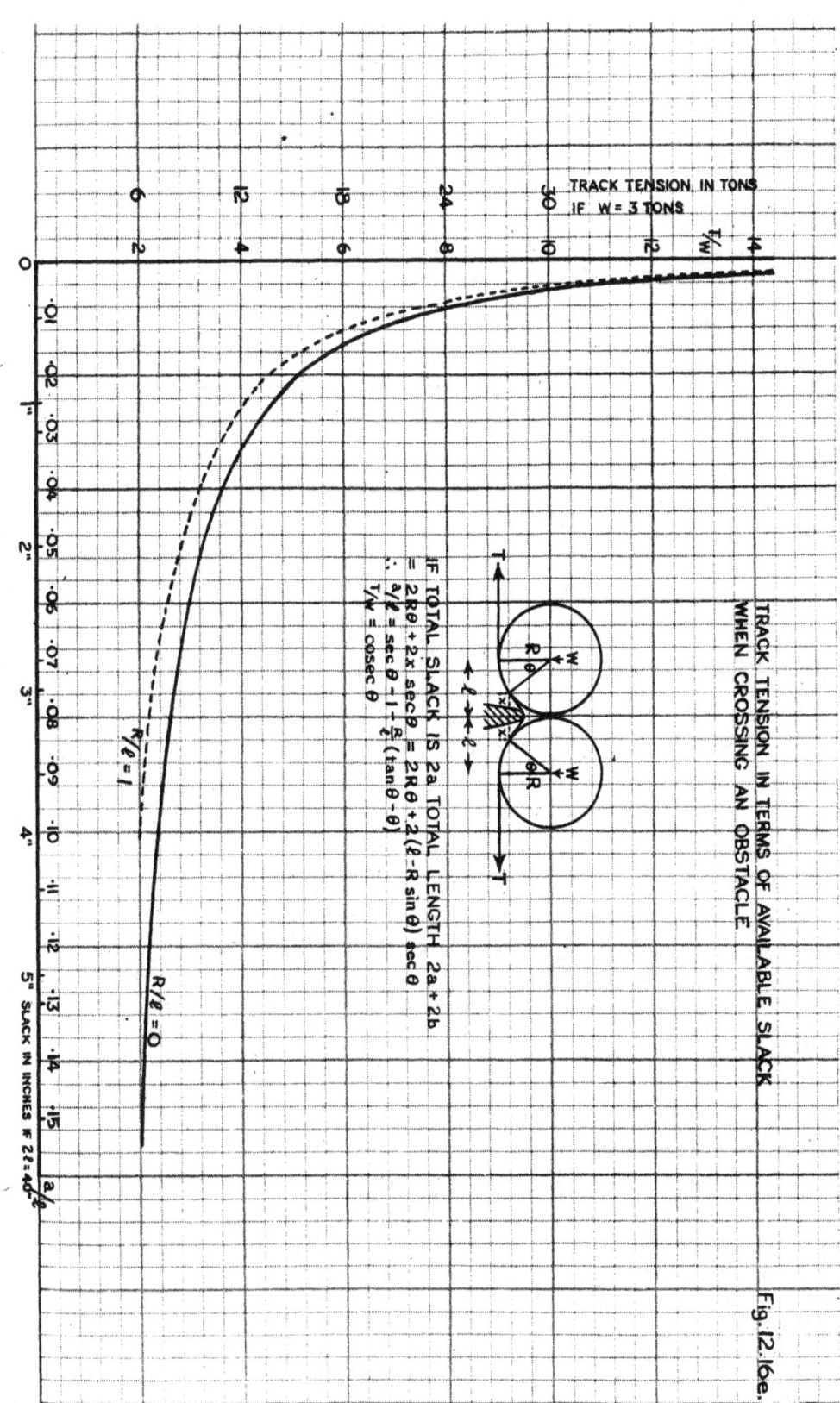

Fig. 12.16e.

In other words, looking upon a track as a roll of carpet, sufficient carpet would be unrolled to fit easily over the obstacle, provided, of course, that there were plenty of carpet available. It will be realised that the length of track extending between the wheels shown in Figure 12.16d. is considerably more than the distance between the wheels and consequently the condition shown in Figure 12.16d. can only arise if there is sufficient slack available in the track. If on the other hand all the slack is taken up the position will be more like that indicated in Figure 12.16a.

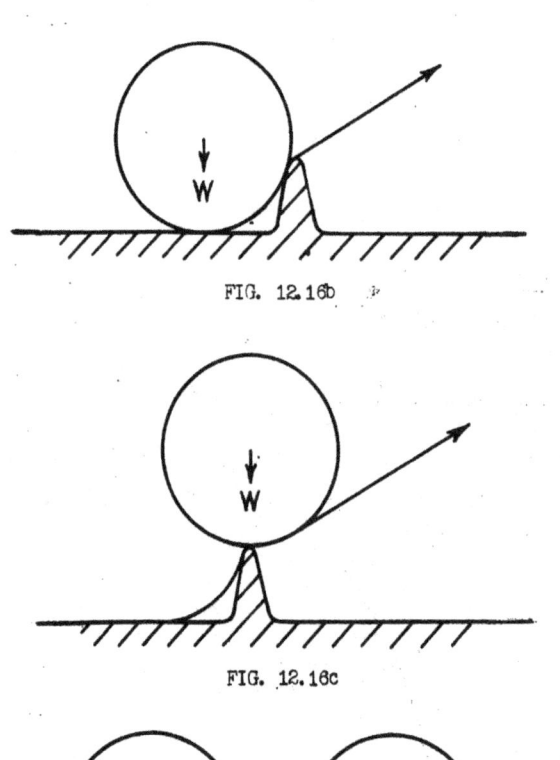

FIG. 12.16b

FIG. 12.16c

Consider now the condition indicated in Figure 12.16a. If the inclination of each portion of the track passing over the obstacle is θ then the

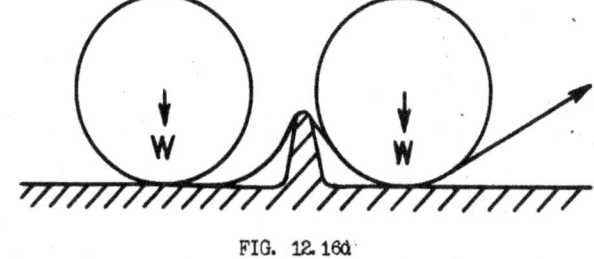

FIG. 12.16d

total length of the track from the bottom of one wheel to the bottom of the other is $2a + 2l = 2r\theta + 2(l-r\sin\theta)\sec\theta$ where the total distance between the wheel centres is $2l$. Hence $a/l = \sec\theta - 1 - r/l\ (\tan\theta - \theta)$.

If the weight on each wheel is W and the tension in the track is T then $\frac{T}{W} = \operatorname{cosec}\theta$. Figure 12.16e shows values of T plotted against values of a/l. In normal cases (except for overlapping wheels like those of the Pz.Kpfw.VI) the values of r/l will lie somewhere between 0 and 1 (corresponding to very small wheels and wheels so big that they touch) and accordingly curves have been plotted for these two limiting values in Figure 12.16e. For these curves scales are marked not only of a/l and $\frac{T}{W}$ but also for values of the actual slack if the wheels are spaced 40" apart, and the actual track tension if the weight carried by each wheel is 3 tons.

From these curves it will be seen that in these circumstances if an inch of slack is available the tension due to passing over an obstacle of this sort may be over 12 tons. If in certain circumstances only about one third of an inch of slack were available the tension might amount to 20 or 30 tons. For crossing an obstacle of this sort the amount of slack provided in the top run of the track by the normal adjustment would not prevent the tension from rising to considerable values, but the absorption of the suspension would provide enough slack to do so. It must of course be born in mind that in some cases the whole weight of the tank would be taken, through the track, by an obstacle of this sort. In such a case the track tension would be considerable in spite of the slack made available by the suspension.

For example, in the case considered in Section 12.13 it was calculated that a tension of the order of 12 tons would make available some 4.8" of slack. Figure 12.16e shows that with this amount of slack $\frac{T}{W}$ is about 2 so that a tension of 12 tons would only support a weight of 6 tons. If in fact the weight to be supported were half that of the tank, say 15 tons, the tension would have to be something of the order of 20 or 30 tons.

To ascertain the exact value it would be necessary to examine the geometry of the suspension in detail and by a tedious process of trial and error strike a balance between the slack released by the suspension at a given tension.

Enough has however been said to indicate that substantial tension may exist in a track quite apart from tractive effort and in fact when the tractive effort is zero.

Moreover it is worth comparing the above figures with those of Section 12.15 in which we saw that with a coefficient of adhesion of .7 the tractive effort per track could not exceed $8\frac{1}{2}$ tons on a limiting slope or $10\frac{1}{2}$ tons on the level.

12.17. OBSTACLE CROSSING. EFFECT OF TENSIONS.

In Section 2.10 the front inclined portion of the track was compared with a ramp. This was a relatively close analogy in the case of the heavy tanks of the 1914 - 1918 war since this portion of the track was backed up by quite a number of wheels. In the case of many modern tanks there are no intermediate wheels between the front idler or sprocket and the front road wheel, and with a flexible short-pitch track the latter becomes an exceedingly flexible ramp. If the track is unduly slack and wraps itself over a vertical step which the front idler or sprocket has passed over or surmounted the front bogie wheel will then have to climb up a vertical face instead of running up an oblique ramp. In fact on certain of the American Tanks where the front sprocket drive tends to accumulate the slack of the track at this point, the front wheel has become blocked against this step owing to the fact that the suspension arm on which it is carried slopes down forwardly from its pivot, and consequently the backward force on the wheel tends to push it down rather than up. Such "wheel block", as it is called, clearly constitutes a serious limitation of step climbing performance. (1)

Thus as regards forming a ramp to assist the tank in climbing an obstacle the track may afford useful help provided it is under adequate tension but it will be of little or no assistance if it is unduly slack. In Figure 12.17a, the effect of the track bearing on the obstacle provides a useful force helping the front wheel to climb up the track on to the obstacle. But in Figure 12.17b. the track can ride slackly over an obstacle and wheel-block is likely to occur.

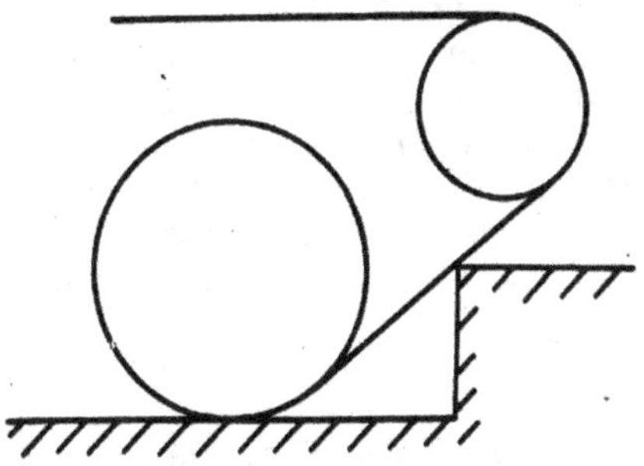

FIG. 12.17a 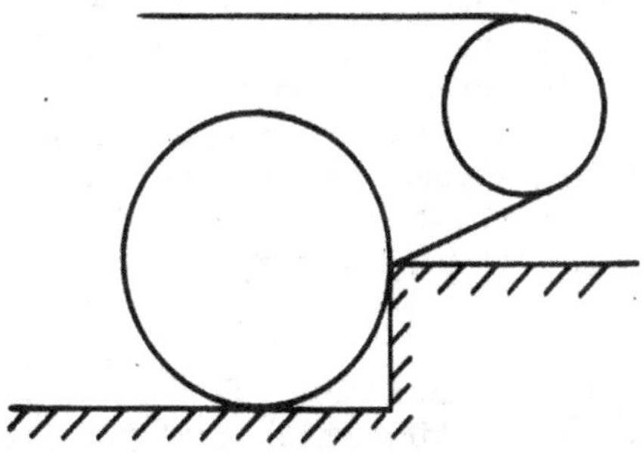   FIG. 12.17b

Apart from the provision of a ramp for climbing obstacles, adequate tension in the track is essential in order to prevent it from jumping sprockets or idlers as discussed in Chapter 14.

---

(1) See for example D.T.D. Report No. F.T. 218/1

12.18. TRACK TENSION DUE TO MUD PACKING.

If mud or gravel packs between the track and the rear sprocket or idler it is a simple matter to calculate the length of track which will be absorbed for a given thickness of mud, and from the calculations in preceding sections it is possible to calculate what will be the effect of this on track tension.

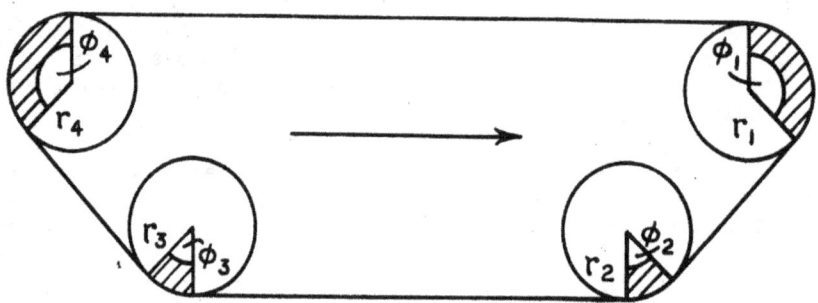

FIG. 12.18a

Thus, in Figure 12.18a. the angles which the track extends round the front sprocket or idler, the front road wheel, the rear road wheel and the rear sprocket or idler are respectively φ_1, φ_2, φ_3, and φ_4. Where, as is usual, the top run of track is roughly horizontal it will be clear that $\varphi_1 + \varphi_2 = 180°$ and $\varphi_3 + \varphi_4 = 180°$. In each case, the length of track wrapped round the wheel will be φr. Hence if the value of r is increased by an amount t corresponding to the average thickness of mud the length of the arc or track length wrapped round will be increased by φt. Hence, if mud packing occurs round the rear road wheel and the rear sprocket or idler to a thickness t the additional length of track required will be πt.

Considering the same Cruiser tank having an angle of attack of 28° and an angle of departure 21° we calculated in Section 12.12 that to produce a length of track of .8" would require a downward bounce of the whole tank of 1". Hence, to produce a length of $t\pi$ will require a downward movement $\dfrac{t\pi}{.8}$ = approximately $4t$

Consequently if a layer of mud ½" thick packs between the track and the rear road wheel and the sprocket or idler the whole suspension will have to yield 2" to supply the necessary extra length of track. If the packing extended also round the front sprocket or idler and road wheel, the length required would be doubled and the suspension would have to yield 4" all the way along for a ½" layer of mud. A similar calculation could be made for an occasional stone.

In the Mechanisation Board Annual Report for 1936 it was reported that the track fitted to the Dragon Mark IV and Tank Infantry Mark I (A.11) gave trouble, owing to stones becoming wedged between the tracks and driving sprockets which resulted in failures in track pins and shoes and also in distortion of the assemblies carrying the idler wheels. This was considered due to the fact that the suspension did not provide sufficient absorption to enable a stone to pass round the sprocket without producing stresses of a high order and also to the contour and design of the track which appeared to invite ingress of stones, etc. To remedy the trouble the sprocket was raised 5 inches in the production model.

In connection with the figures given above for the amount of suspension absorption which must be allocated to counter-acting the effect of mud packing it will be realised that the suspension must still be capable of performing its normal function and if it is deprived of a large part of the absorption due to packing, the remainder may be insufficient to allow of normal suspension movements or passage over uneven ground without setting up excessive stresses.

12.19. TRACK TENSION, EXPERIMENTAL DATA.

Experimental data on track tension is extremely scarce. Some indirect information is afforded by the breaking tension of various tracks, which can of course be fairly readily tested. In the case of light tank tracks it is generally about 15 to 20 tons while for Cruisers and infantry tanks it may be 50 to 70 tons or more. For example in the case of a particular Cromwell track for which it is about 70 tons it can be said with confidence that the tension never much exceeds 70 tons or it would break the track.

Experiments have been conducted (1) by the Scientific Research Dept. of the Ministry of Supply in conjunction with D.T.D. in which a pair of strain gauges were fitted in a specially constructed Matilda track link. The strain gauges were of scratch type recording on a celluloid scale which was spring-urged to work its way along as the strain fluctuated.

Peak values of 10 to 20 tons per gauge, i.e. 20 to 40 tons per track were recorded when steering, hill climbing or braking, a tension peak usually being followed by a corresponding compression peak of about the same magnitude. The scratch does not give at all a high degree of accuracy and as there is no time scale it gives no idea at what points the various peaks occurred, although it is believed that the highest peaks occurred when going over the sprocket. Without more data it is difficult to say whether this is connected with the fluctuating accelerations discussed in Section 15.13, and little more can be said on the subject.

12.20. TRACK TENSION. CONCLUDING REMARKS. TENSION NOT LIMITED BY ADHESION OR TRACTIVE EFFORT.

There is a prevalent idea that the track tension can in theory never exceed the tractive effort corresponding to the adhesion factor multiplied by half the weight of the tank. It will be clear from the preceding sections that this far from being true. The tractive effort or driving tension produced by the track is limited by the adhesion factor but this merely determines the difference between the tension in different parts of the track. If the amount of slack in the track is insufficient to reach round the particular contour it is forced by circumstances to take up, then additional tension will be produced which at each point is added to any tension that may be due to the tractive effort. The safety valve which serves to prevent this tension from becoming excessive is the suspension which enables the front and/or rear road wheel to be lifted and thereby reduces the perimeter of the contour to which the track has to conform and so makes further slack available at other points.

It is of interest to note that the Germans, in the Pz.Kpfw. III, (2) provide an additional safety measure in the form of a shear ring in the track tension adjusting mechanism. If the tension becomes excessive this ring shears and slackens the adjustment to the full extent.

It might seem that the most satisfactory arrangement for controlling track tension would be a compensated idler and sprocket as in the American T.70 but with a resilient linkage instead of a rigid one. The track would then not interfere with suspension characteristics and yet it would enjoy protection from excess tension irrespective of suspension movement. Provision could perhaps be made for adjusting the tension from inside the vehicle. We are not aware that such a scheme has ever been tried.

---

(1) M. of S. File 287/Gen/517

(2) See Gepanzerte Selbstfahrlafette fur Stu. G. 7.5 cm. Sd.Kfz.142 Praktische Winke Fur das Beheben von Schäden am Laufwerk durch die Truppe, pp.59-60, issued by Artillerieschule II Juterborg.

CHAPTER 13

STRENGTH OF TRACKS.

13.1. INTRODUCTION

In the previous chapter we have outlined some considerations worth bearing in mind in assessing what sort of tension the track should be built to withstand.

This tension is transmitted from one link to another by the contact and pressure between the track pins and the surfaces of the pin holes, and before attempting any consideration of the distribution of stresses in the link it will be convenient to consider the rather simpler problem of the loading of the pin.

13.2. BENDING OF TRACK PINS.

If the distribution of pressure along the pin were known it would be a simple matter to treat the pin as a beam and plot diagrams of load, shearing force, bending moment and deflection by well-known methods (1). The difficulty is to decide how the pressure of the link on the pin will be distributed along the pin.

The simplest assumption is that the pressure exerted by each lug on the pin is applied at the centre of the lug as a concentrated load. With cored pin holes it is not impossible for a slight lump to be left in each pin hole and cause the load, at least initially, to be concentrated at a point, and it is conceivable that by an extraordinary coincidence several such lumps might happen to cause the load to be concentrated at the centre of each lug. Such a coincidence is however so unlikely that it can be ignored except as an indication of the worst possible limit of what the bending moment and deflection of the pin could be.

A less unlikely assumption is that the pressure is distributed uniformly along the width of each lug. This again is in general not a justifiable assumption, since, if the surfaces are perfectly cylindrical and co-axial initially, the slightest bending of the pin will tend to concentrate the pressure towards the edges of the lugs, and from observation of the wear on pins it seems fairly clear that some such concentration of pressure does occur. It is out of the question to attempt to assess the extent to which this concentration of pressure occurs, and even assuming that it could be done by a laborious process of trial and error, the result would be of little value, since the moment wear occurred the pressure would be redistributed and the conditions entirely altered.

It is reasonable to assume that wear will occur wherever the concentration of pressure is the greatest and the tendency will be for the pressure to become automatically distributed uniformly across the lugs. It is fairly clear that the condition for maximum life of the tracks would be that this uniform distribution of pressure should occur with the minimum amount of wear.

It is a simple matter to plot the deflection diagram for the track pin, assuming the load uniformly distributed across each lug, and this should give some indication of the wear that would have to take place to bring about such pressure distribution.

---

(1) *See for example, Case J. "The Strength of Materials."*
Chapters IX, X, XIV, XV, and XVI

Working on this basis Messrs. Rolls Royce have plotted diagrams of bending moment and deflection for various links including the standard 14" Cromwell track and a modification in which the effective widths of the end lugs are reduced by boring out the ends of the pin holes. These diagrams, shown respectively at Figures 13.2a. and 13.2b, indicate that the deflection produced by uniformly distributed loads is very considerably reduced by reducing the effective width of the end lugs.

In arriving at these diagrams it is assumed that the intensity of pressure on the outside lugs is the same as that on the centre lug. It is not clear that this assumption is justifiable, especially as it results in the displacement diagram shown in Figure 13.2a. in which the portions of the pin within the outside lugs are considerably out of line with the portion in the centre lug. It would seem more justifiable to start with the assumption that the portions of the pin in the end lugs must be in line with that in the centre lug, and from this assumption calculate what must be the ratio between the intensity of pressure on the outside lugs and that on the middle lug.

Diagrams corresponding with Figures 13.2a. and 13.2b. have been worked out on this assumption and are shown at Figures 13.2c. and 13.2d. It will be seen that in the case of the standard track the pressure in the centre lug is considerably greater than in the end lugs and the bending moment at the centre of the pin is of opposite sign from that shown in Figure 13.2a. The total deflection, i.e. the difference in level between the highest and lowest point, is very considerably less than that shown in Figure 13.2a.

Comparing Figures 13.2c. and 13.2d. it is seen that narrowing the end lugs still appears to result in a useful reduction of pin bending, although it is far less marked than is suggested by Figures 13.2a. and 13.2b.

Perhaps the most important lesson to be learnt from these diagrams is that the answer obtained depends entirely on the initial assumptions made and hence if there is any doubt about the initial assumptions it is unwise to place undue reliance on the results until they have been checked by actual experiment.

13.3. STRESSES IN LUGS OF TRACK LINKS UNDER TENSION

The stresses in lugs can be assessed on the basis of various different assumptions none of which are true and some of which are further from the truth than others.

In the past it has been assumed that the stress across the cross section of the lug is uniform. Hence if the internal and external diameters are d and D respectively, the length l, and the load, W, the stress p is given by the formula

$$p = \frac{W}{l(D-d)} \qquad \ldots \ldots \ldots \ldots \ldots (i)$$

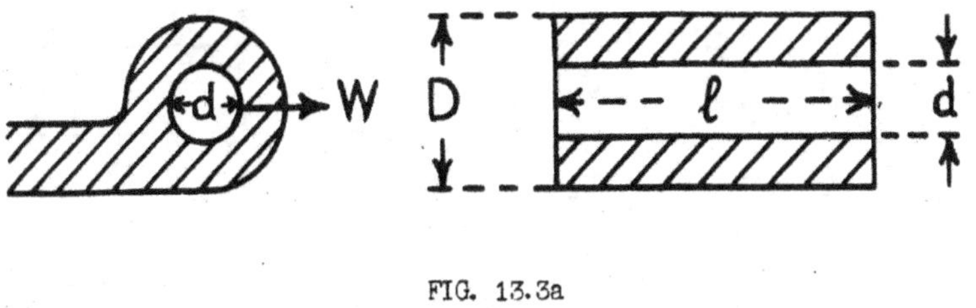

FIG. 13.3a

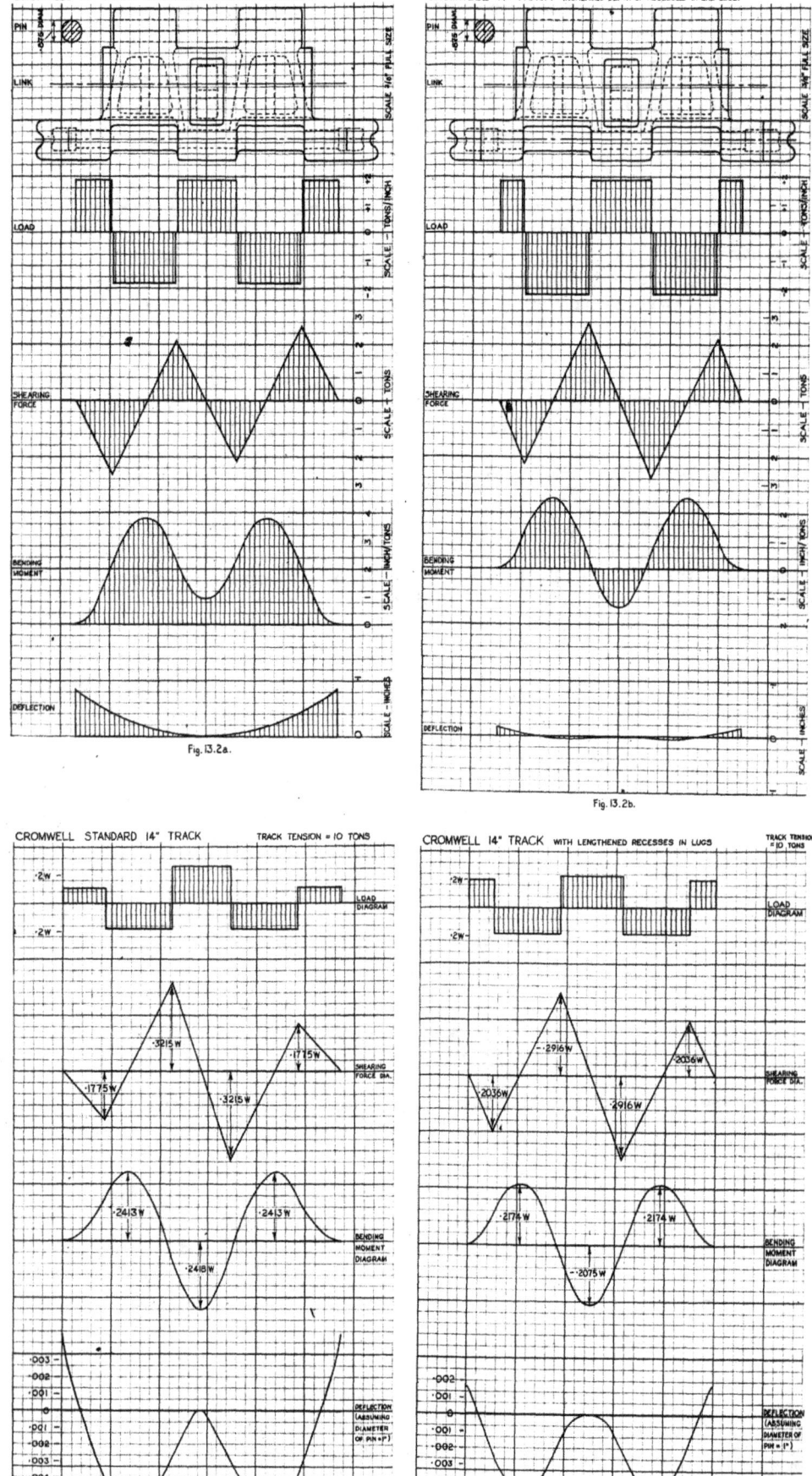

Fig. 13.2a.

Fig. 13.2b.

Fig. 13.2c.

Fig. 13.2d.

Capt. Iliffe (1) has gone into the matter a good deal more fully on the assumption that the load is applied along a line through the pin axis and the lug acts as a curved beam with its ends encastred (fixed firmly so that they cannot rock or move in any way). His investigation is based on Winkler's theory of curved beams (2) and as the mathematics and tabulation are rather tedious we will be content with reproducing the results.

TABLE 13.3b.

D/d	α_2	k, α_1 = 120°	130°	140°	150°	160°
1.5	90°	6.80	7.42	8.08	8.82	9.49
	100°	6.49	7.10	7.77	8.51	9.21
	110°	6.33	6.93	7.56	8.23	8.88
	120°	6.10	6.67	7.31	7.98	8.66
1.6	90°	5.79	6.28	6.78	7.38	7.97
	100°	5.55	6.03	6.56	7.16	7.74
	110°	5.42	5.86	6.39	6.97	7.48
	120°	5.22	5.69	6.20	6.73	7.27
1.7	90°	5.06	5.46	5.89	6.37	6.88
	100°	4.89	5.29	5.72	6.21	6.70
	110°	4.75	5.13	5.57	6.06	6.48
	120°	4.62	4.98	5.40	5.86	6.31
1.8	90°	4.51	4.83	5.19	5.60	6.03
	100°	4.38	4.70	5.06	5.47	5.89
	110°	4.25	4.56	4.94	5.35	5.71
	120°	4.13	4.45	4.79	5.19	5.56
1.9	90°	4.06	4.33	4.64	4.64	5.37
	100°	3.97	4.24	4.54	4.89	5.26
	110°	3.85	4.12	4.44	4.80	5.10
	120°	3.77	4.02	4.31	4.65	4.99
2.0	90°	3.78	4.00	4.28	4.58	4.93
	100°	3.71	3.94	4.20	4.51	4.85
	110°	3.59	3.83	4.12	4.43	4.71
	120°	3.52	3.75	4.00	4.31	4.60

These are given in Table 13.3b. which gives the values of a factor k by which the above formula $p = \dfrac{W}{l(D-d)}$ must be multiplied to give the true stress in various conditions. α_1 and α_2 are the angles from the point of application of the load to the two ends of the beam i.e. the parts of the lug which can be regarded as rigidly held against bending.

It will be seen that the values of k vary from about $3\tfrac{1}{2}$ to about $9\tfrac{1}{2}$ so that in Iliffe's view the true stresses are many times the value given by the formula $p = \dfrac{W}{l(D-d)}$.

It may be argued that Iliffe has been unduly pessimistic in assuming that the load is concentrated at a point, when in fact the pressure is bound to be to some extent distributed over an arc of the circumference.

---

(1) Iliffe, Capt. C. *Analytical Research Report No. 4.* "Stresses in lugs of track links under tension."
(2) See Case, J. "Strength of Materials". pp. 398 onwards.

To what extent this distribution occurs it is difficult to say, but, even if it were complete, the stress would not by any means be uniform over the cross section.

Admittedly Iliffe's figures in this respect would tend to err on the conservative side but there is another respect in which the opposite is true. It has been assumed that the load is uniformly distributed along the length of the pin. This no doubt is the ideal to aim at but as indicated in Section 13.2 it is far from being achieved in existing designs. The discussion in Section 13.2 is from the point of view of the track pin, but sauce for the goose is sauce for the gander, and, if the pressure on the pin is not uniform, the stress at certain parts of the lug must be more than the mean stress.

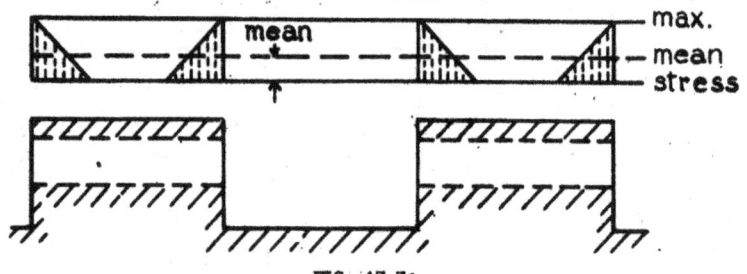

FIG. 13.3c

For example Figure 13.3c. indicates diagrammatically the sort of distribution with a new link where the observed wear indicates that the pressure is concentrated on the end portion of the lugs.

13.4. REVERSE BEND.

Normally one assumes that a track is free to take any degree of reverse bend, but it is desirable to consider for a moment what happens when the limit is reached, and in particular what sort of bending moment the track may then have to withstand. Figure 13.4a. contains some calculations and curves showing how this bending moment varies with reverse bend radius R for a number of different values of r/l, wheel radius divided by half the distance between wheel centres.

It will be seen that the bending moment is of the same order as that in a rigid girder track, except that the bending moment theoretically approaches infinity when $(R+r)$ is nearly equal to l, i.e. when the reverse bend diameter is such as to jam in the gap between the two wheels, a circumstance that would hardly be likely to arise in practice. In general the figures shown would probably be somewhat reduced by track tension and other factors but they appear to indicate that the track should be capable of withstanding a bending moment about equal to that imposed on a rigid girder track if there is any chance of its taking a load at the limit of its reverse bend.

In some existing tracks it is difficult to be sure exactly what surfaces are intended to limit back bend and it rather appears that such surfaces are unnecessarily small and near the pin axis. For example, if the weight W were 3 tons, half the distance between wheel centres were 20", and the abutting surfaces were 1" from the pin axis, the tension on the hinge, corresponding to the rigid girder bending moment, would be $\frac{3 \times 20}{1} = 60$ tons, and in view of the neighbouring equal compression this might well stress the lugs more severely than a pure track tension of 60 tons.

Table 4.24a. shows figures of reverse bend angle for a number of existing tracks.

13.5. BENDING MOMENT ABOUT HORIZONTAL AXES IN TRACK LINKS.

Where a track link extends laterally to a width considerably greater than that of the road wheels, it must be looked upon as a beam in which there may be bending moment about a fore and aft axis.

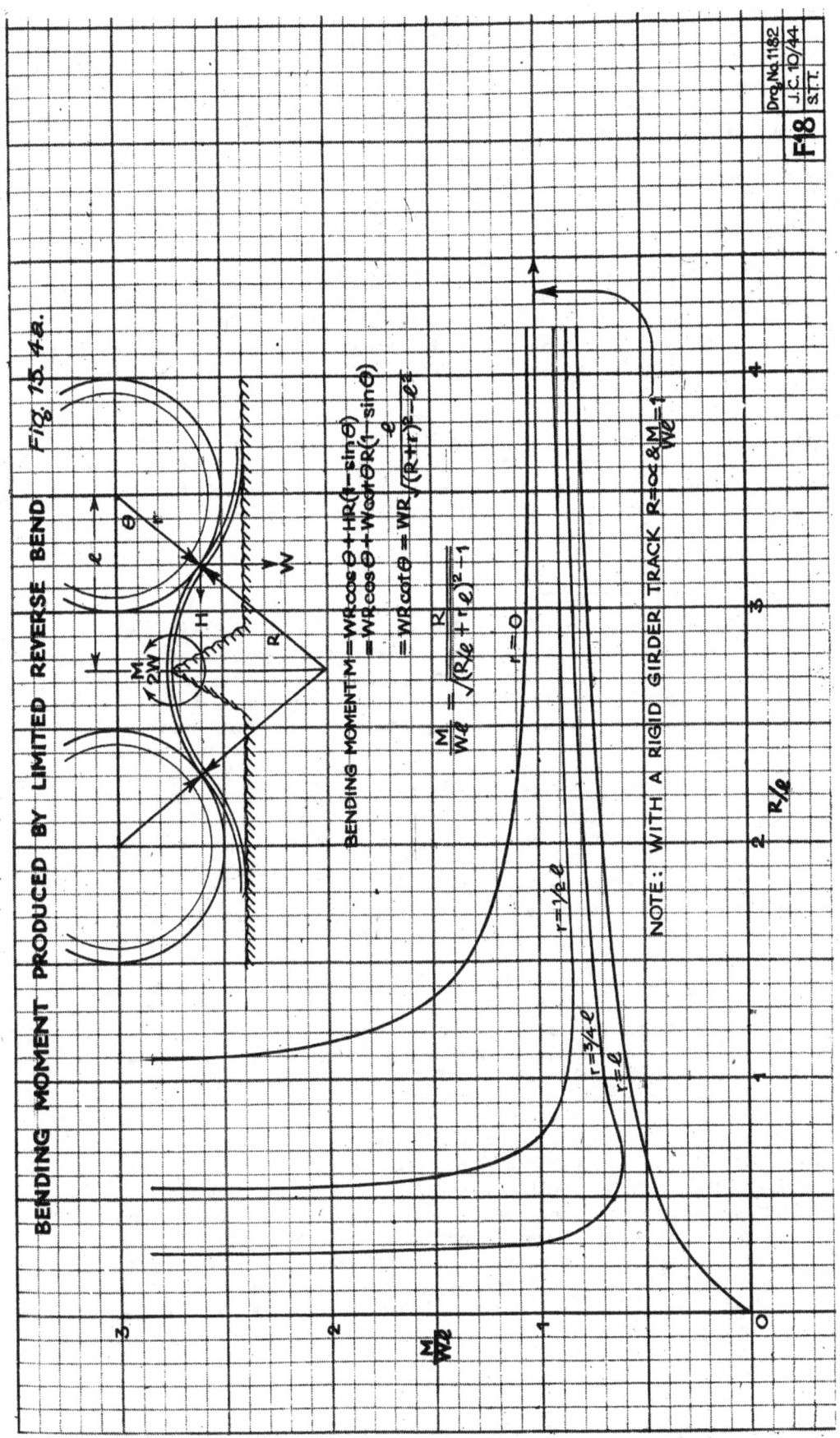

In general, where rubber tyred road wheels are used it is necessary to make them fairly broad in order that they will not be excessively stressed, and in these circumstances the overhanging length of the beam will be comparatively short. The ability of tracks to withstand this form of loading is measured by means of bend tests.

When a track link is supported by spuds at both ends (for example, by its own spud at one end, and that of a neighbouring link at the other end) it acts as a bridge or beam and it will be necessary to consider the bending moment produced in it by a travelling load.

13.6. TWISTING.

If a track passes over a projection such as a stone which only supports one edge of it the effect will be to produce a twisting stress in the length of track. As indicated previously the supporting pressure communicated to portions of the track when they are between two wheels is not likely to be very great, a fact that will tend to mitigate the torsional stress.

With really wide tracks (say over 30") the problem becomes more critical in view of the heavy loading on suspension arms if the load is concentrated at one side of the track, and it becomes necessary to consider whether the suspension and track should be designed to permit local twisting about a fore and aft axis.

13.7. BENDING ABOUT VERTICAL AXIS.

Finally it is necessary to consider the problem of bending about a vertical axis. This tendency will, of course, occur when steering takes place and the road wheels run on a curve and tend to run off the track. The guide horns force the length of track on the ground to skid sideways by the application of a sideways pressure to the particular point where the wheel makes contact with it, and the guide horns must of course be strong enough to produce this sideways skidding. Fortunately for the hinges, it is precisely at this point that the maximum resistance to skidding occurs because this is where the pressure is exerted on the ground, and hence the bending moment occasioned by forcing the intermediate portions to skid is not normally serious. The situation will, of course, be different if an attempt is made to turn sharply in deep mud or some other type of ground where the resistance to sideways movement of the track does not entirely depend on the vertical pressure.

Reference has already been made to the fact that in 1941 the number of lugs used was reduced with the object of preventing cracking of the outermost lugs due to oblique loading when steering (1). Although obviously a stout lug can withstand more bending moment than a less stout lug it would seem that the distribution of the load over a number of lugs would compensate for this.

At the time some fatigue tests were initiated which indicated that an oblique load fluctuating from 0 - 8 tons can be relied on to start a crack after from 20,000 to 100,000 applications although many more applications were possible without completely fracturing the lug. The tests showed that such cracking can be produced in a link with 2-3 stout lugs as well as in one with 3-4 smaller lugs but were not entirely conclusive as to whether the original cracks in service were due to faulty material, choice of material, the number of lugs or the size of the lugs and general design of the link.

---

(1) *Ministry of Supply File 287/Gen/517.*

CHAPTER 14.

DESIGN FACTORS AFFECTING TRACK LIFE.

14.1. WEAR OF SOLE PLATE OR SPUD FACE.

In the present chapter consideration will be given to factors which affect track life. This does not include such points as inadequate strength which may cause a track link to fail almost as soon as it is put into service, but merely those factors which determine the distance which a tank can normally travel on a pair of initially satisfactory tracks, before they become worn out to such an extent as to be no further use.

Where a large proportion of the running is done on roads or similar hard abrasive surfaces considerable wear of the sole plates or spud surfaces of the track is likely to be experienced. In certain designs it has been found that the amount of metal at this point was insufficient but if a spud of conventional thickness is used there is not likely to be much difficulty in providing an additional thickness of metal to bring the life of this part up to the limit set by pitch increase.

If, to improve soft ground adhesion, a very thin spud is used the situation may be altered. It is not possible to compensate for lack of thickness by increased depth since a point is reached where the increased scrub or frictional movement enormously increases the rate of wear.

14.2. PITCH INCREASE OF TRACKS RELATIVE TO SPROCKET.

It is probably true that the limit of life of any well designed track is now set by the increase of pitch of the track relative to the sprocket. When a new track is first fitted there is a comparatively rapid initial increase of pitch as the pins wear down any irregularities in the pin holes and bed themselves in. After this the increase of pitch is comparatively gradual although near the end of the life of the track it may become more rapid again if case-hardening of the link or pin becomes worn through to the softer metal. As the pitch increases it is of course necessary to make an adjustment to maintain the track tension at the appropriate figure. When the idler or other track adjusting wheel has been moved as far as it will go it is shifted back again and a link is removed from the track. As far as maintaining the track tension is concerned this process could be carried on indefinitely but a limit is set by other factors. In certain early tracks (and some recent experimental tracks of decarburised manganese iron) (1) the lugs wore away to such an extent that they no longer possessed a sufficient margin of strength for safe operation. In general, however, the lugs can be thickened up so as to prevent this factor from limiting the life of the track. Accordingly the limit of life of modern tracks occurs when the increase of pitch is such that the links no longer mesh properly with the sprocket teeth and jumping of the sprockets starts to take place.

Actually it is found possible to go on using tracks until the pitch increase is of the order of six to eight or even ten per cent before they become unserviceable due to jumping the sprocket teeth.

It is fairly obvious that if the pitch of a track is such that it fits the teeth of the sprocket when it is new, then if the pitch of the track increases it will no longer fit the sprocket.

---

(1) *Birmingham Electric Furnaces Ltd. Report on Birlec Track Links of Decarburised Manganese Iron. 19th May 1942 and Oct. 1942.*

Hence two broad headings suggest themselves for ways of increasing track life, first reducing wear of the track joints and second designing the sprockets so that the maximum pitch increase can occur without rendering the track unserviceable.

As to the first, materials must be carefully chosen. Pins should be case-hardened or of reasonably hard material, and the material of the lugs must offer hardness to resist wear combined with toughness to maintain strength, a work hardening material like manganese steel being preferable to a case-hardened one as the case cannot wear through. Moreover it is to be presumed that the amount of flexing the track undergoes under tension will affect wear. Section 15.6 discusses track joint friction and although the work done against friction may not be directly proportional to the wear it seems that the same factors will affect both.

It would therefore seem that, other things being equal, wear would be reduced by increasing the size of road wheels, sprocket and idler, or by eliminating the separate sprocket or idler or both. Anything that can be done to reduce flap or wave motion of the track, whether due to dynamic forces or to passage over return rollers etc. will also tend to reduce wear.

With regard to the design of sprockets it will be desirable to examine the relationship between the sprocket and the track in more detail.

14.3. SPROCKET PITCH, PITCH POLYGON, AND PITCH CIRCLE.

In considering the action of a sprocket on a track it is essential to realise that it has little in common with the action of gear teeth which have to be designed so that each point of them in turn meshes with the corresponding tooth of the pinion so as to give a constant velocity ratio. In the case of a sprocket and chain this is impossible since the distance of a link of a chain from the sprocket axis is not accurately controlled and precise sliding between the surfaces cannot be ensured. Nor is the action equivalent to that of a flexible belt and an ordinary pulley. This latter comparison becomes more accurate and helpful if the belt is regarded as passing round a pulley of polygonal and not circular cross section.

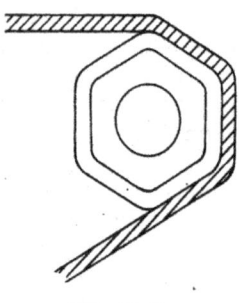
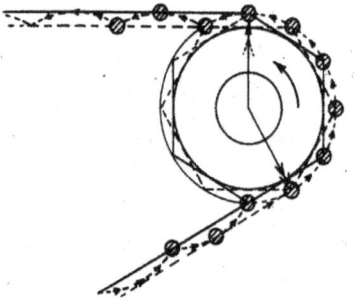

FIG. 14.3a   FIG. 14.3b

In fact as indicated in Figures 14.3a. and b the motion of most tracks is closely similar to that of a flexible belt passing round a polygonal pulley corresponding with the polygon joining the centres of the track pins as they pass round the sprocket. This polygon is known as the pitch polygon of the sprocket, and its circumscribed circle, i.e. the circle through the track pin centres, as the pitch circle.

It will be realised that if the sprocket rotates uniformly both the speed and line of the track will fluctuate as each corner of the pitch polygon comes round. Thus at one moment the line of track coming on to the sprocket will be tangential to the pitch circle or circumscribed circle of the pitch polygon and its speed will be equal to the peripheral speed of this circle, and a moment later, when it has travelled half a pitch further, its line will be tangential to the inscribed circle and its speed equal to the peripheral speed of this circle.

At this moment the next link will strike the sprocket and as a result of the impact its radial component of velocity will be suddenly reversed. The speed and line of the length of track leaving the sprocket will fluctuate similarly but the fluctuations will not necessarily be in phase with those of the part approaching the sprocket.

The mean speed of the track relatively to the vehicle, and of the vehicle relatively to the ground, will of course be equal to the length of track paid out per unit of time, and will therefore be equal to the periphery of the pitch polygon multiplied by the rotational speed (e.g. in revs per sec) of the sprocket.

With a long pitched track and small sprocket this fluctuation of speed and line is important mainly on account of the vibration and noise it occasions, although Figure 14.3a. is of course diagrammatic and the actual flap or wave motion of the track may be quite complex. With a short pitched track and a large sprocket the periphery of the polygon is almost exactly equal to the circumference of its circumscribing circle and the speed of the vehicle can be taken as being the peripheral speed of this circle i.e. of the pitch circle.

The pitch of the sprocket is defined as the distance between corresponding points of neighbouring teeth on the pitch circle. Sometimes, to reduce sprocket wear, there are two teeth to each track link and an odd number of teeth in all, so that each tooth works in alternate revolutions. In this case (sometimes known as a hunting tooth arrangement) the sprocket pitch is measured between points on alternate teeth.

It has been assumed above that the sprocket and track pitches are equal and that each pin has a fixed place on the sprocket and once it reaches it no sliding or other relative movement occurs. In practice this is subject to certain variations and we must now examine the shapes of sprocket teeth and how they mesh with tracks in various circumstances.

14.4. SHAPES OF SPROCKET TEETH.

Anyone who becomes enthusiastic over the exact shape of a new sprocket tooth will be sadly disillusioned at the way it loses its youthful figure in later life.

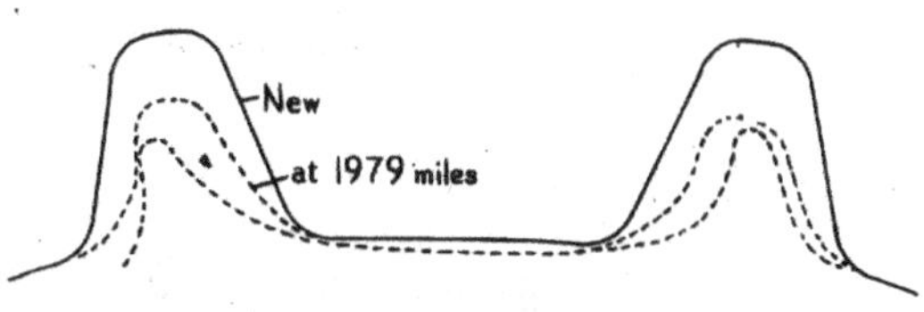

FIG. 14.4a

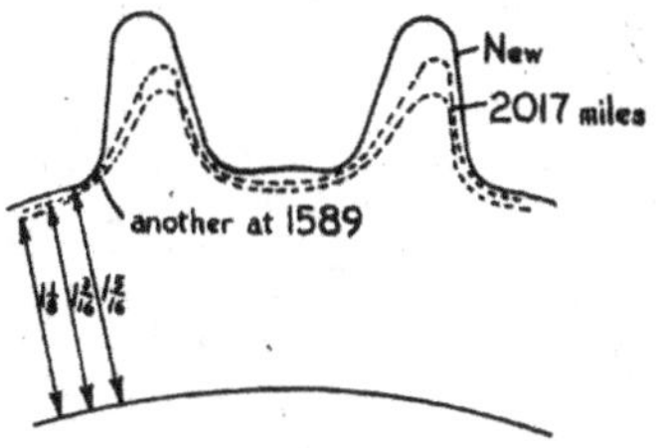

FIG. 14.4b

Figure 14.4a. shows the shape of the Crusader sprocket when new and some of the shapes to which it was reduced after something less than 2,000 miles running, whilst Figure 14.4b. shows a similar type of thing with Carrier sprockets. In some of these cases the wear is regarded as normal although in other cases it is admittedly excessive. (1)

As indicated above the design of sprocket teeth has nothing in common with that of gear teeth and the circumstances which govern the choice, for example, of an involute curve for gear teeth do not arise in the case of a sprocket.

---

(1) D.T.D. Reports F.T. 520 and F.T. 607.

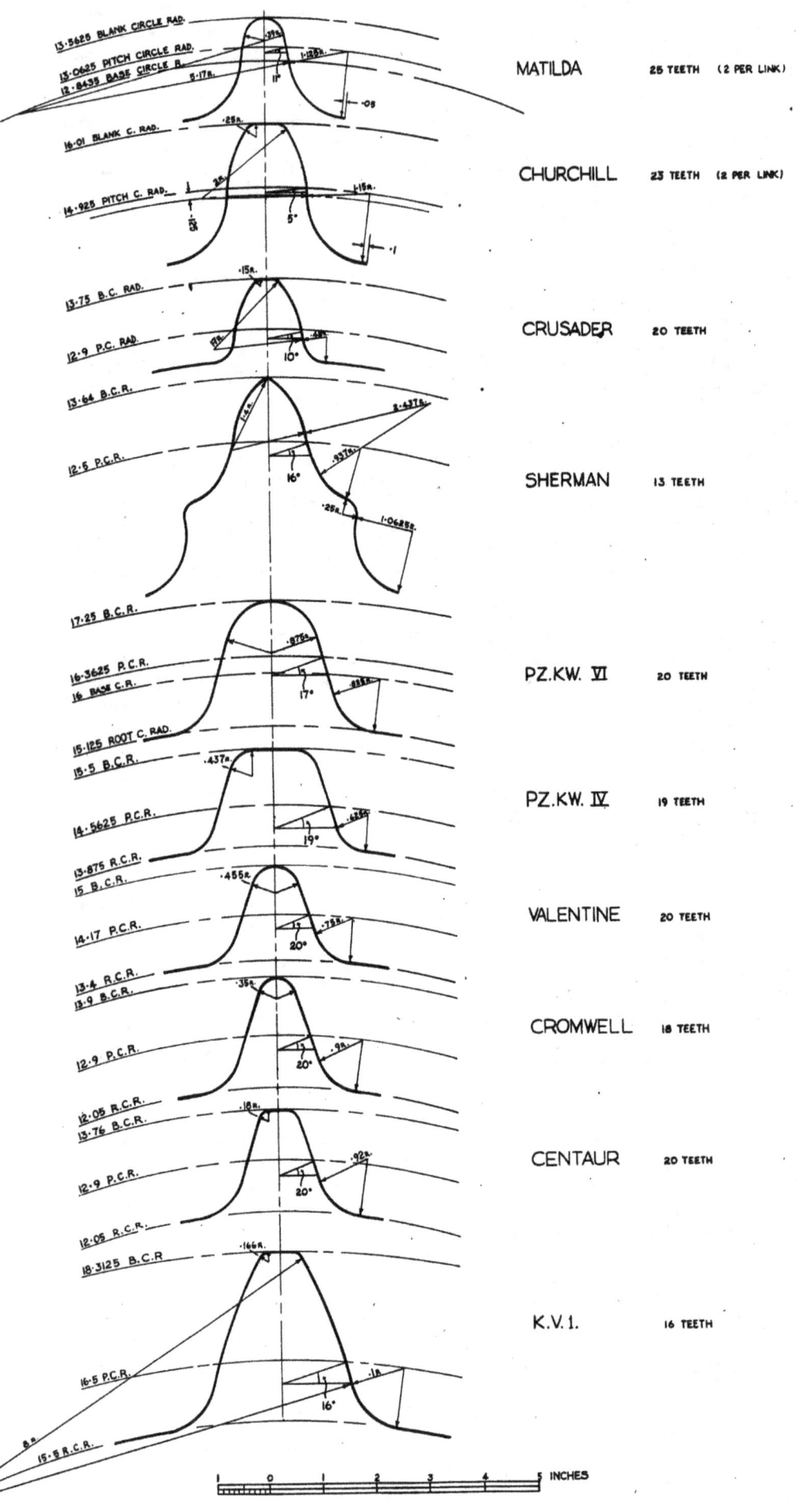

14.5

In fact, the choice of shape is a comparatively free one and Figure 14.4c. which shows the contour of the sprocket teeth of Matilda, Churchill, Crusader, Sherman, Pz.Kpfw.VI. Pz.Kpfw.IV. Valentine, Cromwell, Centaur and Russian K.V.1. indicates that there is considerable divergence in the practice actually adopted.

14.5. MESHING OF TRACKS AND SPROCKETS.

The meshing of tracks with sprockets has to be considered in a number of different conditions, indicated diagrammatically in Figures 14.5a to i.

The track may be underpitched or overpitched. An underpitched track is one in which the pitch of the track is shorter than that of the sprocket i.e. it is shorter than it would need to be to fit the sprocket exactly, and conversely an overpitched track is one where the pitch is greater than that of the sprocket. As wear takes place the track being in tension its pitch will increase and at the same time the diameter of the sprocket will be slightly reduced so that a track which is initially underpitched will pass through its correct pitch and become more and more overpitched till it is of no further use.

Besides considering underpitched, correctly pitched and overpitched tracks we have to consider each when the sprocket is idling or slack, when it is driving the track, and when it is being driven or braking, whether for steering, slowing down, or descending a slope.

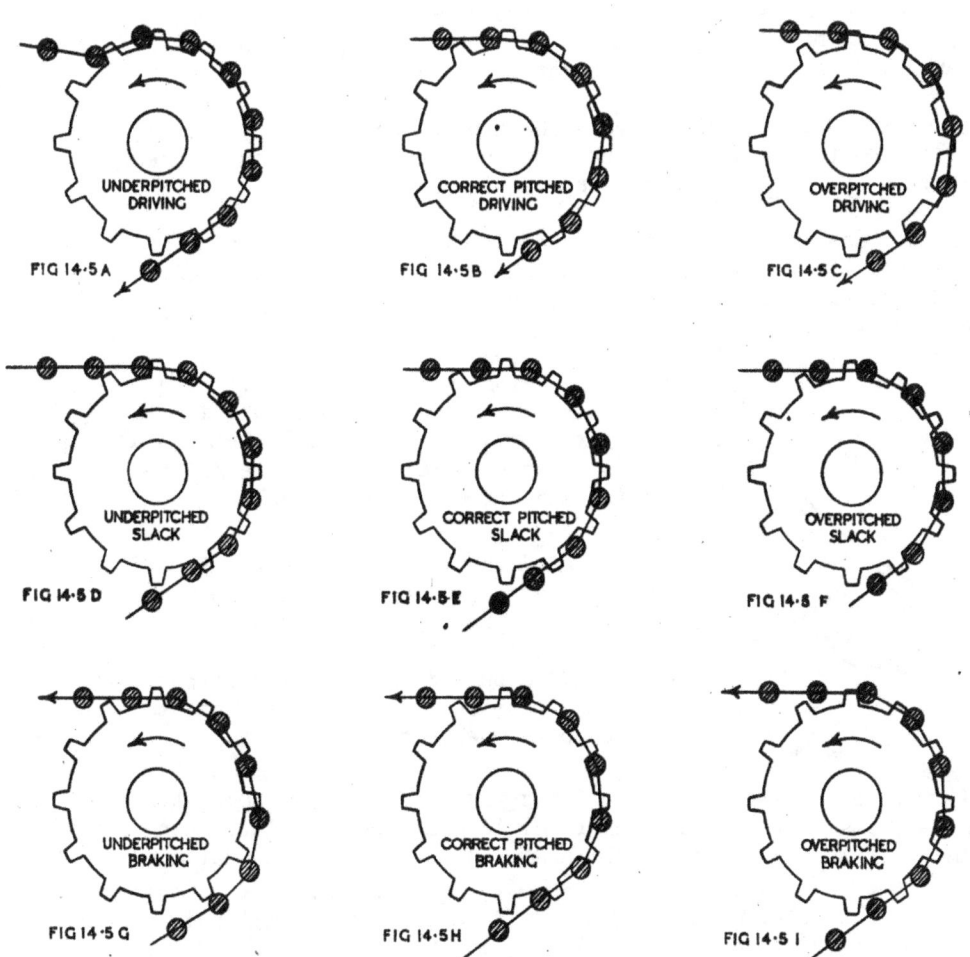

14.6. OVERPITCHED TRACK. SLACK.

The most familiar situation is that of Figure 14.5f. in which an overpitched track rests freely round the sprocket. The arriving link may rest against the adjacent tooth face, each subsequent link being a little further from its tooth face until towards the leaving link contact may be made with the rear face of the tooth.

14.7. OVERPITCHED TRACK. DRIVING.

We are accustomed to seeing tanks standing about with the track hanging round the sprocket and exerting no tractive effort and in fact when a tank is moving at any appreciable speed nobody with normal eyesight can follow how the track links mesh with the sprocket teeth. It must therefore be emphasised that the position of the track links resting obligingly between the teeth of the sprocket is not necessarily their natural position when they are transmitting a drive, and if the tooth face is inclined to the radius the tractive effort will tend to make the links ride up over the tips of the teeth, unless there is something to prevent them from doing so. The thing that prevents any particular link from riding up the sprocket tooth in this way is the tension exerted on it by the previous link i.e. the one which reached the sprocket just before it, helped or hindered by friction according to circumstances.

Neglecting friction we show in 14.7. Appendix 1. that in the case of any one link the ratio between the tension on the taut side and the tension on the slack side is limited by two angles, one depending on the inclination of the tooth surface to the radius and the other on the track pitch and sprocket radius.

For reasons discussed later a very square tooth (with sides almost radial) is not desirable and if the tooth is tapered to a fairly typical angle the ratio referred to may be about $2\frac{1}{2}$.

In other words in this case if the tension taken by any one link is more than about $2\frac{1}{2}$ times that taken by the previous link the tendency will be for the former link to ride up the tooth towards its tip.

In the case of one particular link friction may enable it to retain the position in which it has ensconced itself at the root of the tooth. But consider the next link to arrive, and how it could take over the tractive effort.

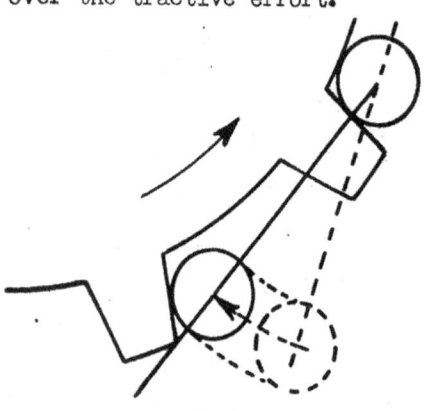

FIG. 14.7a.

Being overpitched, as it swings in relatively to the sprocket it will make initial contact with the tooth at a point some way up from the root as indicated in Figure 14.7a.

And there it will stay. For if it started to move down to the root it would have to take the whole tractive effort, which would then tend to pull it away from the root, and friction will of course tend to keep it where it is.

It will be noted that if the links take up positions some way up from the roots of the teeth the effect is equivalent to increasing the diameter of the sprocket. The number of teeth remains unaltered and hence the effective pitch is increased. Consequently the effective overpitching will be reduced and the next link to arrive will not be laid so much further towards the tooth tip and very soon the links will find a position at which the overpitching is compensated by the increased effective sprocket diameter as shown in Figure 14.5c.

Actually this represents an extreme condition with high tractive effort and very low tension on the slack side. In most cases the links will tend to slide towards the roots of the teeth in the later stages of their passage round the sprocket. Figure 14.7b is from a film showing this actually happening.

In either case the tractive effort will be to some extent distributed over a number of teeth although not equally.

FIG. 14.7b

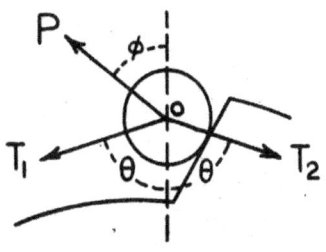

FIG. 14.7.1a

APPENDIX 1.

In Figure 14.7.1a. the surface of the track link engaged by the sprocket tooth is represented by a circle whose centre is at O. If the slope of the sprocket tooth surface is such that the force P exerted on the link is inclined to the radius at an angle φ whilst the track tensions exerted on the link on the taut side T_2 and the slack side T_1 are each inclined to the radius at an angle θ, then we can resolve these forces radially and tangentially.

Resolving radially we have $P \cos\varphi = (T_1 + T_2) \cos\theta$

Resolving tangentially we have $P \sin\varphi + T_1 \sin\theta = T_2 \sin\theta$

Eliminating P from these equations gives us

$$P = (T_1 + T_2)\frac{\cos\theta}{\cos\varphi} = (T_2 - T_1)\frac{\sin\theta}{\sin\varphi}$$

$$(T_2 - T_1) \tan\theta = (T_2 + T_1) \tan\varphi$$

$$\frac{T_2}{T_1} = 1 + \frac{2 \tan\varphi}{\tan\theta - \tan\varphi} = 1 + \left(\frac{2}{\frac{\cot\varphi}{\cot\theta} - 1}\right)$$

For example, in the case of the Crusader and Cromwell the radius is approximately 13" and the pitch 4" so that $\tan\theta = \frac{13}{2} = 6\frac{1}{2}$

We can work out values of $\frac{T_2}{T_1}$ for various values of φ which are approximately thus:-

φ	T_2/T_1
45	$1\frac{3}{8}$
60	$1\frac{3}{4}$
70	$2\frac{1}{2}$
80	15

For the actual Crusader sprocket the value of φ is in the region of 70° so that the maximum ratio of the tension which can be taken in one link without tending to make it ride off the sprocket is of the order of $2\frac{1}{2}$.

14.8. OVERPITCHED TRACK. BRAKING.

With an overpitched track when braking, a similar situation arises except that the arriving link will normally be laid at the root of the tooth and friction will tend to keep it there. Consequently the whole braking effort may be taken by one tooth or, if the braking effort is many times the tension on the slack side and the teeth are very sloping, it may be shared by a number of teeth in the region of the leaving position, by these few links sliding towards the tips of the teeth against the action of friction, as shown in Figure 14.5i.

14.9. UNDERPITCHED TRACK. SLACK.

The position of an underpitched track when exerting no tractive effort is shown in Figure 14.5d. and calls for no comment.

14.10. UNDERPITCHED TRACK. DRIVING.

When the sprocket starts to drive an underpitched track no difficulty arises at the arrival end as here the arriving link is laid neatly into the space between two teeth and can gradually creep back to the tooth face as it goes along.

But at the leaving end things are not quite so easy as the leaving link is taking the whole of the tractive effort. In the case of the overpitched track it could be shared out by the links sliding towards the tooth tips, but the opposite cannot happen with an underpitched track.

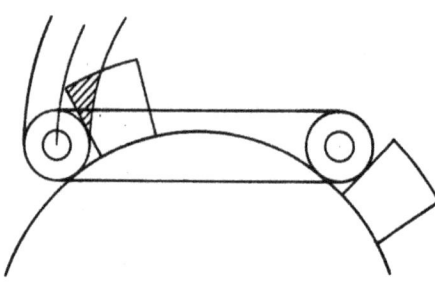

FIG. 14.10a

This difficulty will also arise with tracks of correct pitch if the teeth are too square (surfaces nearly radial) in which case Figure 14.10a. clearly shows how a link pivoting about the next pin will foul the corner of the tooth shown shaded.

When the track is correct or underpitched, there will be pressure on the tooth surface by the link that is leaving it and it will not be good enough to have the tooth surface curved to the arc shown as in this case the link would scrape along it and require a substantial force to get it off the tooth. In fact with correct pitch the actual profile of the tooth should be well within the arc so that immediately the link starts to swing round it parts from the tooth and a slight jerk is sufficient to transfer any tension there may be to the next tooth. If the profile can be inclined to the arc at an angle greater than the angle of friction the link will come away without the need for any force to be exerted, even in the case of slight underpitching.

This does not of course mean that the profile need be arcuate, as a straight line sloped sufficiently to clear the shaded area of Figure 14.10a would give the inclination required at the point of contact and the link would not come into contact with the rest of the tooth surface. A straight line profile has the advantage that the inclination of the contact surface to the radius does not alter appreciably as overpitching occurs and the link rides out towards the tip of the tooth. With a curved profile it would be to be expected that with a new track the links would have difficulty in leaving the tooth and with an old track the tendency to jump the sprocket would be accentuated.

14.11. UNDERPITCHED TRACKS. BRAKING.

The situation when driving is nothing much to worry about but when braking it is distinctly more serious.

Here the link arriving contacts the rear face of the tooth at a distance from its root and there is nothing to pull it down except the tension on the slack side of the sprocket (which is opposed by friction.) Moreover whereas the overpitched track when driving reaches a stable state by riding up the teeth the underpitched track when braking gets worse and worse. For as a link rides out to a greater radius the effect is to exaggerate the extent of underpitching, and the next link goes much further. In fact it only takes a very few links to reach the stage of jumping the sprocket teeth as indicated in Figure 14.5g. Hence the track must be kept very tight and the braking force cannot exceed perhaps one or two times the tension on the slack side (if that) without causing the track to jump the sprocket teeth.

Largely for this reason the extent to which tracks are underpitched when new, to extend their life, is very limited. In general the amount of underpitching is chosen so that after the comparatively rapid initial stretch due to bedding down of the pins the pitch will be correct.

14.12. CORRECTLY PITCHED TRACK. DRIVING, SLACK, AND BRAKING.

The positions of a correctly pitched track shown in Figures 14.5b. e, and h call for little comment beyond pointing out that in the slack condition the track can of course remain in the driving or the braking position instead of an intermediate position such as that shown in Figure 14.5e.

14.13. SPROCKET TOOTH DESIGN; REVERSIBILITY, STRENGTH.

In considering the spacing between the teeth in relation to the form of the surfaces they engage on the track the effect of reversal of torque must be borne in mind. If the space between the teeth is much longer (circumferentially) than the thickness of the boss or trunnion on the track there will be a lot of play or lost motion and consequently shock when torque is reversed and a boss travels from the face of one tooth to the back of the next. This is at its worst in the correctly pitched condition. On the other hand some play is desirable to prevent an overpitched track from engaging the backs of the teeth near its slack part when it is running light.

The above discussion gives some points to be borne in mind in deciding on a tooth profile. Since the vehicle must be capable of reversing, what applies to the front of the tooth must apply to the back also. Admittedly the tank would be travelling forwards most of the time and hence the wear would tend to be on one side of the tooth. No advantage has thitherto been taken of this in the shaping of sprocket teeth although sprocket rings are sometimes taken off and reversed after a certain mileage so that the back of the tooth becomes the front.

The strength of the tooth must be sufficient to take the tractive effort, including a factor of safety to allow for shock loading, and bearing in mind that towards the end of its life the section will be reduced by wear and the load will be applied near the tip.

The above remarks apply of course to ordinary toothed sprockets engaging a boss or roughly cylindrical surface on a link. The conditions which arise with the type of sprocket having, instead of teeth, rollers which engage teeth on the links (as used on Christie tanks, including the Russian T34, German semi-tracked carriers, and some Roadless Traction Tractors) are quite different and it is understood that substantial underpitching of such tracks can be adopted with no ill effects.

14.14. WRAP TEST.

This is perhaps an appropriate point to refer to the wrap test, a test used on production links to determine whether their pitch is on an average within specified limits.

14.14

The details of the test are different for each track but the principle in each case is that a length of track is wrapped round a sprocket with the first link pulled hard up against the adjacent tooth. Then the space between say the sixth link (or some other specified link) and the adjacent tooth must be within certain limits usually tested by pushing in a go and no-go gauge in the form of a strip of metal of the specified thicknesses. Thus the test takes the rough with the smooth and if some links are a little over-pitch and others under they can still pass the test. The number of links varies as does the clearance specified, which is sometimes measured from the face of the tooth and sometimes from the back of the next tooth.

Figure 14.14a. shows a wrap diagram for Cruiser links T.D.507.

ASSEMBLIES OF TWELVE LINKS SHALL BE TRIED ON THE SPROCKET OF THE WRAP TEST FIXTURE AND EACH ASSEMBLY MUST CONFORM TO THE TOLERANCES SHOWN ON THE DIAGRAM BELOW.

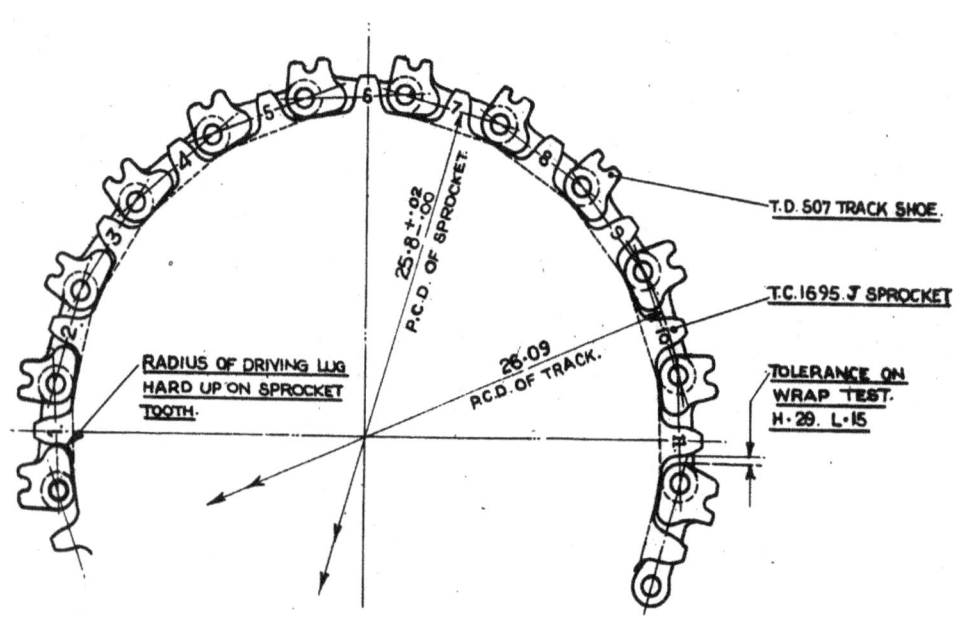

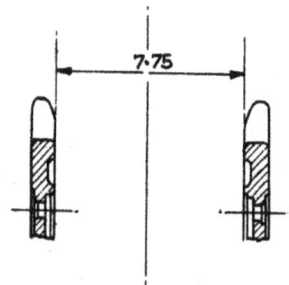

PART SECTION.

SHOWING DISTANCE BETWEEN SPROCKETS.

FIG. 14.14a

CHAPTER 15.

ROLLING RESISTANCE ON HARD GROUND, VIBRATION & NOISE

15.1. RELATION OF POWER/WEIGHT RATIO TO SPEED ROLLING RESISTANCE AND SLOPE-CLIMBING PERFORMANCE.

Rolling resistance or tractive resistance is normally expressed in lb./ton or as a percentage, and as indicated later its order of magnitude on a hard surface such as concrete is roughly 30-40 lbs./ton ($1\frac{1}{2}$ - 2%) for a wheeled vehicle and 80 - 120 lbs./ton (4 - 6%) for a tank. Each of these figures is equivalent to a definite gradient, whether expressed as an angle, a percentage or an incline of one in so many, and to a definite acceleration whether expressed in units such as ft/sec^2 or as a fraction of g, the acceleration due to gravity. Moreover each of these things corresponds to a definite power-weight ratio at any given speed. So before going into details it is important to have a clear idea of these various ways of expressing the required ratio of tractive effort to weight, which we shall refer to as the tractive ratio (sometimes also referred to as gradient factor).

Gradients are usually expressed in terms of the ratio of vertical to horizontal distance travelled. If the inclination of the slope to the horizontal is θ, the usual British method is to refer to a gradient of say 1 in 5 meaning that $\cot \theta = 5$ while in the U.S.A. it is referred to as a grade of 20% meaning that $100 \tan \theta = 20$, θ in this particular case being $11\frac{1}{3}°$.

The tractive ratio (ratio of tractive effort to weight) necessary to climb a slope is as we saw in Section 12.15 equal to $\sin \theta$, and hence when expressed as a percentage differs slightly from the grade in the same proportion as the horizontal distance differs from the distance measured along the slope. For small angles the difference is negligible, for example $\tan 11.3° = 19.98\%$. Whereas $\sin 11.3° = 19.59\%$. Thus on grades up to 20% the error made by interchanging grade and tractive ratio does not exceed .39% or 2% of the total.

Also from elementary mechanics:

$$\frac{\text{acceleration}}{g} = \frac{\text{tractive effort}}{\text{weight}} = \text{tractive ratio.}$$

Hence, the acceleration produced by a given tractive ratio, when expressed as a percentage of g, is equal to the tractive ratio expressed as a percentage. This of course assumes that the whole tractive ratio is devoted to producing acceleration. In practice it would be necessary to subtract from the total tractive ratio the tractive ratios corresponding to rolling resistance and gradient (to be added if downhill) and the remainder would be the acceleration (or retardation if negative) as a percentage of g.

Figure 15.1a. shows how these various forms and methods of expressing tractive ratio and gradient correspond, and also includes the adhesion factor necessary to produce the tractive effort. We saw in Section 12.15 that on the level $\mu = F/W = $ tractive ratio $= \sin \theta$

whereas on a limiting slope $\mu/\sqrt{\mu^2 + 1} = F/W$ whence $\mu = \tan \theta$.

The power/weight ratio of a vehicle is normally expressed in H.P./ton which is most conveniently linked up with tractive ratio measured in lbs./ton, although of course it is equally definitely related to it when measured in other units.

From elementary mechanics:-

| Speed ft/sec | x | Tractive Effort lbs. | = | Power ft.lbs/sec. | = | 550 x Horsepower |

| Speed ft/sec | x | Tractive Ratio lbs/ton | | = 550 x Power/weight Ratio H.P./ton |

(These relationships hold good whether the ton is the British or long ton of 2240 lbs., the metric tonne (1000 kgs) of 2204.6 lbs. or the U.S. or short ton of 2000 lbs, but the equivalent gradient depends on which ton is concerned.)

From Figure 15.1a one can see at once what power/ weight ratio will be required to climb a certain gradient or overcome a certain resistance at any given speed. For example a resistance of 250 lbs/ short ton is equivalent to a slope of just over 7° or $12\frac{1}{2}\%$ or one in 8, and produces an acceleration $\frac{1}{8}g$ or about 4 ft/sec^2. Following along the level of 250 lbs/ton to the points where it cuts the speed lines it is seen that to overcome this resistance or climb this gradient or produce this acceleration requires 5 H.P./short ton at $7\frac{1}{2}$ m.p.h., 10 H.P./ton at 15 m.p.h., 20 H.P./ton at 30 m.p.h., etc. These figures are assuming that the whole power is devoted to climbing the slope or overcoming the resistance concerned. If for example half of it is lost in other forms of resistance the lower figures apply, corresponding to 50% efficiency and double the power/weight ratio must be actually provided.

15.2. FACTORS CONTRIBUTING TO ROLLING RESISTANCE.

Comparatively little experimental work appears to have been done, at all events in this country, to investigate factors affecting rolling resistance and how it varies with different suspension arrangements and track constructions. The total resistance to forward movement is composed of contributions made by various different causes and this naturally makes it difficult to determine how the portion due to each cause varies with different factors.

Merritt (1) has divided up rolling resistance into the following contributions:-

1. Transmission loss proportional to load.
2. Transmission losses due to oil drag and varying with speed rather than load.
3. Losses between driving sprocket and track.
4. Friction in wheel and supporting roller bearings.
5. Friction in track link joints due to the combination of movement and track tension; the latter made up of initial tension, driving load, and forces due to flap or wave motion in the track.
6. Rolling friction of wheels over the track.
7. Work done in deforming the ground.
8. Air resistance.

15.3. TRANSMISSION AND SPROCKET LOSSES.

With losses in the transmission we are not primarily concerned in the present book. According to Icks (2) such losses may amount to over a third of the net engine power, but normally the loss is much less than this and on a Cromwell out of 510 H.P. at the flywheel the measured power available at the sprocket was 480 H.P., a loss of under 6%. Losses at the sprocket should not be difficult to measure experimentally, but we are not aware that it has been done and it seems useless to tackle the problem by calculation, (except for the hammering losses discussed in Section 15.10).

---

(1) Merritt H.E., "The Design of High Speed Track Vehicles" Proc. I.A.E. 1939.

(2) Icks, Lt.Col. R.J. "Engines for Tanks." S.A.E. Journal, July 1943, Page 39.

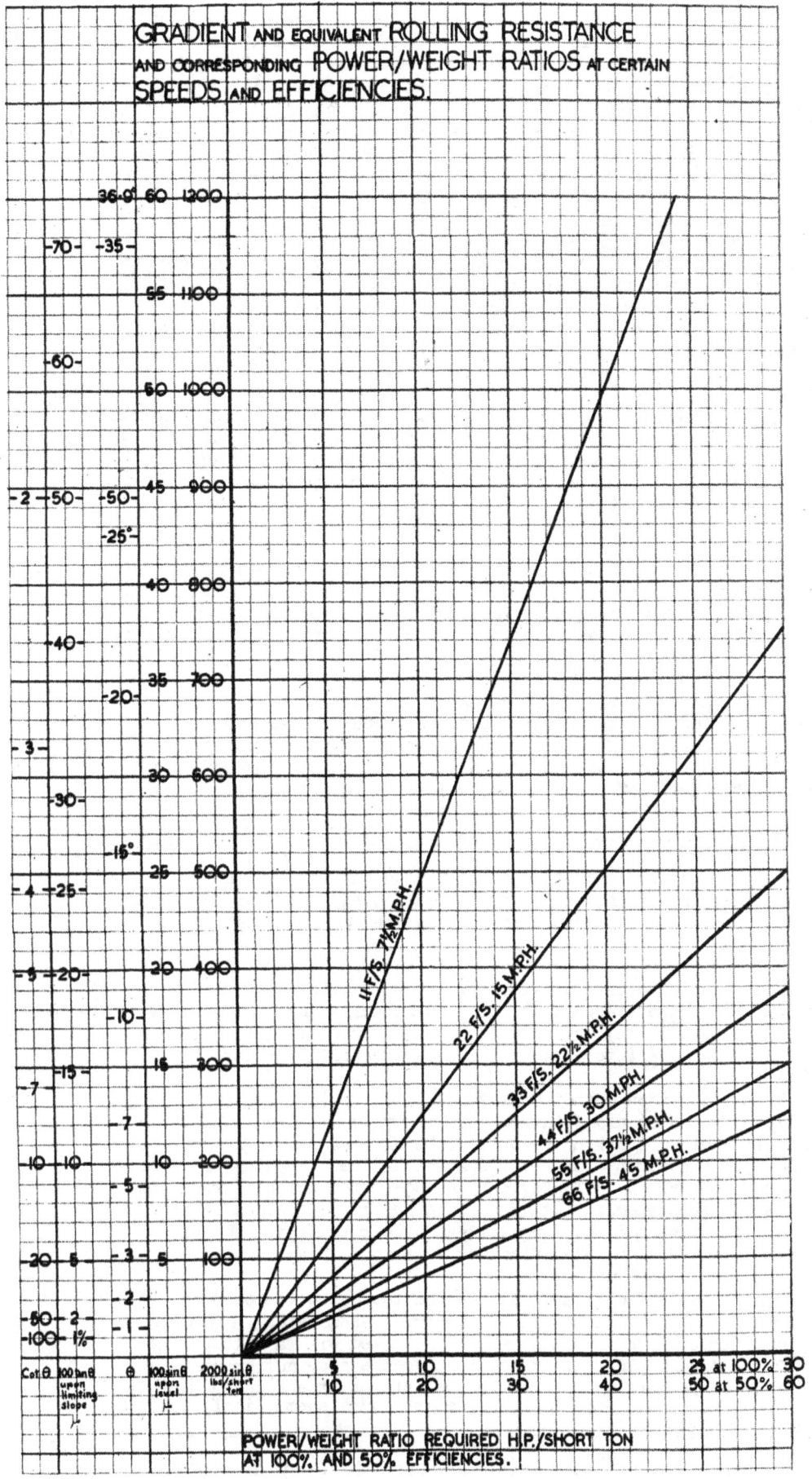

Fig. 15.1a

15.4. ROLLING FRICTION OF WHEELS.

With regard to the rolling friction of wheels over the track it seems permissible to assume that this will be of the same order as the rolling resistance of similar wheels on a hard surface such as a concrete road and a certain amount of experimental material is available from tests on ordinary wheeled vehicles. Of course if the roller path is not smooth, this assumption may have to be reviewed.

Messrs. Dunlop have stated (verbally to the author) that the rolling resistance of a rubber tyre varies considerably with the type of rubber used but as a rough estimate a considerable number of sources seem to agree that a typical figure is between 30 and 40 lbs. per ton. The comparison between a solid tyre and a pneumatic tyre is not quite unanimous. Thus Wolfe (1) gives figures indicating that the resistance of a solid tyre at 10 miles an hour is about the same as that of a pneumatic tyre at 25 miles an hour and rather more than that of a pneumatic tyre at 15 miles an hour, whereas Lockwood (2) gives rather more detailed figures indicating that solid tyres have a rolling resistance something between pneumatic tyres of the cord type and those of the fabric type. These figures include air resistance (which at the speeds concerned would be of minor importance) and hence may be regarded as giving the order of resistance of a tank with its tracks removed. A number of measurements were made on Tetrarch which, having curved track steering, can be run without its tracks, and these results confirm the conclusion that the rolling resistance of a tank without its tracks may be of the order of 30 to 40 lbs/ton ($1\frac{1}{2}$-2%).

The addition of tracks will bring in friction in the track link joints, scrub friction as the links are laid on the ground and lifted, and losses due to hammering and vibration at a number of points, including that of engagement between the track and the driving sprocket, due to the finite pitch of the track.

There appear to be no experimental results to indicate the relative importance of these contributions or how they depend on different variable factors, and before attempting to examine this question from a theoretical angle, we will mention some measurements indicating the order of magnitude to which they add up.

15.5. ROLLING RESISTANCE TEST RESULTS, HARD GROUND AND NON-DRIVEN TRACK.

The rolling resistance of a vehicle on hard ground can be measured in several different ways such as towing, coasting downhill, and different forms of deceleration measurement on the level.

Perhaps the most direct method of measuring the rolling resistance of a tank is to tow the tank through a dynamometer. Difficulty is liable to be experienced with fluctuating pull since (as will be clear from Figure 15.1a) the pull required to produce quite a moderate acceleration can completely swamp that due to rolling resistance.

In deceleration methods the tank is run up to a certain speed and then allowed to coast along in neutral, the rate at which it loses speed as a result of rolling resistance being measured in one of various ways. Assuming the road is level a direct reading of deceleration can be given by a Tapley performance meter which works on the principle of a pendulum. But due to the height of the centre of gravity of the tank and the inequality of track tension the whole machine may tilt forward and introduce an error.

In the so-called fifth wheel method the speed is measured by a trailing wheel which may operate an electric speedometer. The time taken over certain speed ranges is then observed with a watch. No doubt this method could be rendered more accurate by autographic recording, but so long as the rolling resistance itself is subject to wide variations due to uncontrolled factors there seems little point in measuring it with great accuracy.

---

(1) Wolfe, A.M. "Practical Tractive Ability Methods".
S.A.E. Journal, December 1930.
(2) Lockwood, Prof. E.H. "Chassis Friction Losses.
S.A.E. Journal, November 1922

15.6

With any deceleration method it is essential to correct the effective weight of the tank to take into account the moment of inertia of rotating parts and the inertia of the track as it travels round its contour, due to which the effective weight may be perhaps 75% more than the true weight.

This correction, and possible source of error, is eliminated or reduced if the speed is kept constant or nearly constant by coasting down a hill, and this is perhaps the method to be preferred provided a sufficient range of hills is available to approximate to each of the figures of rolling resistance to be measured.

All these forms of test are dictated by practical convenience and from a scientific point of view leave much to be desired. In the first place the figure obtained includes a portion of the transmission losses as well as track losses, although the former can usually be separately measured and allowed for. Secondly the track losses must be treated with reserve since the track is not being driven by the sprocket. The latter objection can be removed by fitting torsion dynamometers in the final drives and measuring the torque output on load, but although this has been planned for some time in more than one quarter no results appear so far to have been obtained by this method.

Figure 15.5a. shows a number of curves of rolling resistance at varying speeds, obtained from various sources.

Rolling Resistance on Roads. Figures from M. E. E. Reports.

Report No.	Vehicle	Rolling Resistance lb./ton.
A.27/7	Light Dragon V.8	53.0
F.T.218/1.	General Lee.	75.0
A.45	A. 11. E. 1.	77.5
A.7/6.	Light Tank Mk. V.	78.5
A.T.23/3.	Light M2. A4.	82.7
A. 27/7	Light Dragon Mk. IIC.	87.0
A. 12/12	Tractor Medium experimental	95.2
A.30/20	Light Tank Mk. VIA.	96.2
A.30/15.	Light Tank Mk. VIA.	105.8

Table 15.5b

Table 15.5b. shows some more figures of rolling resistance, obtained from Reports of the Mechanisation Experimental Establishment in which the speed is not mentioned.

Altogether the available figures suggest that rolling resistance is liable to quite wide variations for which the causes cannot be assigned on the basis of tests in which all sorts of factors are varying, and only a thorough experimental investigation could be relied on to assess the precise influence of various factors on rolling resistance. But some background can be established by calculation.

15.6. TRACK JOINT FRICTION

Looking at the question of joint friction from a theoretical angle we can make calculations which suggest that the loss may be quite considerable and indicate the factors on which it must depend but in view of the uncertainty regarding so many factors such calculations should not be relied on to yield any quantitative estimate of the actual loss.

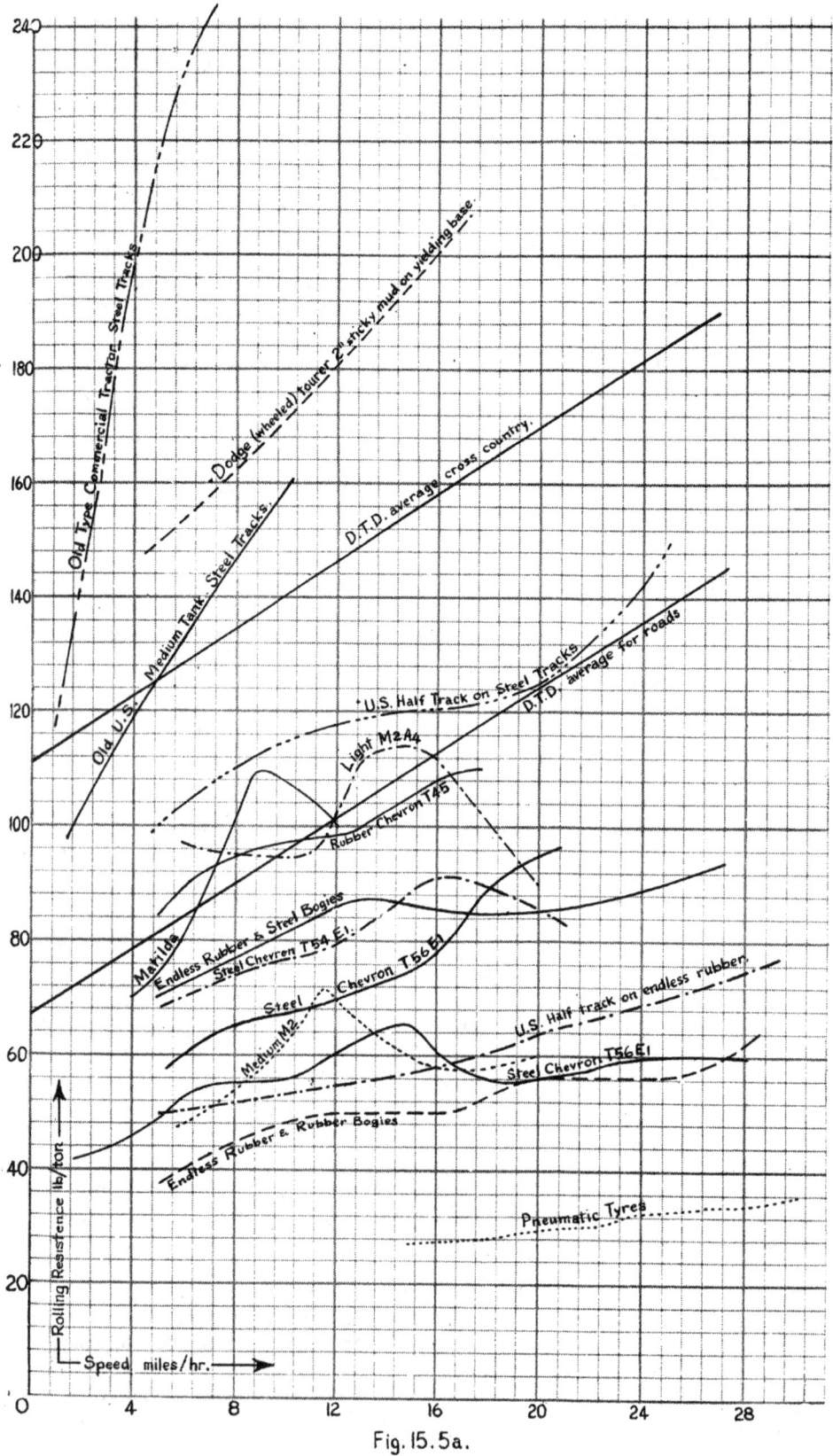

Fig. 15.5a.

In the first place there is considerable uncertainty as to what the co-efficient of friction in the pin joint is likely to be. No doubt figures can be obtained from hand books for the co-efficient of friction between the metal of the pin and the metal of the track link, both surfaces being clean and slightly lubricated. The actual surfaces, so far from being lubricated, would be dirty and might be separated by an abrasive mixture of sand and water. Then again the co-efficient may vary with the actual pressure if this is high so that the friction will depend on whether the pressure is uniformly distributed over the surface or not. In particular if any bending of the pin occurs it may jam in the pinhole or press on opposite sides of it so that the track tension is only the difference between these opposite pressures although the friction of the joint will depend on their sum.

Moreover it is impossible to say through what angle a joint is moved owing to flap or wave motion in the track and owing to rocking of links on the ground.

We will however work out an example neglecting all these points.

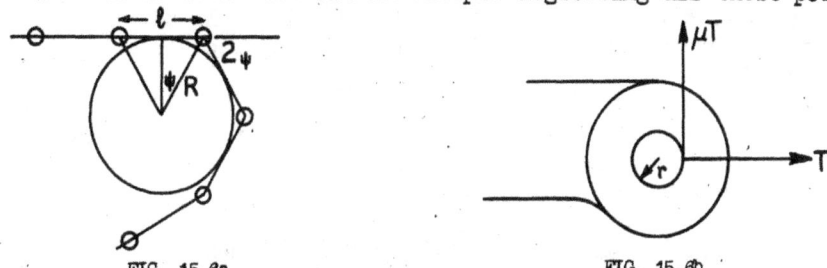

FIG. 15.6a   FIG. 15.6b

If, (in Fig. 15.6a.) l is the pitch, R the radius of a wheel round which the track passes and 2ψ the angle turned through by the joint from the flat position then

$$\sin \psi = l/2R$$

If, (in Fig. 15.6b) T is the track tension in tons, μ the co-efficient of friction between the track and the pin and r the pin radius, then, assuming the pin is an easy fit in its hole when subjected to tension, the torque resisting turning will be

$$\text{Torque} = \mu T r$$

whence the work done in turning through the angle 2ψ will be

$$\text{Work} = \mu T r . 2\psi = 2\mu T r \arcsin l/2R = \text{approx.} \mu T l . \frac{r}{R}$$

If the velocity of the tank is v ft/sec. the rate at which links pass a given point will be v/l links per sec. and if the turning occurs at n points, the power required will be

$$\text{Power} = 2 \mu T r (\arcsin l/2R) \times nv/l \text{ ft. lbs/sec. per track.}$$

If the track pitch is short compared with the wheel radius, $\psi = \sin \psi$ and the power becomes $2 \mu T . nv \frac{r}{R}$ and the rolling resistance

$2 \mu T n \frac{r}{R}$ lbs, for two tracks.

For clean lubricated metals the coefficient of friction is quite low but with dust or dirt and high pressure it would be considerably higher. Suppose we take $\mu = .5$, track tension $T = 1$ long ton, pin radius $r = 1/24$ ft., radius $R = 1$ ft. $n = 8$ (this is a minimum if there is a sprocket and idler as the joint must flex as it reaches and leaves the sprocket, idler, front road wheel and back road wheel) $v = 44$ ft/sec, then:-

$$\text{Power} = 2 \times \tfrac{1}{2} \times 1 \times \tfrac{1}{24} (\arcsin \tfrac{1}{2}) \times \frac{8 \times 44}{\tfrac{1}{3}} \text{ft. tons/sec.}$$

$$= \frac{8 \times 44 \times 3}{24} = .1676 \times \frac{2240}{550} \text{ H.P.}$$

= 30 H.P. per track.

On a 30 ton tank this would be 2 H.P./ton which at 44 ft/sec. represents a rolling resistance of 25 lbs/ton.

This example, though it may be very far from the true figure, indicates that the power lost in flexing the track may be by no means negligible (1), and also enables us to see fairly clearly what factors will influence the power lost in this way.

In the first place obviously the power lost depends on the coefficient of friction and the absence of any binding of the pins in the pinholes due to bending. If lubrication is ruled out, then all that can be done is to ensure absence of binding and choose metals which slide easily with a film of abrasive dirt, whether wet or dry, between them. We have no figures for the resistance to shear of rubber bushings but it seems likely that these may show a considerable advantage due to some of the energy used to bend the hinge being recovered when it straightens out.

The pin radius should be as small as possible consistant with avoiding bending and excess localised pressure (2). This points to a multishear link and careful attention to pin bending.

The angle through which the joint has to turn depends on the radius of wheels it has to pass round. Front and rear road wheels, sprocket and idler should be as big as possible.

The pitch of the track appears to make no difference to the power lost in pin friction since although a short pitch gives a smaller angle of turn there are more joints to turn. We are not of course here speaking of wear in the pin joints.

The number of times a joint has to flex as it passes round the track can be reduced by having the sprocket and idler on the ground, making it unnecessary for the joint to flatten out and then bend again on two occasions. In fact the commercial tractor arrangement employing a very large sprocket and idler on the ground seems almost the ideal in this respect, while the Tetrarch, using the road wheels as sprocket and idler, and various American light tanks having the rear idler on the ground, are likely to be better than the conventional arrangement with a raised sprocket and idler. Additional flexing will occur where the track passes over return wheels and it is possible that the use of a skid (as on Churchill) may reduce losses in this direction.

Perhaps the most important aspect of this rather academic examination is the fact that the power lost varies directly as the track tension and consequently the ordinary test of rolling resistance may give quite a wrong idea of what the real figure will be when a tractive effort is being exerted. Admittedly the tractive effort is likely to reduce the tension somewhat at certain points but it may increase it very greatly at others. It seems desirable to carry out tests of rolling resistance on load to ascertain whether this increase results in a serious loss of efficiency or whether it is actually only a negligible proportion of the resistance represented by the load itself.

---

(1) *This does not mean that track joint friction is necessarily the major cause of rolling resistance, and actually the lubricated tracks of the A.9 and A.10 had a relatively high rolling resistance.*

(2) *For some examples of the effect of pressure on coefficient of friction see Machinery's Handbook. Page 507. also*
Hunter M.C., "Static and Clinging Friction of Pivot Bearings,"
Engineering," Feb. 1944. pp. 120 and 138 - 140.

15.7. POWER LOSS DUE TO FINITE PITCH OF TRACK. SCRUB

The fact that a track consists of a number of rigid links and not a continuously flexible band introduces various further possible sources of loss due either to friction or hammering.

One possible source of frictional loss is scrub, that is to say, friction between the link and the road, especially as the link is laid on the ground.

If a small front road wheel carrying a weight W is approaching a link (arranged spud leading) inclined at an angle of attack θ, and the height of the track pin above the spud face is h then the work done against a coefficient of friction μ will be

$$\mu W h \theta$$

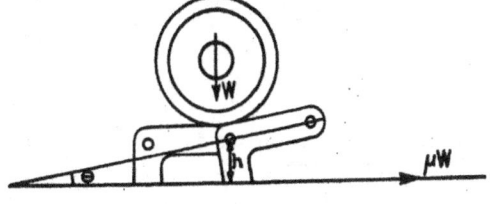

FIG. 15.7a

In the case of certain Churchill tracks the value of h is about $3\frac{3}{4}"$. Taking it as a round figure of $4"$ ($= \frac{1}{3}$ ft) and assuming a coefficient of friction of a half and a load of two long tons, the work done for an angle of attack of $15°$ would be equal to

$$\mu W h \theta = \tfrac{1}{2} \times \frac{2 \times 2240}{3} \times \frac{15 \pi}{180} = \frac{1760}{9} \text{ ft. lbs.}$$

If the pitch is $8"$ at a speed of 15 miles an hour or 22 feet per second each track lays $22 \times 3/2$ links per second, making a total of 66 links per second for the two tracks. Hence the horse-power required for scrub would be $\frac{1760}{9} \times \frac{66}{550} = 23\tfrac{1}{2}$ horse-power. Not only does this represent an appreciable rolling resistance (14.2/3 lbs/ton on a 40 ton tank) but it must also be remembered that the power is devoted entirely to grinding away the material of the tracks and roads.

The example given above does not represent the actual situation on Churchill since a modification made to reduce pitching has had the effect of reducing the angle of attack to a minimum. From the formula given for the work done, namely $\mu W h \theta$, it will be seen that the work can be reduced either by reducing W or by reducing θ. By providing an additional wheel which carries no load but guides the tracks so that the first load-carrying wheel has a very small angle of attack, it is possible to effect a substantial reduction in the wear and loss of power occasioned by scrub.

15.8. LEADING AND TRAILING SPUDS.

One reason for fitting single spud tracks with the spud leading is to minimise disturbance of the ground as the track link is lifted. Another effect of this will be clear from the foregoing section. If the track is fitted with the spud trailing i.e. at the forward end so that it comes last to the front bogie, the link will be entirely free of any load when it slaps the ground. If, on the other hand, it is fitted the other way round as in the tracks on Churchill its spud is carrying the whole weight of the bogie wheel when its opposite end and the spud of the next track is slapping the ground. As a result there will be a very considerable friction moment tending to control the slapping movement and make for gentle laying of each link on the ground, at the expense of wear and loss of power as calculated above.

15.9. POWER LOSS AND NOISE DUE TO VIBRATION AND HAMMERING.

There are a number of points at which a series of impacts occur which are bound to consume power and produce vibration and noise.

15.10

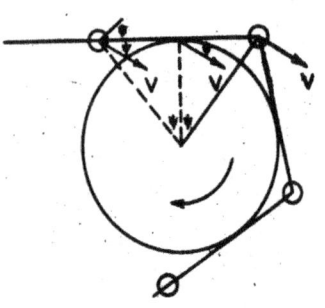

FIG. 15.9a

At any point where the track flexes it forms not a smooth curve but a part of a polygon, as indicated in Figure 15.9a., and already discussed in connection with sprockets in Section 14.3.

Assuming that the links already wrapped round a wheel (whether road wheel, sprocket or idler) move with it at velocity v as if they were fixed to it, then the leading end of a link about to engage the wheel will be moving tangentially.

Hence if the whole link is moving so as to remain parallel to a given direction its centre has a component of velocity $v \sin\psi$ towards the centre of the wheel while its trailing end has a component $v \sin 2\psi$, where ψ is the angle subtended at the centre by half a pitch. In the case of a road wheel or idler the middle of the link will usually strike the wheel whereas in the case of a sprocket the trailing end often does so. In either case the component of velocity referred to is suddenly reduced to nothing by the impact between the surfaces.

In the case of a leading roadwheel of small diameter and a long pitched track the situation may be somewhat different since no links are wrapped round the wheel, but the link previous to the one just being engaged is held down to the ground by the weight of the road wheel as indicated in Figure 15.9b. In this case the relative velocity has

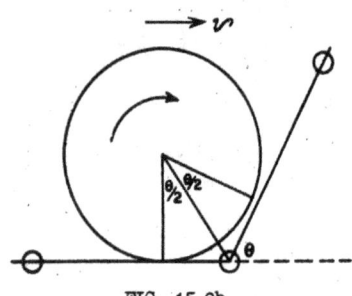

FIG. 15.9b

a component towards the centre $v \sin\theta$ where θ is the angle of attack.

Where the pitch of the track is long it is therefore worth while considering the provision of rubber pads or tyres to cushion these impacts, as is done on the sprocket and idler of Churchill but not on its front road wheel.

In the case of the sprocket there will not only be a transverse relative velocity resulting in a series of impacts but also a longitudinal fluctuation of velocity resulting in a fluctuating track tension superimposed on any steady tension.

15.10. **KINETIC ENERGY LOSS DUE TO HAMMERING ON SPROCKETS ETC.**

If for the moment we imagine the whole mass of the link concentrated at its centre then this mass has a component of velocity $v \sin\psi$ relative to the sprocket and when it strikes the latter the corresponding kinetic energy is dissipated by the impact.

If the weight per link is W and the weight per foot is $w = \dfrac{W}{l}$ where l is the pitch, and R is the radius of the sprocket, then the kinetic energy lost per link will be $\dfrac{Wv^2 \sin^2\psi}{2g} = \dfrac{wlv^2 \sin^2\psi}{2g}$.

The number of links striking the sprocket per second per track will be $\dfrac{v}{l}$ so that the rate of loss of kinetic energy of two track will be

$$2 \frac{v}{l} \frac{wlv^2 \sin^2\psi}{2g} \text{ ft. lbs/sec} = \frac{w v^3 \sin^2\psi}{550} \text{ H.P.}$$

or since $\sin \psi = \dfrac{l}{2R}$

Power lost $= \dfrac{w}{2,200 g} \cdot \dfrac{v^3 l^2}{R^2}$ .... (i)

whence rolling resistance $= \dfrac{wv^2 l^2}{4gR^2}$ .... (ii)

For Churchill $w = 90\ lbs/ft$, $v = 22\ ft/sec$, $l = 2/3\ ft$, $R = 5/4\ ft$

Power lost $= \dfrac{90}{2,200} \cdot \dfrac{22}{32} \cdot \dfrac{22}{1} \cdot \dfrac{22}{1} \cdot \dfrac{4}{9} \cdot \dfrac{16}{25} = \dfrac{1936}{500} = 3.87\ H.P.$

Tractive Effort $= \dfrac{550 \times 1936}{22 \times 500} = 96.8\ lbs.$

on a 40 ton tank this is about $2\frac{1}{2}$ lbs/ton.

We will now discuss these results.

The actual figure for rolling resistance due to hammering may seem negligible, but there are various points we have tacitly neglected. First we have neglected the rotational inertia of the track link which though small will add slightly to the kinetic energy. Secondly we have only considered the link actually striking the sprocket whereas actually the leading end of the next link is bound to be equally affected and probably following links will be to some extent affected. Figure 14.3a. showed diagrammatically the type of path which would be followed by the links if they were travelling slowly in which case the whole row would lose their kinetic energy, but actually it is probable that energy would be dissipated into a wave in the track which would die away by friction in the pin joints and other sources of loss. Finally this phenomenon, in addition to happening at the sprocket, will also happen at the idler and possibly at front and rear road wheels and return wheels. Altogether the loss may actually amount to ten or more times the figure given above.

As to equation (i) it is of interest to note the variables on which the loss of power depends. Obviously anything depending on kinetic energy will vary as the weight of the track. Then it will be seen that the power lost varies as the cube of the velocity so that if for example the speed of Churchill were put up from 15 to 30 miles/hour the power loss would be multiplied 8 times. At the same time it varies as the square of the pitch so if this cause of lost power is of importance we can see why short pitched tracks become almost essential for high speeds.

In this connection it is of interest to recollect that early light dragons could run with either the $3\frac{1}{2}"$ pitch $10\frac{1}{2}"$ wide manganese steel skeleton track or the $1\frac{3}{4}"$ pitch $9\frac{1}{2}"$ wide M.C.I. light tank track. Although the former was appreciably lighter it increased the rolling resistance to such an extent as to reduce the maximum speed by several miles an hour. We saw above that loss due to track joint friction should be independent of pitch, so the loss due to hammering, varying as the square of the pitch, may perhaps have had something to do with this result.

In short to reduce this source of rolling resistance we want a light track but more important a short pitch, big wheels, and as few bends as possible.

15.11. **SLAP**

The engagement of a small front road wheel with a long pitched track is of the same nature as that referred to above, although differing in detail, and will not be separately discussed.

There remains however the question of the track link striking the ground.

15.11

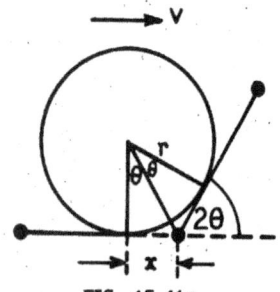

FIG. 15.11a

Figure 15.11a. represents diagrammatically a wheel resting on one link of a track which is flat on the ground, while the adjacent link slopes up at an angle of 2θ. It will be obvious that the angle between the line joining the centre of the wheel to the hinge and each of the radii to the points of contact will be equal to θ.

If x is the distance from the hinge to the point of contact with either link the velocity of the Tank $\underline{v}$ will be equal to $\frac{dx}{dt}$. What we want to find out is the angular velocity of the inclined link and as the angle of inclination is 2θ its angular velocity will be:- $2\frac{d\theta}{dt}$ but $\tan\theta = \frac{x}{R}$ (where R is the radius of the wheel.))

$$\therefore \frac{d}{dt}(\tan\theta) = \frac{d}{dt}\left(\frac{x}{R}\right)$$

$$\therefore \frac{d}{d\theta}(\tan\theta)\cdot\frac{d\theta}{dt} = \frac{1}{R}\cdot\frac{dx}{dt}$$

$$\therefore \sec^2\theta\cdot\frac{d\theta}{dt} = \frac{v}{R}$$

$$\therefore \frac{d\theta}{dt} = \frac{v\cos^2\theta}{R}$$

At the moment when the inclined link slaps the ground the angle θ has become zero so that $\cos^2\theta = 1$. If l is the pitch of the link the velocity of its centre will be the angular velocity multiplied by $l/2$. Hence from the above the velocity of the centre of the link when the latter slaps the ground is $\frac{l}{2}\cdot\frac{2d\theta}{dt} = \frac{lv}{R}$.

Hence assuming the mass concentrated at the centre

Kinetic energy per link = $\frac{wl}{2g}\cdot\frac{l^2v^2}{R^2}$

and since number of links per sec. per two tracks = $2v/l$

Power lost = $2v/l \cdot \frac{wl}{2g} \cdot \frac{l^2v^2}{R^2} \cdot \frac{1}{550} = \frac{wl^2v^3}{550gR^2}$ H.P.

It is interesting to note that this varies in the same way as the hammering losses previously treated, but is four times as great.

It will be seen from the above that in theory the velocity of slap is not dependent on the angle of attack at which the track is led on to the front bogie wheel but varies only directly as the pitch of the track and inversely as the radius of the bogie wheel (and of course directly as the forward speed of the tank). No account has here been taken of the effect of the suspension of the front road wheel and it is possible that if the inclination of the track coming on to it is very slight the suspension may yield as it comes on to each link and enable it to be laid on the ground more gently. If the angle of the track coming to the front wheel is very steep it will be realised from Figure 15.11a. that any such yield is unlikely to occur since the angular velocity of the link builds up quite gradually, varying as $\cos^2\theta$ and hence the momentary yield of the suspension would do little or nothing to reduce it.

It will be realised that if the front wheel is made three times as big and the pitch of the track is halved (as is approximately the case in British Cruiser Tanks) the velocity of slap at the same road-speed will be reduced to one sixth so that even if the speed is doubled it will still be only a third of the figure worked out for the Churchill.

15.12. COMPARISON WITH ACTUAL TRACK BEHAVIOUR.

We have assumed above that the track will move in a certain path and calculated the energy lost when it strikes sprockets etc. on this assumption. At very slow speeds there is no reason to doubt that roughly speaking it really does behave in this way. At high speeds it seems most unlikely. In the absence of experimental evidence it seems useless to try to work out any complex forms of wave or flap. But it seems worth commenting that the peculiar peaks in the curves of rolling resistance at Figure 15.5a. might be due to the fact that up to a certain speed (varying with conditions) the power lost has a hammering component varying as the cube of the speed, but beyond this the track having received a buffet does not come back for more but keeps at a respectful distance travelling as it were in mid-air in a smooth curve which merges gradually with the sprocket periphery. At the moment this is mere surmise.

15.13. LONGITUDINAL ACCELERATION DUE TO SPROCKET TOOTH ACTION.

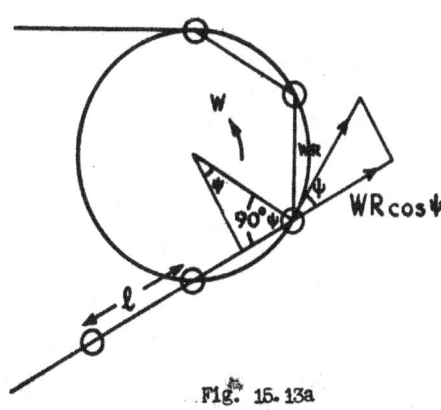

Fig. 15.13a

We saw in Section 14.3. that the movement of a track and sprocket is like a belt on a polygonal pulley.

Hence at any instant as indicated in Fig. 15.13a the component of velocity along the track is equal to $\omega R \cos \psi$ where $(90° - \psi)$ is the angle between the length of track and the radius of the pitch circle, and ω is the angular velocity

Hence the longitudinal acceleration is

$$-\omega R \sin \psi \cdot \frac{d\psi}{dt} = -\omega^2 R \sin \psi$$

since $\frac{d\psi}{dt} = \omega$

The maximum value of $\sin \psi$ is equal to $\frac{l}{2R}$ where l is the pitch of the track, whilst the maximum velocity of the track, which is approximately equal to the mean velocity is $\omega R = v$

Hence the maximum longitudinal acceleration

$$= \omega^2 R \cdot \frac{l}{2R}$$

$$= \frac{v^2}{R^2} \cdot R \cdot \frac{l}{2R} = \frac{lv^2}{2R^2}$$

15.13

Hence the maximum longitudinal acceleration is proportional to the pitch and the square of the speed and inversely proportional to the square of the radius of the sprocket.

In the case of the Churchill for example the sprocket has 23 teeth, two per link, and we can take the pitch as about 8". Whence $R = 4 \times \operatorname{cosec} \frac{360°}{23} = 14.83"$.

if $v = 15$ m/h $= 22$ f/s.

$$\text{acceleration} = \frac{v^2 l}{2R^2} = \frac{8 \cdot 22^2 \cdot 12}{2 \cdot 14.83^2} = 106 \text{ f/sec.}^2$$

$$= 3.3 \text{ g.}$$

In the case of a cruiser with twice the speed and half the pitch it would be double this, i.e. over six and a half g. This pulsating acceleration occurs at a frequency of 33 vibrations per sec. (corresponding to the lowest C on the piano).

It has been assumed above that the angular velocity of the sprocket remains constant and the track speed fluctuates. When a tractive effort is being exerted this is likely to be impossible (as it would involve an extra fluctuating tractive effort up to over $6\frac{1}{2}$ times the weight of the tank) in which case the fluctuation gets thrown back on the transmission.

It would be interesting to know whether a resilient connection between the sprocket ring and the final drive would give smoother running, by allowing slight angular oscillation between them. The actual movement need only be small. (1)

---

(1) Since this was written an article has appeared discussing the phenomenon but not attempting to assess the peak acceleration on a fast fighting vehicle.

See Fiegehen E.G.; "Track-Laying Vehicle Design "Engineering" July 14th and 21st 1944. pp. 21-2 and 43-4.

PART III

CHAPTER 21

SOIL MECHANICS IN RELATION TO TRACKS

MECHANICAL PROPERTIES OF SOILS

21.1 ITS IMPORTANCE

As indicated previously (Section 2.9) two of the most important functions of a track are to provide support and adhesion on soft ground, i.e. to prevent the wheels from sinking in and to enable them to obtain a driving grip. Clearly these functions cannot be studied without a knowledge of the properties of soils.

In the case of adhesion the problem and its importance are both fairly obvious, as the maximum possible adhesion is required for climbing slippery slopes, getting out of shell holes or ditches, or surmounting similar obstacles. It is also obvious that the question must depend on the properties of the earth at least as much as on the design of the track for if the ground gives way clearly the track cannot get a grip. (1) The problem is therefore to examine how a given area of ground can be used to the best advantage to resist tractive effort, and whether any advantage is gained by extending the area of ground used.

As regards support the problem and its importance are perhaps less obvious. It is clear that the length and width of track on the ground necessary to support a given weight are among the most important and fundamental dimensions in the design of a tank. Limitations such as the Railway Loading Gauge have set an upper limit to the overall width of the vehicle and as designers usually wanted the hull to be wider than it could be (to accommodate an adequate turret ring) the width of the individual tracks usually got squeezed out. If the ratio of the length of track on the ground to the width between track centres is excessive it gives an awkward general shape and makes steering difficult, so this limited the length of track resting on the ground.

To protect the track against being excessively squeezed out it became customary to specify a certain soft ground pressure (which we shall refer to as the mean ground pressure), obtained by dividing the weight of the tank by the total projected area of a length of track equal to the distance between the centres of the front and rear road wheels. There is some divergence of views as to whether the calculations should be based on the overall width of track or whether variations of width should be taken into account. It is suggested that the influence of other factors makes any great accuracy of little importance.

Specifying a certain mean ground pressure amounts to saying that for a given weight of tank there must not be less than a certain area of track resting on the ground, but it does not indicate how efficiently that area is to be made use of to transmit the weight to the ground. For example if some of the intermediate road wheels of a tank were removed it would made a considerable, probably disastrous, difference to its soft ground performance but it would make no difference at all to its mean ground pressure.

---

(1) *A recently suggested requirement that tanks for the South West Pacific Area should be capable of climbing a slope of $45°$ (adhesion factor 1.0) not merely involves certain track characteristics, but also amounts to a demand that all ground of moderate shearing strength in that region should be removed and replaced by something stronger, or at least prevented from getting wet.*

What we want if possible to investigate is the extent to which the ground is squashed down when a tank passes over it. If at a certain point (under a wheel) the pressure is much greater than the mean ground pressure the ground will be squashed down to a corresponding maximum depth and as the point of maximum pressure moves along, each point in the ground will be squashed down to this depth, and the depth will not be reduced merely because the pressure is less at other points. Hence in considering how far the ground is squashed down, the mean ground pressure is of no consequence and what we need to get at is the maximum pressure.

It is sometimes imagined that the mere provision of a track, however flexible it is, will, due to the tension in it, distribute the weight of the tank uniformly over the whole area of ground with which the track is in contact.

On the other hand Merritt (1) has remarked that "As a basis for calculating track pressure (i.e. a drawing-board comparison) the theoretical length of track profile in contact with the ground can be quite misleading. The actual pressures are probably but little different from those which would result if a length of track were wrapped round each wheel............". As a generalisation this probably goes too far but the calculations made later indicate that normally, even on soft ground, the pressure is only distributed over a fraction of the area of track in contact with the ground and the mean ground pressure is no indication at all of the maximum pressure, on which the squashing of the ground depends.

This squashing of the ground is of importance for two reasons. In the first place obviously if the tracks sink in beyond a certain depth the tank will become bellied. Equally important, however, is the effect on the speed and range of action of the tank on softish ground. The squashing of the ground demands a large amount of power and this power can only come from the engine of the tank via the transmission, so that if the sinkage can be reduced it will result in a direct increase of cross country speed and range of action.

It will be realised that a figure for the maximum ground pressure cannot conveniently be used as a basis for design or comparison of vehicles since it depends on, and may be largely determined by, the particular soil concerned, and there appears to be a need for some criterion of the vehicle which will take into account not merely the area of track resting on the ground but the area over which the weight is actually distributed. In the absence of experimental data it would be rash to dogmatise but we suggest tentatively, for consideration, that a useful comparative figure might be what we may term the "diametral ground pressure". This would be defined as the weight of the tank divided by the projected area of a length of track equal to the sum of the diameters of the road wheels. This is a dimension that can easily be assessed for a given vehicle and it will be seen later that in certain of the calculations and subject to certain assumptions, it goes some way towards indicating what will be the sinkage on a given soil, for a given track tension per ton weight per wheel.

Before going into these questions it is necessary to have some general knowledge of the characteristics and properties of soils, and these are briefly discussed in this chapter and the next. Chapter 23 is concerned with adhesion, chapter 24 goes into questions of bearing capacity, the results being applied in chapter 25 to the assessment of ground pressure, and rolling resistance.

21.2. SOIL AS AN ENGINEERING MATERIAL

Looking round for any information that is available about the properties of the soil we find that a good deal of attention has been given to the subject at one time and another from various points of view but not from the point of view of tracks.

---

(1) Merritt, H.E. "The Design of High Speed Track Vehicles."
Proc. I.A.E. 1939.

The fertility of the soil has been studied from the agricultural point of view, and its origin from the geological point of view. These aspects are of no interest to the track designer and only of secondary interest to the track user (as giving him a clue to the type of soil he is likely to encounter). (1).

Of more interest, however, from our point of view is the considerable attention that has recently been given to soil mechanics, i.e. the study of the soil as an engineering material, and the various papers and books that have been written on the subject mainly in Germany and America (2). But even this work needs to be interpreted with reserve from the point of view of track design for two reasons. First much of it has not really got beyond the controversial stage and more work is required to reconcile different methods of approach and clear up obscurities, and second it has not been done from the point of view of the man designing a track but of men building foundations, dams, or roads.

The track designer is interested in knowing how far the earth will sink down under a track link in a fraction of a second and not in the settlement that occurs under the Washington Memorial in a period of half a century. Moreover the engineer who excavates a foundation can confine his attention to the particular type of soil that happens to be there, and the highway engineer may even be able to choose his soil. The tank designer on the other hand has to cater for all possible conditions and cannot even call for spuds to be attached when soft ground is encountered. Lastly the civil engineer will generally remove the top layer of the soil as he finds it, whereas the track designer may encounter turf, heather, loose stones, or mud on the surface and must take it as he finds it.

Hence we are not concerned with the particular properties of an individual soil but more with properties which are common to all soils or typical of many. We are concerned more with how two tanks compare on any one typical soil than with how two soils compare when traversed by one or more typical tanks.

With further study it may become possible to narrow down the range of soils we need to consider by eliminating certain types (such as completely cohesionless sand, wet silts, or almost liquid clay), either because they are rarely encountered or because it is out of the question to attempt to compete with them except perhaps with a track designed specially for the purpose.

This is perhaps a suitable point at which to emphasise the importance of keeping accurate records of the mechanical analysis and state or properties of the soil on which soft ground trials are carried out.

Even if we could make all our tests on the same day, which we clearly cannot, every test would leave the ground in a different state for the next test. If there is to be any hope of correlating results obtained say in America in winter, with others obtained in this country in summer, it can only possibly be from a good knowledge of the properties of soils and a record of the particular soils and their state at the time of the test. An exact record of soil conditions is important since a small change in the moisture content of a clay soil may make far more difference to performance than a change of tracks of the most widely divergent types.

---

(1) See "Tank Country". 1943. (General Staff Pamphlet)

(2) Geologically the term "soil" is reserved for the upper layer of particles which can support plant life, while lower layers are known as mantle or regolith, being composed of rock particles. Engineering literature on soil mechanics is primarily concerned with the lower layers which may be suitable for foundations, etc. and are referred to as soil, and in the present book the term soil or earth is used to cover all layers of particles between the track and the solid rock.

21.3. CHARACTERISTICS OF SOILS.

Soils of course differ widely in their chemical composition and other properties but the characteristics which concern us and on which their mechanical properties chiefly depend are the size and shape of the particles of which a soil is composed. In addition to depending on these permanent characteristics the properties of a particular soil may vary enormously from day to day depending on the arrangement of the particles and the amount of moisture in the soil

21.4. SIZE OF SOIL PARTICLES

Under the International Classification the size of the particles of which a soil is composed is indicated by its name as follows (1) :-

Gravel	2.0 mm. upwards
Coarse Sand	0.2 mm. to 2.0 mm.
Fine Sand	0.02 mm. to 0.2 mm.
Silt	0.002 mm. to 0.02 mm.
Clay	finer than 0.002 mm.

Naturally occurring soils are not of course confined to one particle size, for example, a clay soil would contain a proportion of silt and fine sand particles as well as clay particles, and the relative proportions of the different sized particles would give a useful indication of the mechanical properties to be expected of the soil (2).

21.5. SHAPE OF SOIL PARTICLES.

In the case of the larger particles the shape has a considerable bearing on the ease with which the particles can flow over one another. The shingle on beaches which has been knocked together by the tide for years or centuries consists of rounded and polished pebbles which flow far more easily than the sharper gravel found in the beds of mountain rivers. Similarly what is known as a sharp sand consists of relatively angular particles which offer a high degree of internal friction or resistance to flow or shear (See Section 23.4.).

21.6. MOISTURE CONTENT

In most places if you dig a deep hole it will fill with water up to a certain level. In fact the soil is saturated with water up to a certain level known as the water table, which is a long way below the surface in some places whilst in other places such as bogs it comes above the surface.

Above the water table the soil contains a varying amount of moisture depending on many factors such as rainfall, drainage permeability of the soil, transpiration through plants and direct evaporation etc. When and why a soil acquires a given moisture content are matters that can be left to the geologist and meteorologist, but the profound effect of moisture content on the mechanical properties of a soil is a matter of direct interest to the track designer.

The effect of moisture is of a capillary nature. If two glass plates with a drop of water between them are pressed together the water tends to make them stick together owing to surface tension.

---

(1) *The classification of the U.S. Bureau of Public Roads is somewhat different, namely:-*
Gravel, over 2 mm; Coarse sand, 0.42 to 2 mm; Fine sand, 0.05 to 0.42 mm; Silt, 0.005 to 0.05 mm; Clay, finer than 0.005mm.
(2) *For some mechanical analysis curves for typical soils see:-*
Markwick A.H.D., "Soil Mechanics in Road & Aerodrome Construction".
Jnl. Inst. C.E. March 1942, p. 64.

In the same way a minute drop of water between two particles of soil tends to hold them together, the effect being known as cohesion. The effect is greater with a moderate amount of moisture than with very little or very much. This is easy to understand since with very little moisture relatively few particles get wetted, whereas with very much moisture the particles are completely immersed, and there is no surface tension. Cohesion is only pronounced in the case of clay soils the small particles of which can get close together giving numerous thin water films; in the case of sands cohesion is relatively slight.

The above gives only a very rough idea of the effect of moisture in producing cohesion, which is discussed far more fully by Keen (1)

Another extremely important property of moisture in a soil is its capacity to exert a neutral or hydrostatic pressure. If a saturated soil is loaded, a part of the load is taken by the water until the latter has time to percolate or be squeezed away. This part of the load adds nothing to the shear strength of the soil and is therefore wasted as far as producing adhesion is concerned, as discussed in Chapter 23.

21.7. ARRANGEMENT OF PARTICLES

The spacing and arrangement of particles also have a marked effect on the properties of a soil.

When soil has been disturbed, as by digging, or when it is deposited by wind or water, it will generally be in a loose open structure, whereas the action of rain or of pressure and vibration tends to consolidate it to a close compact structure.

Hence, two forms of consolidation, or squashing down soil from a loose to a compact structure, need to be distinguished. When the ground is dry consolidation merely squeezes out air, and occurs relatively quickly, and there does not seem to be much information as to the laws governing it. By bringing the particles into a tighter mass it increases the limiting shear strength but the moment shear starts the particles revert to a sort of uniform spacing and the increase is lost. On the other hand with a moist soil moisture is squeezed out. This takes time in any case and in addition it is opposed by capillary action. Hence a load put on a moist soil is initially supported on the water and as the latter is gradually squeezed out at a rate depending on the load, the sinkage is a function both of the load and the time.

Apart from this sinkage by consolidation, if a greater load is applied the soil may fail by a shearing action, the soil in effect flowing bodily outwards from under the load without necessarily suffering any further decrease of volume. The load per unit area that a particular soil will support when it fails by shear is termed the bearing capacity of the soil.

---

(1) Keen, B.A. "The Physical Properties of the Soil". Chapters 3 and 4

CHAPTER 22.

SOILS ACTUALLY ENCOUNTERED

22.1. INTRODUCTORY

In a series of articles (1) entitled "Ground surface conditions throughout the world" Messrs. Roadless Traction have discussed some of the types of natural surface most likely to be encountered, from the point of view of their use as routes by vehicles. These articles were written some years ago and in some cases the theoretical explanations or observations may require qualification in view of recent theory, but from the practical point of view it is thought useful to outline some of the gist of their contents.

The types of surface considered are divided into the following:-

a) Shingle
b) Sand
c) Wind blown sand
d) Volcanic soil
e) Laterite
f) Loam
g) Clay
h) Ice
i) Snow.

22.2 SHINGLE

Shingle is included mainly because in mountainous districts, such as the north west frontier, roads tend to be rare, and often the only routes at all possible for vehicles are river beds with a shingle surface.

The bearing capacity of shingle varies little with weather conditions but it is considerably affected by the shape of the pebbles and whether or not they are mixed with sand or earth, grass etc. which tend to bind them together.

With shingle composed of well-rounded pebbles and no binder, such as is found on many beaches, the bearing capacity is very poor, of the order of 4 to 5 lbs/sq.in. or even as low as 3 lbs/sq.in., owing to the tendency of the shingle to flow from under the loaded area. The bearing capacity is increased by increasing the loaded area. This the article attributes to the fact that the edges of the area are ineffective.

Moreover the bearing capacity is improved by a high coefficient of sliding friction between the track and the shingle, tending to resist outward flow, and is reduced by any rocking of the track, or other action tending to disturb the shingle. In these respects a wooden surface was found to be much better than a smooth steel one, and the implication is that a rigid girder track would be much better than an ordinary freely pivoted track.

It is also stated that the provision of spuds gives no advantage compared with a smooth surface.

22.3. SAND.

Sand is in general a difficult surface for transport and varies considerably with the shape and arrangement of the particles and the amount of moisture present. A sharp sand, i.e. where the grains are not so rounded and polished that they flow easily, gives better bearing capacity than a more polished one.

---

(1) *Roadless News.* June, July, Sept., Oct., Nov. and Dec., *1932*, and Jan. and Feb., *1933.*

A little moisture is most desirable as it acts as a binder but if the sand is immersed it tends to behave as quicksand. This the article attributes to the lubricating effect of the water but it seems probable that buoyancy plays an important part in reducing the effective weight of the sand, upon which, in the absence of cohesion or surcharge, its bearing capacity depends. (1).

For dry loose but not windblown sand the pressure should not exceed 20 lbs/sq.in. and preferably be as low as 15 lbs/sq.in. A smooth surface is best for a trailer but for a driven track a slight roughening is desirable but no pronounced spud. As in the case of shingle, but to a lesser extent, any convexity or any rocking of the track surface tends to encourage flow, and the larger the unbroken area of surface the greater will be the bearing capacity in lbs/sq.in.

22.4. WINDBLOWN SAND

Windblown sand differs strikingly in its character from ordinary sand and is well-known to those familiar with the desert districts where it occurs. It consists of grains so small, well rounded and highly polished that even a slight wind keeps them continually in motion rolling over one another.

The pressure should never exceed at most 15 lbs/sq.in. and for good results should be below 5 lbs/sq.in. Uniform distribution over a flat or even slightly concave area without even slight projections, absence of rocking, and distribution over a large area are of great importance. The difficulties of negotiating a gradient are particularly marked.

(The characteristics of naturally occuring sand surfaces are discussed in some detail by Bagnold). (2).

22.5. VOLCANIC SOIL

Although actual deposits of lava are limited to the relatively close vicinity of volcanoes, the volcanic dust comprising a highly abrasive and penetrating pumice power is windblown to great distances (occasionally up to 2000 miles) and vast areas in North America and parts of Asia are covered with this dust. This is easily disturbed to form a choking cloud and little can be done to improve going conditions on it beyond adopting the same precautions as for windblown sand.

In course of time and under favourable climatic conditions volcanic soil may by a process of weathering be converted into or replaced by a very fertile rich loam, (as in the Hawaiian Islands). Such soils are included under the heading Loam.

22.6. LATERITE

Laterite is a form of decomposed rock, which often retains a characteristic structure resulting from that of the rock modified by the decomposition, and is very abundant in tropical countries such as Ceylon, India, Burma, Africa, America, etc. Laterite, unlike the materials already dealt with, will consolidate and harden under pressure provided this is not excessive. Under dry conditions a uniformly distributed 20 to 25 lbs/sq.in. can be borne without disintegration but if wet a limit of 15 to 20 is desirable.

Rocking of the track is less serious than on the soils already discussed and some projections on the surface may be desirable, especially under wet conditions, to penetrate a lubricating surface film. A large unbroken area of pressure is not essential provided the actual pressure does not exceed the figures specified.

---

(1) See Hogentogler C.A., "Engineering Properties of Soils", P.162,
Also Section 24.5
(2) Bagnold, Lt.Col. R.A., "The Physics of Blown Sand and Desert Dunes"

22.7. LOAM

Loam is far and away the most important of the natural soil surfaces as it is the most prevalent throughout the world. It comprises a mixture of sand, clay and decomposed vegetable matter or humus. In a heavy loam the predominating material is the clay whilst in a light loam it is the sand. Loam can be considerably consolidated and hardened by moderate pressure, as occurs in footpaths for instance, but will fail under excessive pressure especially if the formation of ruts encourages subsequent vehicles to use the same wheel tracks, and causes water to lie in them.

The pressure should not exceed 15 or at most 20 lbs/sq.in. uniformly distributed. The tendency to flow is not pronounced but there is little tendency towards the formation of a lubricating film so that projections on the track surface are harmless but not particularly necessary. Rocking of loaded track links is undesirable but less serious than with some other surfaces.

22.8. LOESS (1)

Though geologically a form of loam, loess can be described as a soft porous rock, pale yellowish or buff in colour, which may form vertical or overhanging cliffs and which occurs eastward from north west France, in China and in parts of America. In mechanical properties it resembles something between loam and clay.

When dry, loess will withstand pressures of 25 or even 30 lbs/sq.in. In wet weather a lubricating film is liable to form and a tread pattern is desirable. In other respects it calls for no special treatment.

22.9. CLAY

Clay has very special characteristics and is very widely distributed. For the passage of vehicles one clay differs but little from another but the characteristics of any clay are completely transformed by a change of moisture content. In fact the article suggests that transportation over wet clay is out of the question and that passage over clay in wet weather can only be practicable where the route chosen is drained so that the water runs off it.

Provided clay is dry pressures as high as 50 - 60 lbs/sq.in. can be supported although about half these figures are preferable. It is desirable but not of great importance that the track surface should be entirely smooth or flat, since the hard, cement-like nature of dry clay enables it to stand up to traffic which would destroy a softer surface.

22.10. ICE

The main difficulty on ice is of course to obtain adhesion and it is suggested that this is only possible by the use of special spikes which bite into the ice, care being taken that these are self-clearing so that they do not become choked and masked by accumulations of ice. Mechanical transport over ice cannot be achieved without damage to the surface.

22.11. SNOW.

Freshly fallen snow will only support 1 to 1½ lbs/sq.in. without appreciable sinkage taking place. After a few hours its own weight compacts it till it will support 1 to 2 lbs., and when really compacted and hardened by traffic its properties are in many ways similar to those of ice and it may support 100 lbs/sq.in. or more without appreciable sinkage.

---

(1) *Similar to the British soil known as brick-earth.*

As with ice, projections must be used to gain adhesion, and it is even more important that these should be self cleaning, especially when the snow is thawing. (1)

22.12. GENERAL REMARKS

A final article summarises the conclusions arrived at and includes some comments on the question of speed, to the effect that in general higher speed involves less economical working.

Throughout the series the primary viewpoint is that of regular commercial transport over routes where the construction of proper roads would not be economic, and various references are made to the use of binders for stabilising the natural surface. From this point of view damage to the surface is clearly bad in itself as rendering the route progressively less and less satisfactory for traffic.

From the military point of view these considerations appear in rather different perspective. For a fighting vehicle speed has advantages entirely unconnected with economy. On the other hand damage to cross country routes (other than those used regularly) is not likely to matter much apart from the secondary effect that the power required to do the damage detracts from the range and performance of the machine.

---

(1) See also
Mech. Board. 1st Annual Report 1934. para. 28 and
Mark, Dr. H. "Report and Curves on Snow Conditions, The Studebaker Corporation Cargo Carrier Light T.15. O.S.R.D. Report 1187"

CHAPTER 23

ADHESION AND SHEARING STRENGTH OF SOILS

23.1. INTRODUCTORY

The limit of adhesion, when track slip occurs, may arise either when the material of the track slides over the supporting surface, as for instance on a concrete road, or when spuds on the track, having dug into the ground, cause failure of the earth by a shearing action between one part of the earth and another. The former type of slip is governed by the laws of solid friction and the latter by laws in some ways similar and it will be convenient first briefly to recall the main points of these laws.

23.2. ELEMENTARY LAWS OF FRICTION. COEFFICIENT OF FRICTION

If two flat surfaces are in contact and a force is built up tending to make one slide over the other no movement takes place until this force reaches a certain limiting value. This value varies with the material, nature and state of the surfaces, and is also directly proportional to the normal force pressing the surfaces together. Within limits it is independent of the area of the surfaces in contact (for a given total normal force).

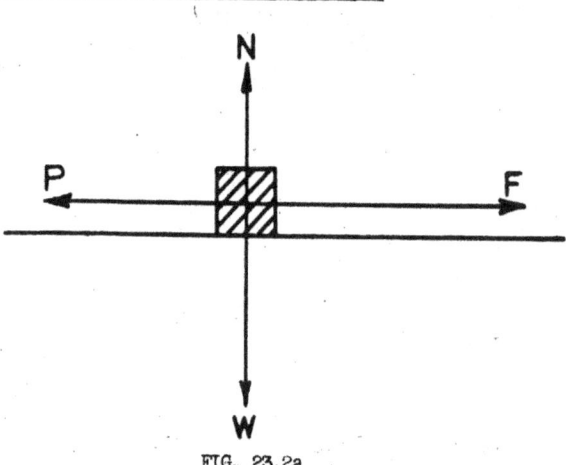

FIG. 23.2a

Thus if F is the friction and N the normal force and $F/N = \mu$, then within limits μ is a constant. This constant is known as the coefficient of friction for the particular surfaces.

23.3. ADHESION FACTOR

Whether the slip occurs between the material of the track and the soil, or between two layers of soil, the ratio of the frictional or shearing force to the normal force is known as the adhesion factor. Thus in the case of solid friction between the track and for example a concrete road, the coefficient of friction and the adhesion factor are the same thing, and within limits are independent of the area of contact.

Where the track is provided with spuds which dig into the ground it generally follows that slip can only occur if there is some shearing of the upper layer of the ground between the spuds and as we shall see later the adhesion factor in these circumstances will (on a cohesive soil) be dependent on the area of contact. It is as well to bear in mind that, as indicated later with reference to Figure 23.8a. to e., both shear and surface friction may be present together, especially on hardish ground where the bulk of the weight is carried on the spuds.

23.4. SHEARING OF SOILS : COULOMB'S EQUATION

The law governing the friction of the kind that arises when a sample of earth is sheared is somewhat similar but not identical to the laws of solid friction, the resemblance varying with the type of soil. In this case the force required to produce shearing (per unit area) is given by Coulomb's equation namely.

$$s = p \tan \varphi + c$$

where p is the normal pressure, φ the angle of internal friction (1) and c the cohesion.

Since $s = c$ when $p = 0$, the cohesion is equal to the shearing resistance when the normal pressure is zero.

Internal friction is primarily associated with granular particles such as sand, whilst cohesion is associated with binders such as clays.

Hogentogler (2) illustrates these effects thus:-
"The effect of the granular material may be illustrated by two pieces of sandpaper when pressed together. They will exert no resistance to being pulled apart but will resist efforts to slide one over the other, this resistance increasing as the force with which they are pressed together increases.

The effect of binders is illustrated by the performance of two sheets of sticky flypaper when pressed together. Under these conditions they exert high resistance to being pulled apart owing to the cohesion of the glue-like materials brought into contact with each other."

TABLE 23.4a.

	Cohesive strength c lbs/sq.in.	Angle of internal friction φ	$\tan \varphi$
Silts wet	0	10°	.176
Sands dry	0	34°	.674
tightly compacted	0	40-50°	.839-1.92
Sands immersed	0	34°	.674
Clay liquid	.7	0°	0
" very soft	1.4	2°	.035
" soft	2.8	4°	.070
" fairly stiff	7.0	6°	.105
" very stiff	14.0	12°	.213
Cemented sand and gravel wet	3.5	34°	.674
Cemented sand and gravel	7.0	34°	.674

Table 23.4a. gives typical figures of internal friction and cohesion for some different types of soil. These figures are shown in graphic form in Figure 23.9a.

From the above it will be realised that in the case of a cohesionless material like dry sand the adhesion follows the laws of solid friction referred to above.

The resistance to shear, like solid friction, is directly proportional to the normal pressure. A cohesive material on the other hand can offer a resistance to shear even when there is no normal pressure, in which case the adhesion factor would theoretically be infinite.

---

(1) *Strictly speaking this angle is the angle of shearing resistance which is only in certain circumstances the same as the angle of internal friction. The distinction is elaborated by Terzaghi but is beyond the scope of the present treatment. See Terzaghi K., "Theoretical Soil Mechanics," Chapter 2.*

(2) *Hogentogler, C.A. "The Engineering Properties of Soils".*

It has already been remarked that moisture content and the spacing and arrangement of particles affect the properties of a soil, and it must be realised that the values of c and φ are not absolute constants for a given soil but vary with factors such as those mentioned.

Even in the case of a cohesionless material like dry sand the initial resistance to shear can be affected by compaction. It generally happens that a loose material fails gradually while a tightly compacted one fails suddenly. Hence the shear stress required to start failure of sand in a tight state is greater than in a loose state, but once flow has started the loose sand gets tighter and the tight sand gets looser until their resistance to shear are about equal, as indicated diagrammatically in Figure 23.4b. Due to this compaction the value of φ for a given sand may vary as much as $15°$.

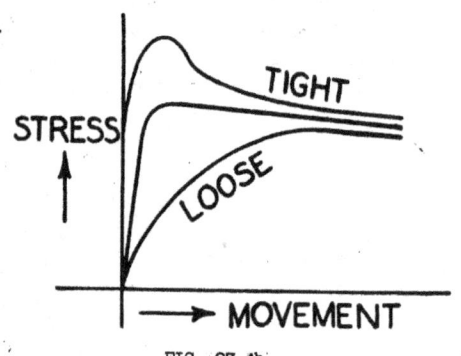

FIG. 23.4b

In the case of cohesive materials like clay the situation is very complex, particularly due to the part played by moisture.

For example if we start with three samples of a clay of different moisture contents and make a rapid series of shear tests we may obtain the dotted curves I, II and III of Figure 23.4c. If now we take sample I and make a slow series of shear tests, leaving it subjected to each value of normal pressure for a day or so before measuring the shear strength, we get a curve something like the full line I'. When the sample has been left subjected to the normal pressure p_{II} for a time moisture will have been squeezed out until its moisture content and shear strength are the same as those of sample II.

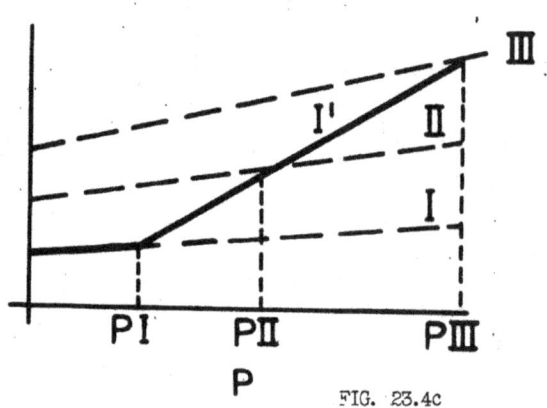

FIG. 23.4c

A rapid series of shear tests made now on sample I will result in the curve II being obtained. Moreover if the water has been allowed to drain away so that it cannot return to the sample when pressure is relieved, a subsequent slow series of shear tests will still give the lower part of curve II.

In the same way sample I or sample II can be brought to the moisture content and shear strength of sample III by further consolidation.

For our purposes it is probably best to regard materials in different states as different materials at any rate in quoting values of c and φ for wet clay, dry clay etc. In view of the short time taken by a tank to pass a given point the loading will be extremely rapid, and will have little opportunity to make much difference to moisture content although the state of the ground may be materially altered by the passage of a succession of vehicles.

An allied question is the difference between effective and neutral stresses. A load on a moist soil is partly taken on the water which it places under hydrostatic or neutral pressure. This part of the load makes no contribution to the shear strength of the soil which is determined solely by the effective load or difference between the total pressure and the neutral pressure. This is of great importance in connection with suddenly applied loads such as those due to a moving vehicle since the water will have little chance to escape.

Hence we must presume that the resistance to shear and bearing capacity of a soil, especially of a moist soil, will depend on the rate of application of the load. Owing to lack of information regarding the conditions arising with a rapidly applied load the following chapters are on the basis of slowly applied loads. It must however be borne in mind that even if the results are applicable qualitatively the values of shearing resistance and bearing capacity that apply for rapid loading may differ considerably from those that apply for slow loading of the same soil in the same condition.

It is not even possible to be quite certain whether these values will decrease or increase with increased speed of loading although it is believed that in general the adhesion will decrease and the bearing capacity increase, with increased speed of loading. Thus the hydrostatic or neutral pressure, balancing part of the load, should directly increase the bearing capacity while resulting in an adhesion corresponding to only a part of the load, so representing a reduced adhesion factor. The lack of time for consolidation and squeezing out of moisture would in certain circumstances result in reduced shear strength at high normal pressures, and hence a reduction both of adhesion and of bearing capacity.

23.5. SHEARING OF SOIL IN PLANE INCLINED AT $(45^\circ - \varphi/2)$ TO HORIZONTAL

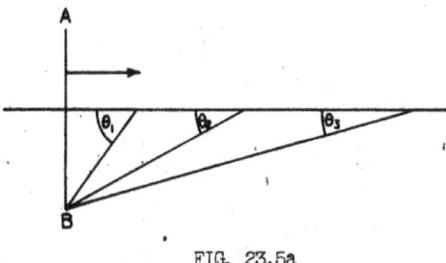

FIG. 23.5a

A complication which arises in connection with shearing of soil but not in connection with friction between two surfaces is that in the case of solid surfaces the plane in which sliding takes place is fixed beforehand, whereas in the case of shearing of soils the shearing might take place in any plane from the vertical to the horizontal (or along a curved surface). Thus in Figure 23.5a. if a vertical blade AB (like the blade of a hoe) were driven down into the earth and then forced horizontally it would be quite possible for the ground to shear along any of the planes indicated by the angles $\theta_1 \theta_2 \theta_3$ etc., although obviously it could shear along some of these planes more easily than along others. If the plane of rupture were very nearly vertical the horizontal force would be pushing the two surfaces towards one another and hence producing a high normal pressure between them whilst only a very small component of it would be in a direction tending to cause shear.

At the other end of the scale if the plane of rupture were very nearly horizontal it would mean that an enormously long wedge of soil would have to be shifted. The opposition to the shifting depends on the force due to internal friction which in turn depends on the weight of the wedge plus any loading of its upper surface, and also on the cohesion which is proportional to the length of the sliding surface. Hence both these components get bigger and bigger as the sliding surface gets more and more nearly horizontal. Accordingly we may expect that between the vertical and the horizontal there is some inclination of the sliding surface at which the horizontal force required to produce shear will be a minimum.

In section 24.4 Appendices 1 to 8 we examine the stresses in an earth which is in a state of plastic flow or shear according to Coulomb's equation and we show that at every point the surfaces of rupture are inclined to the plane on which acts the major principal stress, at angles of $(45^\circ + \varphi/2)$.

If the force applied to our vertical hoe blade is horizontal it has no shear component and hence the major principal stress in the adjacent ground acts on vertical planes, whence the lines of rupture are inclined to the vertical at angles of $(45° + \varphi/2)$ or to the horizontal at $(45° - \varphi/2)$ see Figure 23.5b.

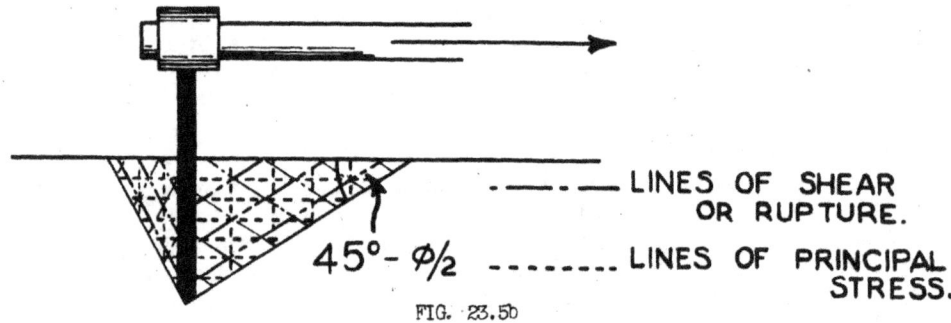

FIG. 23.5b

Hence if a vertical blade such as a hoe is driven into the ground and then moved horizontally the earth will shear in a plane inclined at an angle $(45° - \varphi/2)$ to the horizontal, where φ is the angle of internal friction. This angle of rupture is independent of the cohesion of the soil and also of any surcharge or surface loading that may be applied on top of the soil.

23.6. CONDITIONS FOR SHEAR IN HORIZONTAL PLANE OR PLANE INCLINED AT $(45° - \varphi/2)$.

In the foregoing section we saw that if a vertical blade is thrust into the ground and then moved horizontally the ground will shear not in a horizontal direction but in a plane inclined to the horizontal at an angle $\beta = (45° - \varphi/2)$ where φ is the angle of internal friction. β will vary from $45°$ for liquid clay or other liquid for which $\varphi = 0$ to less than $30°$ for a granular material like sand for which $\varphi = 30°$ or more.

It may be asked how this is reconciled with the action of a spudded track which appears to shear the ground in a horizontal plane.

If the spuds are far apart or are only dug in to a slight depth the ground will actually shear or flow in planes inclined to the horizontal and the surface will pile up roughly in the manner indicated in Figure 23.6a.

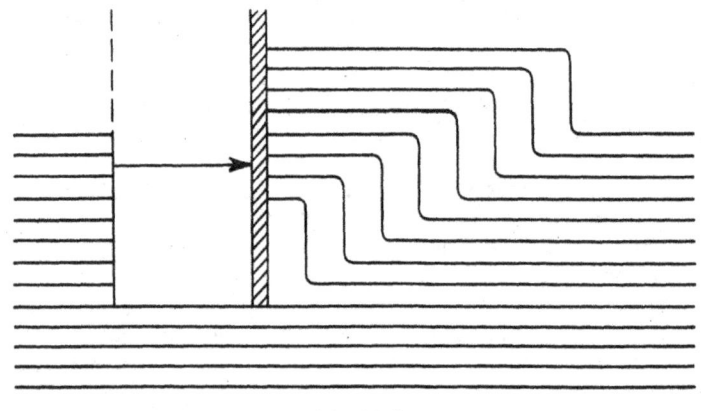

FIG. 23.6a

In calculating the angle at which the earth would shear it was assumed that the area of earth subjected to shear was backed up by a backing of earth in compression extending away to infinity behind it and for shear in a horizontal plane the blade would have to move an infinitely long wedge of earth. This is not the case when there are a number of spuds close together, as in this case if the shear is horizontal each spud only has to move the block of earth between itself and the next spud.

23.6

It is possible to calculate the force required to shear this block of earth in a horizontal plane, and compare it with the force required to shear it in an inclined plane, for various values of the ratio between the length of the block and its height, i.e. the depth to which the spud is embedded. This has been done in 23.6. Appendix 1 in which the horizontal forces needed to produce shear in a horizontal plane and in a plane inclined at $(45° - \varphi/2)$ are worked out and compared, and in which the limiting conditions are examined in which the two forces are equal. Curves are plotted at Figure 23.7a. giving the results for various conditions of cohesion and applied pressure. Above the particular curve concerned the shear will be inclined whilst below the curve it will be horizontal.

It should be realised that these calculations are only intended to give a rough idea of the conditions governing the transition from inclined rupture to horizontal rupture. In both cases it is assumed that the pressure exerted by the spud acts in a horizontal direction whereas due to friction it may well be inclined, thereby producing a shear stress in the adjacent soil surface.

Again although the calculations are not affected by a uniformly applied surcharge pressure it may well be that in a case such as that of Figure 23.6a. the surcharge due to a track link would be applied only on the wedge shaped portion and not on the adjacent area.

It has also been tacitly assumed that the surfaces of rupture are plane. This is true for a horizontal force acting on a vertical blade in a semi-infinite mass but is generally not true otherwise.

But it is believed that the error is on the safe side since if the soil can shear more easily in a horizontal plane than an inclined plane it will presumably not shear in the latter even if it actually starts to shear along some curved surface slightly different from the horizontal plane.

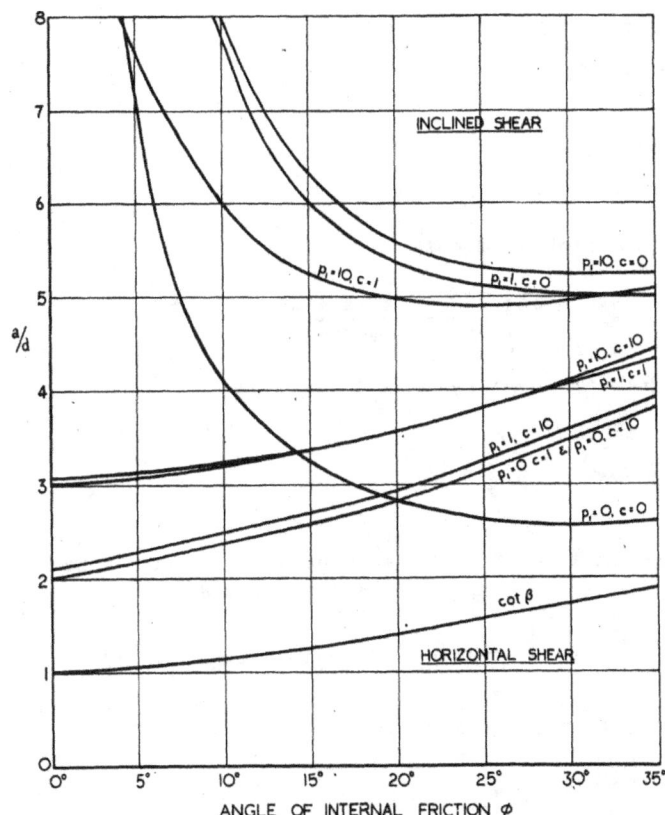

a/d. SPACING/DEPTH OF SPUDS GIVING HORIZONTAL SHEAR ON VARIOUS SOILS

FIG. 23.7a

APPENDIX 1.

23.6.1.

In considering whether rupture will occur more easily in a horizontal plane or in a plane inclined at an angle $\beta = (45° - \varphi/2)$ two cases have to be worked out separately namely where the ratio of length (or spacing of spuds) to depth $a/d > \cot \beta$ and where $a/d < \cot \beta$

Case 1. $a/d > \cot \beta$

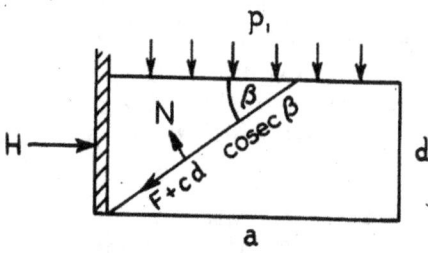

FIG. 23.6.1a

The horizontal force H_0 required to produce rupture in a horizontal plane is given by:-

$$H_0 = (ap_1 + \gamma ad) \tan\varphi + ca$$

To find the horizontal force H_β required to produce rupture in a plane inclined at the angle β, we can resolve vertically and horizontally. Equating vertical forces on a plane inclined at β to the horizontal:-

$$N \cos\beta - (F + cd \csc\beta) \sin\beta = W + p_1 a = \frac{\gamma d^2}{2} \cot\beta + dp_1 \cot\beta$$

Putting $F = N \tan\varphi$

$$N(\cos\beta - \tan\varphi \sin\beta) = \left(\frac{\gamma d^2}{2} + p_1 d\right) \cot\beta + cd$$

$$N = \frac{\left(\frac{\gamma d^2}{2} + p_1 d\right) \cot\beta + cd}{\cos\beta - \tan\varphi \sin\beta}$$

Equating horizontal forces:-

$$H_\beta = (F + cd \csc\beta) \cos\beta + N \sin\beta$$

$$= N(\tan\varphi \cos\beta + \sin\beta) + cd \cot\beta$$

$$= \left\{\left(\frac{\gamma d^2}{2} + p_1 d\right) \cot\beta + cd\right\} \frac{\tan\varphi \cos\beta + \sin\beta}{\cos\beta - \tan\varphi \sin\beta} + cd \cot\beta$$

$$= \left\{\frac{\gamma d^2}{2} + p_1 d\right) \cot\beta + cd\right\} \tan(\beta+\varphi) + cd \cot\beta$$

$$= \left(\frac{\gamma d^2}{2} + p_1 d\right) \cot^2\beta + 2cd \cot\beta$$

The limiting condition in which rupture is equally easy in a horizontal plane and in a plane inclined at angle β is that $H = H_0$ i.e.

$$H_\beta - H_0 = 0 = \left(\frac{\gamma d^2}{2} + p_1 d\right) \cot^2\beta - (ap_1 + \gamma ad) \tan\varphi + 2cd \cot\beta - ca$$

$$a(p_1 + \gamma d) \tan\varphi + ac = \left(\frac{\gamma d^2}{2} + p_1 d\right) \cot^2\beta + 2cd \cot\beta$$

$$\therefore \frac{a}{d} = \frac{2c \cot\beta + \left(\frac{\gamma d}{2} + p_1\right) \cot^2\beta}{c + (\gamma d + p_1) \tan\varphi}$$

Hence if a/d is less than this, the rupture will occur more readily in a horizontal plane.

23.6.1.

Case 2. $a/d < \cot\beta$

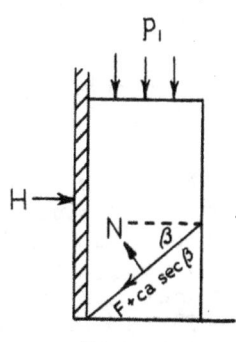

FIG. 23.6.1b

$H_0 = (ap_1 + \gamma ad) \tan\varphi + ca$

Equating vertical forces on plane inclined at β

$N \cos\beta - (F+ca \sec\beta) \sin\beta = W + p_1 a = \gamma ad - \dfrac{\gamma a^2}{2} \tan\beta + p_1 a$

putting $F = N \tan\varphi$

$N(\cos\beta - \tan\varphi \sin\beta) = \gamma ad + p_1 a - \dfrac{\gamma a^2}{2} \tan\beta + ca \tan\beta$

$N = \dfrac{a(\gamma d + p_1) - \left(\dfrac{\gamma a^2}{2} - ca\right) \tan\beta}{\cos\beta - \tan\varphi \sin\beta}$

Equating horizontal forces

$H_\beta = (F + ca \sec\beta) \cos\beta + N \sin\beta$

$\quad = N(\tan\varphi \cos\beta + \sin\beta) + ca$

$\quad = \left\{ a(\gamma d + p_1) - \left(\dfrac{\gamma a^2}{2} - ca\right) \tan\beta \right\} \dfrac{\tan\varphi \cos\beta + \sin\beta}{\cos\beta - \tan\varphi \sin\beta} + ca$

$\quad = \left\{ a(\gamma d + p_1) - \left(\dfrac{\gamma a^2}{2} - ca\right) \tan\beta \right\} \tan(\beta + \varphi) + ca$

$\quad = a(\gamma d + p_1) \tan(45° + \varphi/2) - \dfrac{(\gamma a^2 - ca)}{2} \tan(45° - \varphi/2) \tan(45° + \varphi/2) + ca$

$\quad = a(\gamma d + p_1) \cot\beta - \dfrac{\gamma a^2}{2} + ca + ca$

$H_\beta - H_0 =$

$(\gamma ad + ap_1)(\cot\beta - \tan\varphi) - \dfrac{\gamma a^2}{2} + 2ca - ca$

$\quad = (\gamma ad + ap_1) \sec\varphi - \dfrac{\gamma a^2}{2} + ca = a\gamma\left(d \sec\varphi - \dfrac{a}{2}\right) + ap_1 \sec\varphi + ca$

but it can be shown $\dfrac{\cot\beta}{\sec\varphi} = 1 + \sin\varphi$

which cannot exceed 2 so that $\sec\varphi < \tfrac{1}{2}\cot\beta$, and in the case we are considering $d\cot\beta > a$ whence $d\sec\varphi > a/2$ and the above expression is always positive.

Hence in this case $(a/d \leq \cot\beta)$ rupture will always occur more readily in a horizontal plane.

23.7. APPLICATION TO SPUD DISTRIBUTION; LIMIT TO INCREASE OF ADHESION BY ADDING SPUDS

These calculations provide some basis for a theory as to the required distribution and depth of spuds. It would seem that so long as the shear takes place in an inclined plane it would be possible to get more adhesion from the same track by using a greater number of spuds arranged closer together. If this is done a point will be reached (corresponding to the curves of Figure 23.7a.) at which shear will occur in a horizontal plane. When this is so it is fairly obvious that no further adhesion will be gained by providing additional spuds since the adhesion of each block of earth will be proportional to its length and this is being reduced just as fast as the number of spuds is being increased (it will be noted that in 23.6 Appendix 1 the expression for H_0 is proportional to a whereas the expression for H_β is not). This is true in the case of a spud of negligible thickness, but with a thick spud the spacing should be wider apart for two reasons. First the thickness of the spuds reduces the area of earth subjected to shear, and the proportion of the load applied to this area, and secondly, as indicated in section 24.4, the penetration of the spuds disturbs a volume of soil depending on the number and size of the spuds and this disturbance will tend to reduce the shear strength of the soil disturbed.

Examining Figure 23.7a. in more detail it will be seen first of all that if a/d is less than two, i.e. if the effective depth of the spud is greater than half the distance between neighbouring spuds, the shear will be horizontal in all conditions. With non-cohesive soils the limiting value of a/d is very high for small values of internal friction and diminishes as the internal friction increases. On the other hand if the cohesion is the predominating factor the limiting value increases with increase of internal friction. Perhaps the simplest way of extracting useful data from Figure 23.7a. is to tabulate limiting values of a/d for various types of soil since the curves of Figure 23.7a. include all conditions such as soils with no cohesion and no internal friction, which are of no practical interest. Table 23.7b. shows limiting values of a/d for various types of soil. From this it will be seen that the minimum value is about $2\frac{1}{2}$ for dry sand or stiff clay and about 2 for soft clay subject to no surcharge.

TABLE 23.7b

Type of Soil	Angle of Internal Friction φ	Cohesive Strength c	Spacing/depth of spuds to give horizontal shear, a/d if $P_i =$		
			0	1	10
Sand & Cement	34	10	$3\frac{3}{4}$	$3\frac{3}{4}$	$4\frac{1}{2}$
Hard Clay	10	10	$2\frac{1}{2}$	$2\frac{1}{2}$	$3\frac{1}{4}$
Soft Clay	2	1	2	3	9
Sand	34	0	$2\frac{1}{2}$	5	$5\frac{1}{4}$
Wet Silt	10	0	4	$7\frac{3}{4}$	8

23.8. ADHESION BY COMBINATION OF SHEARING AND SURFACE FRICTION DEPENDING ON SPUD DESIGN

Figures 23.8a. to e are sketches indicating a number of different ways in which a spud may obtain adhesion.

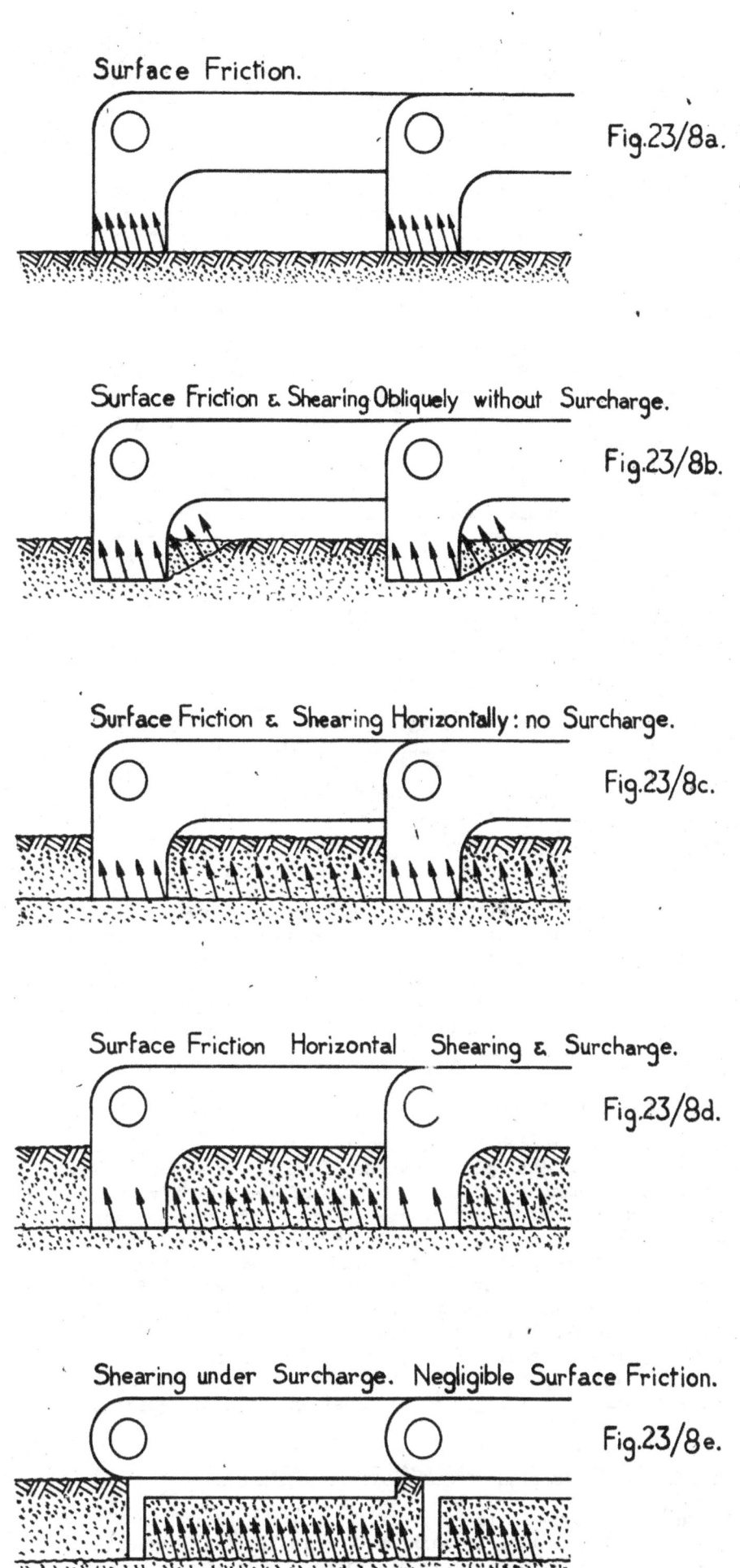

Fig. 23/8a. Surface Friction.

Fig. 23/8b. Surface Friction & Shearing Obliquely without Surcharge.

Fig. 23/8c. Surface Friction & Shearing Horizontally: no Surcharge.

Fig. 23/8d. Surface Friction Horizontal Shearing & Surcharge.

Fig. 23/8e. Shearing under Surcharge. Negligible Surface Friction.

It is perhaps not generally recognised that the mere presence of a spud of a type suitable for running on roads, does not of itself raise the adhesion from that corresponding to sliding friction to that corresponding to shearing of the ground.

The first diagram 23.8a. indicates the situation of a track having fairly wide spuds resting on a hard surface such as concrete. Here the adhesion is obtained entirely by surface friction between the track and the concrete if the track does not appreciably sink into the surface. The adhesion therefore is determined by the coefficient of surface friction between the track and the supporting surface.

In the second diagram 23.8b. the spuds of the same track have sunk some way into the ground but shear is in an inclined direction. In Figure 23.8c. the depth is such that shear is horizontal and the spuds may even have sunk until the surfaces of the track between them have come into contact with the original ground surface, but the main weight on the track is still being supported by the surfaces of the spuds themselves and the surface loading on the intervening ground is negligible. In these circumstances the adhesion obtained by the shearing action on the ground between the spuds is confined to cohesion and the majority of the adhesion may still be due to surface friction.

The fourth diagram 23.8d. shows a case in which considerable loading has been imposed on the surface of the ground between the spuds and the adhesion due to shearing is a correspondingly greater proportion of the maximum possible.

The fifth diagram 23.8e. indicates the type of track used on many commercial tractors which has comparatively narrow spuds formed of thin plates which dig into the ground very readily and support only a negligible proportion of the weight of the vehicle. In these circumstances the surface loading of the ground between the spuds is a maximum, while the disturbance caused by their penetration is a minimum.

If, as is usually the case, the adhesion factor for areas of soil rupture is greater than that for areas of surface sliding, then it will be obvious that the thinnest possible spud should be used to get the maximum total adhesion factor. For example, if the factor for areas of soil rupture is 0.7 and that for areas of surface friction is 0.4, then if half the weight W is taken on each the total adhesion force is $\frac{0.7W}{2} + \frac{0.4W}{2}$ whereas if the whole weight is taken on the areas of ruptured soil the adhesion factor is 0.7.

A compromise is demanded by the need to operate on roads, which sets a certain minimum to the spud thickness, from the viewpoints both of spud wear and road damage. The seriousness of these points was perhaps formerly overestimated, and if the tracks of the cruiser series are examined it will be seen that the pre 1939 tracks generally had a wide flat face with no spud, the single-spudded box-section track had a spud thickness about half the pitch, while the spud thickness of the ribbed track which superseded them was only about half as great. On the latest Cromwell series tracks the spud has recesses in its face to give an improved grip on roads. Purely from the point of view of soft ground adhesion it would apparently be preferable to reduce the spud thickness rather than maintaining the thickness and forming recesses in the face.

23.9. RELATION BETWEEN ADHESION AND MEAN GROUND PRESSURE.

The adhesion factor provided by solid surface friction or by shear of a completely cohesionless soil is (within limits) independent of the area over which a given load is distributed, i.e. the adhesion factor is independent of the normal pressure.

On the other hand as we have already remarked a cohesive soil will theoretically give an infinite adhesion factor if the normal pressure is zero.

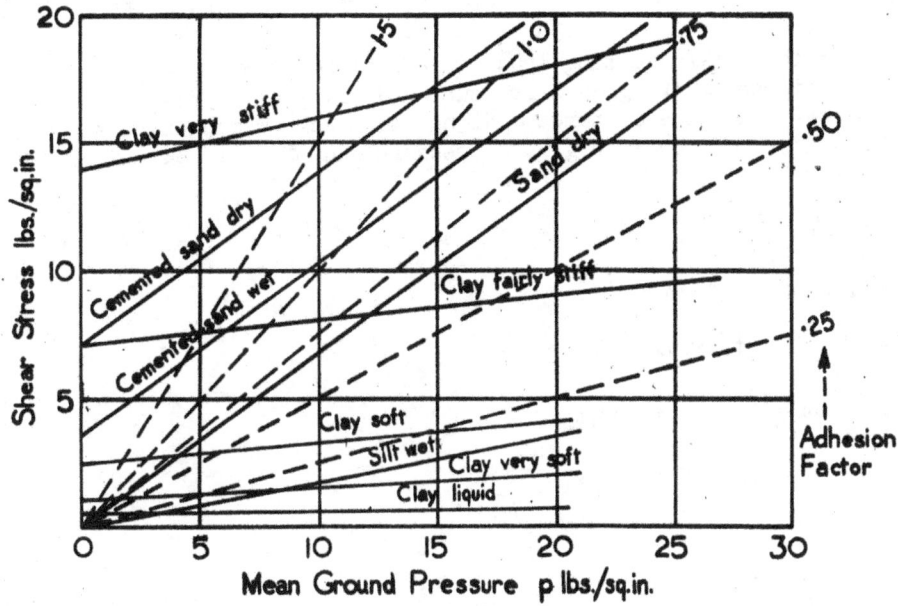

FIG. 23.9a.

Figure 23.9a. shows the figures of table 23.4a. in graphical form and by extending this figure it can be gathered that at normal pressures above about 70 lbs/sq.in. the adhesion due to internal friction is greater than that represented by cohesion even with a very stiff clay. With sandy soils the effect of cohesion is negligible.

On the other hand if the ground pressure is low, as it is under a considerable part of the track between the wheels, the part played by cohesion is far more important.

Assuming the cohesive strength and angle of internal friction are constant it can be shown (23.9 Appendix 1) that these results are equally applicable if the pressure is not uniformly distributed, and that the adhesion factor depends on the angle of internal friction φ, the cohesive strength c, and the mean ground pressure p_m thus:-

$$P/W = \tan\varphi + c/p_m \qquad \qquad 23.9.1(i)$$

Adhesion factor = tan angle of internal friction + cohesive strength ÷ mean ground pressure.

In fact in Figure 23.9a. if we take the mean ground pressure along the x axis and find the corresponding point on the line for the soil concerned, then the slope of the line joining this point to the origin will be the adhesion factor. A number of adhesion factors are shown dotted, from which it will be seen that on a cohesive soil the lower the mean ground pressure the higher will be the adhesion factor.

APPENDIX 1.

23.9. RELATION BETWEEN ADHESION FACTOR, INTERNAL FRICTION, COHESIVE STRENGTH AND MEAN GROUND PRESSURE.

If P is the total limiting tractive effort (of two tracks) W the total weight, and p the ground pressure and s the unit shear strength at any point at a distance x along the track (which extends from $x=0$ to $x=x_1$), p_m the mean ground pressure and b the track width, then:-

$$P = 2b \int_0^{x_1} s \, dx$$

putting $s = p \tan\varphi + c$

$$P = 2b \int_0^{x_1} p \tan\varphi \, dx + 2bx_1 c$$

$$= \tan\varphi \cdot 2b \int_0^{x_1} p \, dx + 2bx_1 c$$

but $2b \int_0^{x_1} p \, dx = W$ and $2bx_1 = \dfrac{W}{p_m}$

$$\therefore P = W \tan\varphi + \frac{Wc}{p_m}$$

Hence the adhesion factor $\dfrac{P}{W} = \tan\varphi + \dfrac{c}{p_m}$ . . . . (i)

23.10

23.10. EFFECT ON ADHESION OF DISTURBANCE OF THE GROUND AS BY ROCKING OR SNAKING OF TRACK LINKS.

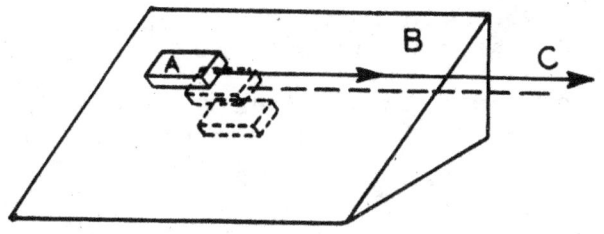

FIG. 23.10.a

Figure 23.10a. illustrates a simple experiment showing the effect on frictional resistance of a "second front". A block A is placed on a surface B which slopes but not enough to make the block slide down it. No movement occurs. Now the block is pulled by a string C in a direction horizontally along the slope but it moves obliquely, its movement having a component down the slope as well as along it.

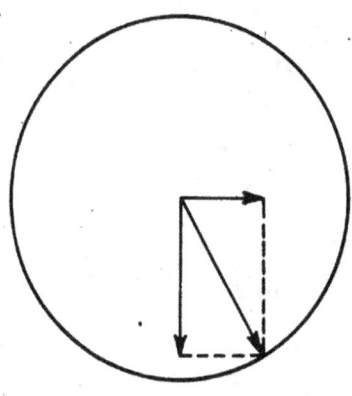

FIG. 23.10.b

The reason for this will be clear from Figure 23.10b. The components of force along and down the slope are each alone less than the limiting friction represented by the radius of the circle. But their resultant is equal to the radius and hence when they act together they produce movement in the direction of their resultant.

In the case of soil shear, it is difficult to get such a clear picture but the principle is the same, namely that when soil is being sheared in one direction it will offer a decreased resistance to shear in another direction. In particular if soil is being sheared downwards or outwards by the weight or snaking of the tracks, the tractive effort will probably take the opportunity of shearing it longitudinally, even if it would not be sufficient to do so unaided. Moreover even an inherently non-cohesive soil like sand may acquire some cohesion or at least increased shear strength if it is firmly compacted, especially if it is damp or if it is mixed with other materials, as it is in an ordinary sandy soil. Any disturbance of the soil whether by rocking of spuds embedded in it or by skidding due to a harsh gear change or operation of steering controls, will tend to destroy this cohesive strength almost as a metal bar loses its strength when fractured. A similar effect may be produced by the pulsating pull due to the polygonal pitch line of the sprocket discussed in Section 15.13.

The mere penetration of the spuds into the soil will tend to cause some disturbance especially if the spuds are relatively broad.

Such rocking of track links is of course minimised in the rigid girder type of track and Messrs. Roadless Traction (1) have made the following statement as regards the adhesion obtainable with this type of track, when fitted with spuds:- "Recent experiments for instance, have shown that it is quite possible to obtain in drawbar pull 150% of the weight of the machine and it appears that this is by no means the limit attainable.

Figure 23.9a. indicates that this is possible theoretically on a cohesive soil provided the mean ground pressure does not exceed say 5 or 10 lbs/sq.in.

---

(1) *The Roadless News*. Oct. 1943, p 24.

23.11. PRACTICAL SPUD DESIGN

So much for the theoretical background of the spud situation. In practice opinions differ as to whether spuds are desirable at all.

In the articles referred to in Chapter 12 Col. Johnson concludes that on a number of surfaces their disturbing effect in breaking up the surface more than offsets any advantage they may give. The strongest case for some irregularities is on soils which get a lubricating surface film of moisture.

Other authorities also argue that a tank is not a tractor having only to propel itself and therefore should not require any spuds.

In this connection it seems that there is a distinction between military and commerical transport applications. Whatever may be the case with a commercial vehicle, a military vehicle will often be compelled by tactical considerations to take a route other than the easiest route between two places, and make journeys which commercially could never be a paying proposition. Quite apart from surmounting slopes and natural or artificial barriers, the maximum possible adhesion may be needed to overcome the rolling resistance due to deep sinkage into soft ground.

It therefore seems clear that a tank track must have the maximum possible longitudinal adhesion and the only question is what arrangement of spuds will secure this.

In the first place even if there were no spuds the top surface of the earth could shear if the coefficient of sliding friction were greater than the shear strength of the soil. In fact this might happen with say rubber tracks on dry gravel. Hence if the top surface is compelled by spuds to shear, other things being equal, the maximum adhesion cannot be reduced and will almost always be increased.

Trials made in 1940 at Bovington showed that the fitting of quite a few spuds to the A.9 track made a marked improvement to the adhesion.

Moreover it is worth bearing in mind that when climbing an obstacle a spud may obtain a positive grip for example on a tree root, the reinforcement of a broken concrete obstacle, or a projecting rock.

From the discussion of Section 23.8 it seems clear that the best adhesion will be obtained when the whole load is applied on the sheared area. Hence the spuds should be as thin as possible, the limit normally being set by the damage to roads. As to the requisite depth of spud, section 23.6 suggests that the space between thin spuds can be between 2 and 3 times the depth of spud and on many soils may be more than this without reducing adhesion, and with thick spuds the spacing should definitely be wider apart than this.

In actual practice a spud depth of about 1" to $1\frac{1}{4}$" has been used in the past with a pitch up to 4" - 5" whilst $2\frac{1}{2}$" has been used with a pitch of 7" or 8". (The space between spuds would of course be less than the pitch).

An important practical function of spuds is to penetrate a layer of soil having a poor shear strength and get a grip on a lower layer having a better shear strength. In particular when rain falls on a moderately dry clay soil the surface layer may be reduced to almost liquid mud, while, an inch or two below, the soil remains firm and hard. With a smooth faced track the mud can form a lubricating film and greatly reduce the adhesion. For such conditions a track is needed which will encourage the mud to escape from under it or will penetrate it to get a grip on firmer ground beneath.

23.12

This requirement conflicts with that arising on level soils with poor bearing capacity where it is desirable to prevent the soil from escaping and to avoid penetrating or otherwise disturbing it.

This raises the question of skeleton tracks, and here two conflicting factors arise. On the one hand they are theoretically bad for adhesion as the sheared areas do not bear the weight. On the other hand they have the great advantage of letting mud escape through the holes so that instead of floating on a lubricating cushion of mud the track can sink down till it grips the firm ground (if any) beneath. This effect could probably be obtained with relatively small holes which would not destroy the loading of the sheared areas.

It is understood that racing motorists, entering for cross-country reliability trials, fit quite different tyres according to the type of soil and state of the course, one condition calling for thin high pressure tyres with a smooth tread, while another condition demands low pressure, and a pronounced tread pattern.

The same thing probably applies to tracks. For example a layer of slippery mud on a good firm bottom on a slope might be insuperable to anything but a skeleton track with deep spuds to bite through the mud into the firm ground. On the other hand on a level crust of dry soil turf etc. over a bottomless bog, a completely smooth undersurface might be the best arrangement.

In practice it is obviously quite impossible to provide different tracks for different soils, and in these circumstances it seems important to collect data as to what types and states of soil are most prevalent or likely to present most difficulty in anticipated battle areas.

It would then be possible to decide what conditions would present no difficulty, what conditions could not be attempted, what conditions would be very rare, and in what conditions the designer should aim at giving the best possible performance.

23.12. POSITIONING OF SPUDS. SNAKING

FIG. 23.12a

The positioning of spuds in the length of the link is determined largely by the necessity to give the link stable support on a hard surface such as a road. If the link is not supported by a spud at each end, for example if it has a single spud or two spuds spaced away from the ends, then when a wheel presses on the overhanging end the link will behave like a seesaw and its opposite end will be lifted off the ground. Fig. 23.12a. is from a film showing this snaking occurring with the link of the Italian M.13/40.

Hence in the case of any spudded link at least a part of the spud should be under the pin.

23.13. SHAPE OF SPUDS

It is obviously desirable as far as possible to shape the spud so that it will enter and leave the ground with a minimum of disturbance. On a track like the Char B having a single spud in the middle of the link, it is possible to radius each face of the spud about one of the pins, but with most tracks where the spud is at one end, this is not possible. Clearly as the spud enters the earth the latter is bound to be disturbed to some extent and the most one can do is to ensure that it does not dig a bigger hole than the minimum set by the need to provide a given depth of spud and a given area of spud face for road work.

The same thing applies to leaving the ground namely that the spud should be lifted out of the hole it has made for itself without enlarging it or disturbing its sides.

The shape needed to achieve this will clearly depend on the direction of movement of each link as it is laid and lifted. If the track is arranged spud leading the spud will start to lift out of the hole when the opposite end of the link is held by the following link. Hence if the spud lies wholly within a radius struck about this pin axis it will not enlarge the hole. On the other hand if the track is arranged spud trailing the initial pivoting occurs about the pin directly above the spud and it is impossible to prevent some enlargement of the hole. This movement does not lift the spud and the best that can be done is to ensure that the subsequent movement as the spud is lifted about the next pin, does not further enlarge the hole. This involves shaping the leading face of the spud so that when inclined to the following link as it is when wrapped round a road wheel, the leading spud face will be within the radius struck about the following pin axis.

The form of the spud and adjacent surfaces will also largely influence the self cleaning properties of the link. In a double spudded link mud can collect between the two spuds and as there is no relative movement between them there is nothing to disturb it. On the other hand with single spudded links neighbouring spuds move towards and away from each other as the track bends to pass round its contour and this tends to dislodge the mud. The Germans claim that this self cleaning is improved by adopting an interrupted construction, but whether of the spud or of the link as a whole is not quite clear. (1).

---

(1) See Section 4.19

CHAPTER 24

BEARING CAPACITY OF SOILS: CONSOLIDATION

24.1. WHAT HAPPENS WHEN A SOIL IS LOADED

The work that has been done on the bearing capacity of soils has been wholly or mainly from the point of view of foundations for buildings and other structures which are intended to be permanent. In that case two things particularly interest the designer, namely whether the building will fail and whether the foundations will fail. Even if the foundations remain fully capable of supporting their load they may still settle unevenly as much as a foot or more over a period of years and this may cause the building to give way.

The study of soils as engineering materials is comparatively recent and much remains to be done in collating and checking experimental results. Different investigators have considered different factors and the results seem often to show disagreement which is sometimes real and sometimes only apparent.

Briefly it seems that when an area of soil is loaded up sinkage can occur by squeezing out air, earth or water thus:-

1. The ground under the load is consolidated; that is to say, its apparent volume is reduced by squeezing out air and forcing the particles closer together, the sinkage increasing with the applied load.

2. WHen the load reaches a certain figure, known as the yield point, failure occurs and additional sinkage takes place with little or no additional load. Failure is by a shearing or flow of the particles of earth away from the area under the load and does not involve any further reduction of apparent volume.

3. Both the above things normally happen quite rapidly if they are going to happen at all. In addition sinkage can occur with certain soils due to water being pressed out. Theoretically there is an equilibrium between the loading and the amount of water that remains, but it takes an infinite time to reach this equilibrium and in practice settlement often goes on for many years; for example that of the Washington Memorial has been recorded since 1879, and is apparently still going strong. But the variation of this last form of sinkage with time is of asymptotic form. Thus Hogentogler shows a curve of consolidation plotted against time in which if the consolidation achieved in 1440 minutes is taken as 100%, then 50% is achieved in as little as 4 minutes. Hence although the track designer is not interested in consolidation over a period of years there may yet be some initial sinkage due to squeezing out water, which takes place sufficiently rapidly to be of interest. This will introduce an important time factor which must be borne in mind both in considering tanks travelling at widely differing speeds and also in comparing soil data for foundations with soil data for vehicles.

24.2. APPARATUS FOR RECORDING RELATION OF SINKAGE TO PRESSURE

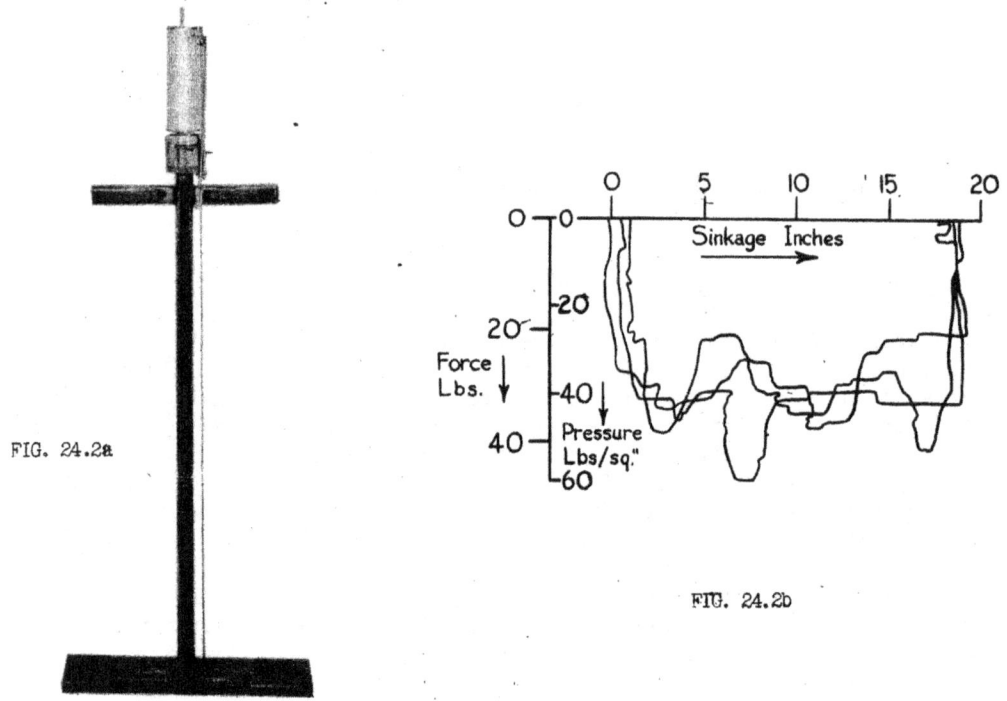

FIG. 24.2a

FIG. 24.2b

Figure 24.2a is a picture of an experimental "bogstick" made by the author for measuring the variation of pressure with sinkage. It comprises a vertical tube, the closed lower end of which constitutes a base (actually 1" diameter), which can be loaded up through a coil spring by pressing down on the handles, (which slide in slots). The sinkage is measured in relation to a datum platform which rests on the ground round the loaded area and is held down by the users' feet.

At the top of the tube is a recording drum which is rotated by a spring winding in a cord which is paid out in response to relative movement between the rod and the datum platform. Compression of the spring moves a pencil vertically downwards in relation to the drum, so as to give an autographic indicator diagram relating sinkage to pressure.

Sufficient experience has not yet been gained with the instrument to assess its possibilities for predicting how tanks will perform on ground tested by it. It certainly gives some idea of whether a particular piece of ground is harder on top and softer underneath or vice-versa but for comparing different pieces of ground too much depends on the rate at which sinkage is made to occur and therefore on the user.

Figure 24.2b shows three curves obtained with this apparatus, by pressing down slowly and as steadily as possible, on a piece of very soft ground in which even a Churchill became hopelessly bogged.

24.3. CURVES RELATING SINKAGE TO PRESSURE

It is generally accepted that on uniform soil the required load increases with the sinkage up to a point known as the yield point, beyond which failure occurs and additional sinkage takes place with little or no additional load. This failure is by a shearing or flow of earth from the area under the load and does not involve any further reduction of apparent volume.[1] The pressure that a soil will stand before it fails in this way is known as its bearing capacity.

The first stage, consolidation, will probably in practice depend on so many chance variables that it will seldom be possible to make anything like accurate forecasts of its characteristics.

---

[1] See Hogentogler, C.A., "The Engineering Properties of Soils."

As a rough approximation it is usual to assume that this part of the curve is a straight line passing through the origin.

Thus the curve relating sinkage to pressure can be regarded as approximating to a straight line through the origin followed by a straight line representing a constant pressure. Such a curve cannot be represented by a simple mathematical equation and in our subsequent treatment we shall consider two separate cases, one assuming that all the sinkage occurs at constant pressure and the other assuming that it is all directly proportional to the pressure.

The former case is probably a fair approximation for a homogeneous soil when the vehicle is sinking in very deep so that the initial sinkage of perhaps a couple of inches is only a fraction of the total. The latter case, which is less simple and is treated less fully, would probably be nearer the mark for soil giving a sinkage of only an inch or two and also for heterogeneous soil the deeper layers of which have a higher bearing capacity than the surface layer. In any particular practical case of course the situation may not even remotely resemble either of these cases, for example quite a small pressure may suffice to penetrate through a layer of mud to a certain depth at which a rock-hard bottom is reached, or on the contary a surface crust may provide an appreciable bearing capacity while that of a bog beneath it is negligible. We can therefore only hope to establish the general trend of results to be expected under typical conditions, and it will only be a waste of time to aim at meticulous accuracy.

24.4. FORMULAE FOR BEARING CAPACITY IN TERMS OF INTERNAL FRICTION COHESION AND SURCHARGE

Various methods have been tried for expressing the bearing capacity of a soil in terms of its angle of internal friction, cohesive strength and surcharge (if any).

In the method adopted by Prandtl and by Reissner a two-dimensional stress system is assumed (i.e. the load is applied to a long strip extending indefinitely in both directions) and the weight of the soil is neglected.

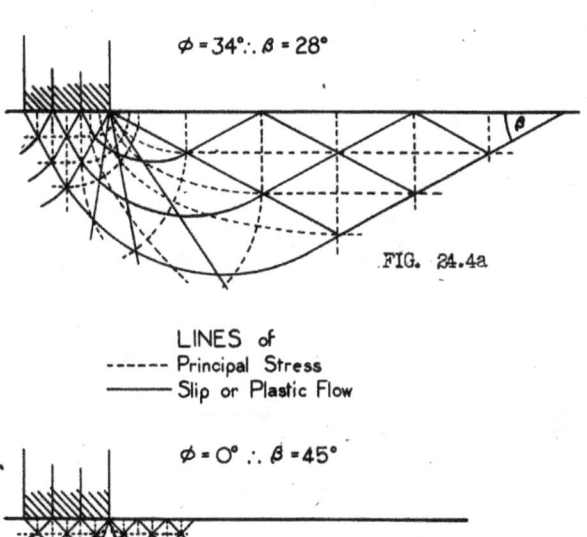

FIG. 24.4a

LINES of
------ Principal Stress
─── Slip or Plastic Flow

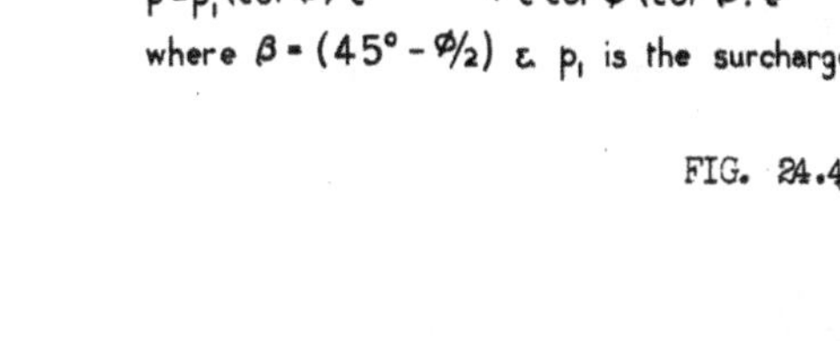

PRANDTL'S THEORY for Effect of Internal Friction on Bearing Capacity of Soil.

$$p = p_1 (\cot^2 \beta) e^{\pi \tan \phi} + c \cot \phi (\cot^2 \beta \cdot e^{\pi \tan \phi} - 1)$$

where $\beta = (45° - \phi/2)$ & p_1 is the surcharge.

FIG. 24.4b

24.4.

On this basis, and assuming the loaded surface is smooth, the lines of rupture and principal stress directions are of the form shown in Figures 24.4a and 24.4b. On each side of the loaded strip the soil which is in a state of flow comprises two wedge shaped regions in which the principal stresses act on vertical and horizontal planes (the major principal stress acting on horizontal planes in the wedge under the load and vertical planes in the other wedge) and between these wedges a sprial sector in which the directions of principal stresses are two sets of logarithmic spirals crossing at right angles.

The flow lines cut the lines of principal stress direction at angles $(45° \pm \varphi/2)$ where φ is the angle of internal friction.

The formula for bearing capacity is

$$p = p_1 \cot^2\beta \, e^{\pi \tan\varphi} + c \cot\varphi \left(\cot^2\beta \, e^{\pi \tan\varphi} - 1\right)$$

where $\beta = (45° - \varphi/2)$

If the loaded surface is assumed to be rough the lines of rupture and principal stress are as shown in Figures 24.4c and 24.4d. and the bearing capacity is increased to

$$p = p_1 (\tfrac{1}{2} \cosec^2\beta) \, e^{(\pi+2\beta)\tan\varphi} + c \cot\varphi \left(\tfrac{1}{2}\cosec^2\beta \, e^{(\pi+2\beta)\tan\varphi} - 1\right)$$

One way in which these curves and formulae can be arrived at is outlined in 24.4 Appendices 1 to 8.

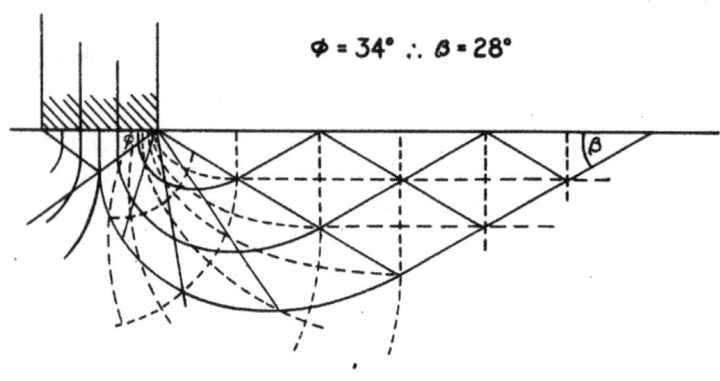

$\phi = 34° \therefore \beta = 28°$

FIG. 24.4c

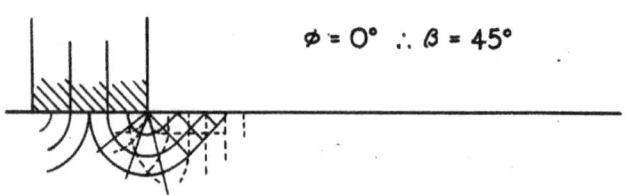

$\phi = 0° \therefore \beta = 45°$

Effect of Internal Friction on
Bearing Capacity of Soil
Rough Footing

$p = p_1 (\tfrac{1}{2}\cosec^2\beta) e^{(\pi+2\beta)\tan\phi} + c \cot\phi (\tfrac{1}{2}\cosec^2\beta e^{(\pi+2\beta)\tan\phi} - 1)$
where $\beta = (45° - \phi/2)$ & p_1 is the surcharge.

FIG. 24.4d

APPENDIX 1.

BEARING CAPACITY OF SOILS, STRESS DISTRIBUTION, - INTRODUCTORY

In order to investigate the distribution of stresses in soils and the general form of the surfaces along which soils will shear, it is necessary to have some knowledge of stress systems in general.

It is shown in text-books on the subject that even when a material is subjected to shear there are certain directions, or imaginary surfaces at right angles to one another in the material, upon which the stress acts normally, that is to say, there is no shear stress on these planes even though there will be shear stress on planes in other directions. These surfaces are known as principal planes and the stresses as principal stresses and it will be assumed that the reader is familiar with them. (1).

In a two dimensional stress system, that is to say one of which a cross section can be represented by a diagram on paper without imagining that any of the stresses act in planes which are not perpendicular to the paper, it is a simple matter to establish a relationship between the principal stresses and the normal and shear stresses on a plane inclined at any given angle to the principal planes. A very convenient way of representing the results of this investigation is by means of a graph relating shear stress to normal stress and this gives a circle known as Mohr's circle.

APPENDIX 2.

MOHR'S CIRCLE DIAGRAM FOR TWO DIMENSIONAL STRESS SYSTEM

Let us consider a small wedge of the material of unit thickness bounded by two principal planes, and a plane inclined to one of them at an angle α. In Figure 24.4.2a. this is represented by the triangle ABC of which it is convenient to assume the hypotenuse is of unit length, in which case the sides AB and BC are respectively $\cos\alpha$ and $\sin\alpha$. If the principal stresses s_1 and s_2 act respectively on the sides AB and BC and a normal stress s and a shear stress t act on the side AC as shown, we can resolve the forces acting on the wedge in directions parallel to the sides AB and BC.

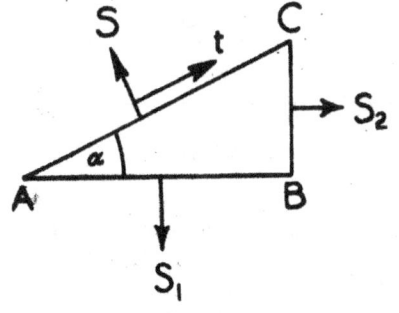

FIG. 24.4.2a

Thus resolving vertically:-

$$s \cos\alpha + t \sin\alpha = s_1 \cos\alpha$$

$$\therefore \quad s + t \tan\alpha = s_1$$

$$\therefore \quad \tan\alpha = \frac{s_1 - s}{t}$$

---

(1) See Case, J. *"Strength of Materials"*, Chap. 5, pages 72 onwards.

24.4.2.

and resolving horizontally:-

$$s \sin\alpha - t \cos\alpha = s_2 \sin\alpha$$

$$\therefore s - t \cot\alpha = s_2 \qquad \therefore \cot\alpha = \frac{s - s_2}{t}$$

$$\therefore t^2 = (s_1 - s)(s - s_2)$$

$$= \left(\frac{s_1-s_2}{2} + \frac{s_1+s_2}{2} - s\right)\left(s + \frac{s_1-s_2}{2} - \frac{s_1+s_2}{2}\right)$$

$$= \left\{\frac{s_1-s_2}{2} - \left(s - \frac{s_1+s_2}{2}\right)\right\}\left\{\frac{s_1-s_2}{2} + \left(s - \frac{s_1+s_2}{2}\right)\right\}$$

$$t^2 = \frac{(s_1-s_2)^2}{2} - \left(s - \frac{s_1+s_2}{2}\right)^2$$

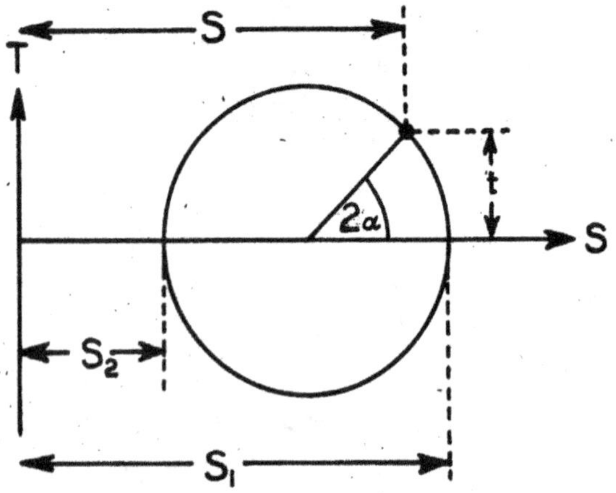

FIG. 24.4.2b

If we plot a graph of t against s according to the above equation we get a circle whose radius is $\frac{s_1-s_2}{2}$ and whose centre is at a point $\left(\frac{s_1+s_2}{2}, 0\right)$

Also if $t = 0$

$$s - \frac{s_1+s_2}{2} = \pm \frac{s_1-s_2}{2}$$

i.e. if $t = 0$ $s = s_1$ or s_2

This means that if we know the principal stresses at any point in a material we can make a diagram from which we can read off the normal and shear stresses acting on a plane in any other direction at that point, and this diagram will be in the form of a circle.

Moreover
$$\tan\alpha = \frac{t}{s-s_2}$$

therefore the inclination of the radius to the s axis is equal to 2α i.e. twice the inclination of the plane considered to the plane on which the major principal stress acts. For example the points at opposite ends of a diameter represent the stresses in two planes at right angles to each other. The shear stresses on any two such planes will be equal and opposite whilst the sum of the direct stresses on the two planes will be equal to the sum of the principal stresses.

The foregoing results apply to any material whether having elastic, plastic or any other properties. We will now consider the particular case of a soil in a state of or on the verge of plastic flow, and therefore satisfying Coulomb's equation.

APPENDIX 3.

APPLICATION OF MOHR'S STRESS CIRCLE TO SOIL

In soil to which Coulomb's equation is applicable this law gives us the relation between normal and limiting shear stress.

$$\pm t = c + s \tan\varphi$$

We can plot this as a graph relating t to s as in Figure 24.4.3a.

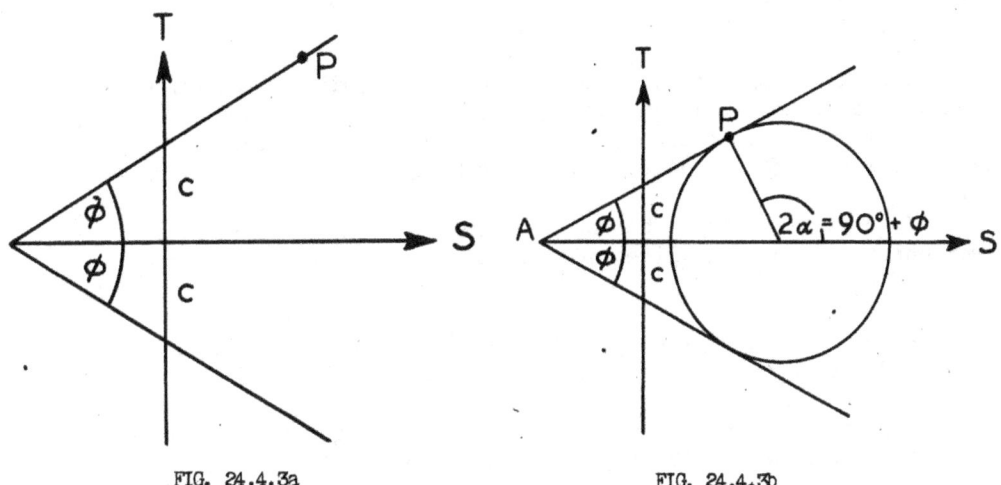

FIG. 24.4.3a   FIG. 24.4.3b

Let us compare this diagram with Mohr's circle diagram given in Figure 24.4.3b. The co-ordinates of a point P represent the normal and shear stresses acting on a certain plane at a certain point in the soil where plastic flow or shear is taking place or on the verge of taking place.

Suppose now that we are interested in the stresses in other directions at that same piece of soil the problem is to put in the appropiate Mohr's circle for the particular piece of earth. Obviously the point P must lie on the circle since its co-ordinates represent the stresses on one of the planes through the piece of earth concerned. Equally no part of the circle must lie beyond the line AP for if it did the tangential stress would exceed the limiting value $c + s \tan\varphi$ specified by Coulomb's equation. Hence the line AP must be a tangent to the circle.

From the geometry of the figure it is therefore clear that
$$2\alpha = 90^\circ + \varphi$$

$$\therefore \alpha = 45^\circ + \varphi/2$$

Now α is the angle between the plane in which the stresses are represented by the point P, and the plane on which the major principal stress acts.

Hence in any earth satisfying Coulomb's equation the planes of shear or plastic flow are inclined to the planes of principal stress at angles $(45^\circ + \varphi/2)$ and $(45^\circ - \varphi/2)$.

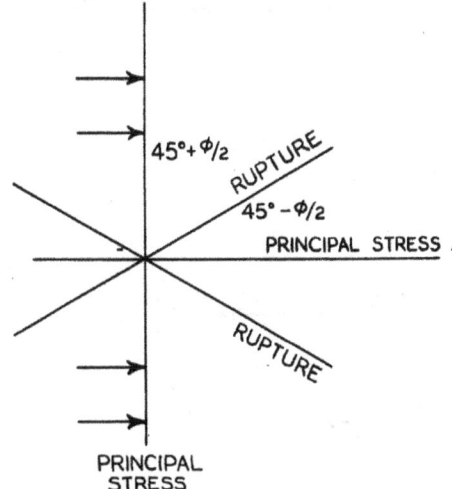

FIG. 24.4.3c

24.4.4.
The slip planes are nearer to the plane on which the smaller principal stress acts than to that on which the bigger principal stress acts, and the principal planes bisect the angles between the slip planes.

This result has already been made use of in Section 23.6.

APPENDIX 4.

VERTICAL PENETRATION BY SHEAR OF SOIL

We can now examine what happens when something, whether it be the spud of a tank track or the foundation of a skyscraper, presses vertically on the ground with such pressure that the ground shears or flows away from under it, or is on the verge of doing so.

Assume that the soil has a level surface extending indefinitely in all directions, the strip supporting the load is long in relation to its width $2b$ and supports (or fails to support) a pressure p, while the rest of the surface is loaded with a surcharge or pressure p_1.

It is clear that when the load descends the earth under it has to go somewhere and the only direction it can go is outwards and then upwards.

Moreover it will be assumed that any elastic compression of the soil is negligible in comparison with the movement due to flow.

Let us consider the stresses in a plane passing through the edge of the load and inclined to the horizontal at an angle θ. In a similar treatment of plastic materials in general Prandtl (1) assumes that the stresses in any such plane are uniform, i.e. the normal stress s and tangential stress t depends only on θ. This assumption is somewhat arbitrary but the results deduced are in general supported by experimental results.

APPENDIX 5.

EQUILIBRIUM OF ELEMENTARY SECTOR. RADIAL LINES SHOWN TO BE SLIP LINES

On this assumption we can consider the equilibrium of a sector of earth like a slice of cake of small angular thickness $\delta\theta$ and radius r, the tangential and radial normal stresses being s_t and s_r and the shear stress t. (Figure 24.4.5a)

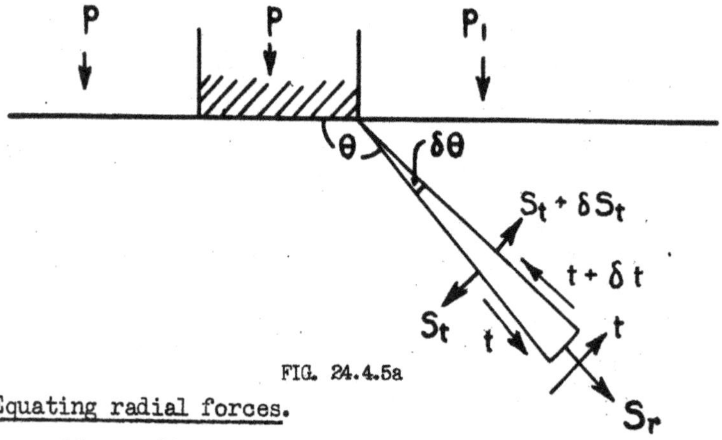

FIG. 24.4.5a

Equating radial forces.

$$r \, s_t \, \delta\theta = r\delta\theta \, s_r \quad -r\delta t$$

$$\therefore \frac{dt}{d\theta} = s_r - s_t$$

---

(1) Prandtl. L. *On the resistance to indentation (hardness) and Strength of Plastic Materials.*
(Z. angew. Math. Mech. 1921. 1(1), 15 – 20).

Taking moments.

$$r \cdot \delta s_t \frac{r}{2} + r\delta\theta t r = 0$$

$$\frac{ds_t}{d\theta} = -2t$$

whence $\dfrac{dt}{ds_t} = \dfrac{s_r - s_t}{-2t}$

Now if we draw a Mohr's circle the planes on which s_t and s_r act are at right angles, so that the points representing them will be at opposite ends of a diameter.

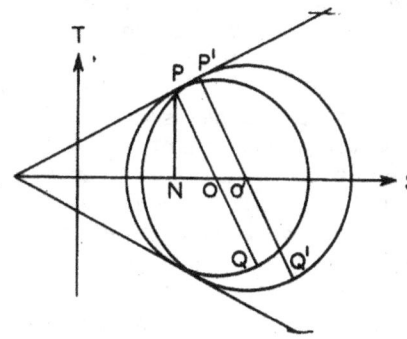

FIG. 24.4.5b

But we do not yet know that either of them is on the line $t = c + s \tan \varphi$ since the slip line may not be either radial or tangential.

But consider two different planes θ and $\theta + \delta\theta$. In each case there is plastic equilibrium or flow and hence there must be a point on the line $t = c + s \tan \varphi$ and a Mohr's circle touching this line.

If, in Figure 24.4.5b, P and P^1 are the points representing tangential stress, s_t, and Q and Q^1 those representing radial stress s_r we saw that

$$\frac{dt}{ds_t} = \frac{s_t - s_r}{2t} = \frac{2ON}{2PN}$$

In other words the slope of the line PP^1 is equal to $\dfrac{ON}{PN}$ which means that PP^1 must be at right angles to OP the radius, i.e. PP^1 must be along the tangent to the circle whose centre is at O. The same applies to the circle whose centre is at O^1 and hence the point P must be on the common tangent i.e. the line $t = c + s \tan \varphi$

This means that the plane in which the point P represents the stresses i.e. the radial plane, is a plane of plastic flow or a slip plane.

24.4 APPENDIX 6.   LINES OF PRINCIPAL STRESS.

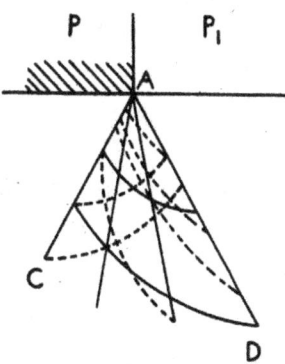

FIG. 24.4.6a

24.4.7.

We saw above that in a soil obeying Coulomb's law for plastic flow the slip lines are inclined to the lines of principal stress at angles $(45° + \varphi/2)$ and $(45° - \varphi/2)$.

Hence, as indicated in Figure 24.4.6a, the lines of principal stress are two families of spirals which are inclined to the radii at these angles and are mutually orthogonal (i.e. they intersect each other at right angles).

The other slip line must also be inclined to the principal stress lines at angles of $(45° + \varphi/2)$ and $(45° - \varphi/2)$ and hence is inclined to the radius at $(90° + \varphi)$ and takes the form of another spiral.

The next question is how far this arrangement of slip lines and principal stress lines extends. Does it come right up to the surface of the earth?

Since the loaded area is assumed smooth it follows that at the surface both of the supporting area and of the neighbouring area the pressure is vertical i.e. it is normal to the surface and there is no shear so that the principal stresses here are vertical and horizontal. Consequently if the principal stresses exerted on the adjacent wedge-shaped piece of earth by the sector shaped piece are also vertical and horizontal the wedge will be in a state of uniform stress.

As the principal stress lines are inclined to the radial lines at $(45° \pm \varphi/2)$ the radial lines AC and AD in which the principal stresses in the sector shaped piece are vertical and horizontal must make angles $(45° + \varphi/2)$ and $(45° - \varphi/2)$ respectively with the horizontal. Therefore angle $CAD = 90°$.

We can therefore fill in the remainder of the diagram as shown in Figure 24.4a, remembering that in the wedges the principal stresses are uniform, vertical and horizontal and the slip lines are inclined to them at angles $(45° \pm \varphi/2)$.

APPENDIX 7.

MAGNITUDE OF STRESSES.

It now remains to find the magnitudes of the stresses.

We saw above that in the sector shaped portion

$$\frac{dt}{d\theta} = s_r - s_t = -2t \tan \varphi$$

Integrating this gives

$$\log_e t = -2 \tan \varphi \cdot \theta + A$$

$$t = B e^{-2\tan\varphi \cdot \theta}$$

$$\therefore \frac{t_2}{t_1} = \frac{B e^{-2\theta_2 \tan\varphi}}{B e^{-2\theta_1 \tan\varphi}}$$

$$\frac{t_2}{t_1} = e^{-2\tan\varphi (\theta_2 - \theta_1)}$$

If θ_2 and θ_1 are the limits of the sector shaped portion

$$\theta_2 - \theta_1 = -90° \text{ or } -\frac{\pi}{2} \text{ radians}$$

$$\frac{t_2}{t_1} = e^{\pi \tan \varphi}$$

24.4.7.

We are now in a position to draw the Mohr's circle diagram for the whole system.

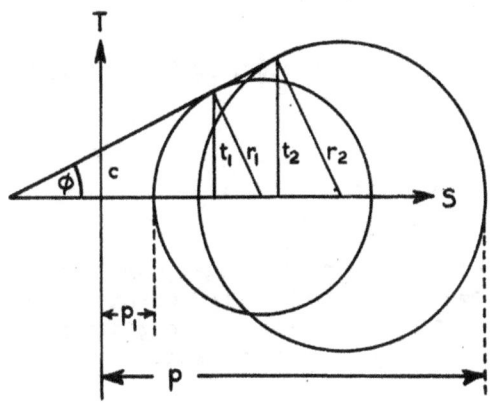

FIG. 24.4.7a

If r_1 and r_2 are the radii of the Mohr's circles for the two wedge shaped portions ADF and ABC respectively (See Fig. 24.4a) we know the minor principal stress in the former is equal to p_1. Hence we draw the circle which cuts the s axis at the point $(p_1, 0)$ and touches the line $t = c + s \tan\varphi$

Clearly the radii of the circles are in the ratio t_1 to t_2

i.e. $\dfrac{r_2}{r_1} = \dfrac{t_2}{t_1} = e^{\pi \tan\varphi}$

This gives us the size and therefore the position of the second circle, and the major principal stress of this is p, the bearing pressure we want to find. From inspection of the diagram it is clear that

$r_1 = (r_1 + p_1 + c \cot\varphi) \sin\varphi$

$r_1 = \dfrac{p_1 + c \cot\varphi}{\operatorname{cosec}\varphi - 1}$

$p = r_2(1 + \operatorname{cosec}\varphi) - c \cot\varphi = r_1 e^{\pi \tan\varphi}(1 + \operatorname{cosec}\varphi) - c \cot\varphi$

$= \dfrac{\operatorname{cosec}\varphi + 1}{\operatorname{cosec}\varphi - 1}(p_1 + c \cot\varphi) e^{\pi \tan\varphi} - c \cot\varphi$

$p = \tan^2(45° + \varphi/2)(p_1 + c \cot\varphi) e^{\pi \tan\varphi} - c \cot\varphi$

$p = p_1 \cot^2\beta \, e^{\pi \tan\varphi} + c \cot\varphi (\cot^2\beta \, e^{\pi \tan\varphi} - 1)$

where $\beta = (45° - \varphi/2)$

APPENDIX 8

ROUGH LOADED AREA

We assumed in Appendix 7 that the loaded area was smooth and the principal planes in the adjacent soil were therefore vertical and horizontal. If now the load is rough the immediately adjacent soil can be regarded as bonded to it and must therefore move vertically. Consequently the sprial sector must be regarded as continuing round until the spiral flow lines have vertical tangents, i.e. the diagram will be as shown in Figures 24.4c and 24.4d.

The total angle of the spiral sector, $(\theta_2 - \theta_1)$ of Appendix 7, will now be

$$\pi - \varphi - \beta = \pi/2 + \beta$$

$$\therefore \frac{t_2}{t_1} = \frac{r_2}{r_1} = e^{(\pi + 2\beta)\tan\varphi}$$

But now the principal planes are no longer horizontal and vertical and we need to consider the equilibrium of the central wedge. If in Figure 24.4.8a. the normal and shear stresses along the sloping surface are p_n and t_2 respectively then resolving vertically

$$p \cos\varphi = p_n \cos\varphi + t_2 \sin\varphi$$

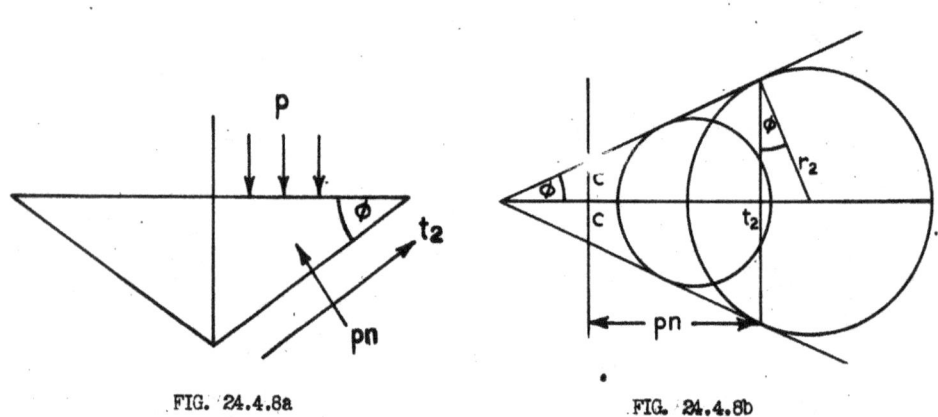

FIG. 24.4.8a   FIG. 24.4.8b

Also from Mohr's diagram (Fig. 24.4.8b) $t_2 = r_2 \cos\varphi$

and $p_n + c \cot\varphi = r_2 \cot\varphi \cos\varphi$

whence $p \cos\varphi = r_2 \cot\varphi \cos^2\varphi + r_2 \sin\varphi\cos\varphi - c \cos\varphi\cot\varphi$

$$p = \frac{r_2}{\sin\varphi}(\cos^2\varphi + \sin^2\varphi) - c \cot\varphi$$

$$= r_2 \csc\varphi - c \cot\varphi$$

Now $r_1 = (r_1 + p_1 + c \cot\varphi)\sin\varphi$

$$= \frac{p_1 + c \cot\varphi}{\csc\varphi - 1}$$

Whence

$$p = \frac{p_1 + c \cot\varphi}{\csc\varphi - 1} e^{(\pi+2\beta)\tan\varphi} \csc\varphi - c \cot\varphi$$

$$= p_1 \left(\frac{e^{(\pi+2\beta)\tan\varphi}}{1 - \sin\varphi}\right) + c \cot\varphi \left(\frac{e^{(\pi+2\beta)\tan\varphi}}{1 - \sin\varphi} - 1\right)$$

$$= p_1 (\tfrac{1}{2}\csc^2\beta) e^{(\pi+2\beta)\tan\varphi} + c \cot\varphi (\tfrac{1}{2}\csc^2\beta \, e^{(\pi+2\beta)\tan\varphi} - 1)$$

24.5. TERZAGHI'S APPROXIMATE FORMULA FOR YIELD BY SHEAR

The actual surfaces along which the shear occurs are probably logarithmic spirals as indicated in Section 24.4 but in that section no account is taken of the weight of the soil. An approximate formula which does so has been worked out by Terzaghi (1) on the assumption that sliding occurs along plane surfaces by substantially wedge-shaped blocks of soil.

This is worked out in 24.5. Appendix 1. from which it will be seen that the formula is :

$$p = \frac{b\gamma}{2}(\cot^5\beta - \cot\beta) + 2c(\cot^3\beta + \cot\beta) + p_1 \cot^4\beta$$

where (as before) p is the bearing capacity, γ the unit weight of the earth, c the cohesion of the earth, p_1 the surcharge, i.e. the pressure on the remaining surface of the earth, and $\beta = (45° - \varphi/2)$ where φ is the angle of internal friction.

APPENDIX 1.

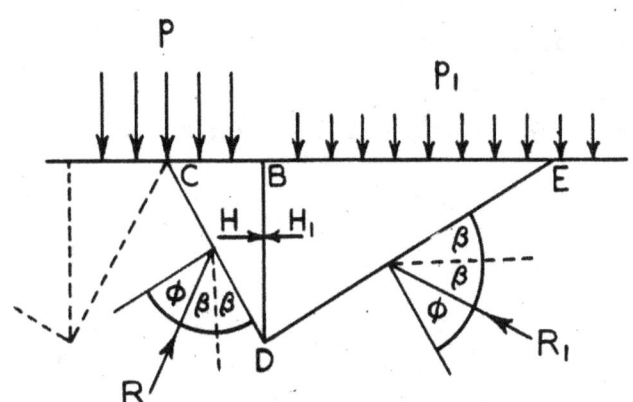

FIG. 24.5.1a

In Figure 24.5.1a. the load causing the failure by shear is assumed to act on a very long strip of width $2b$. Then shearing will occur by downward movement of the wedge shaped block BCD along the surface CD. This will push the wedge shaped block BDE to the right, shearing along the surface DE. The angles CDB and DEB are each $\beta = (45° - \varphi/2)$ where φ is the angle of internal friction of the material.

Suppose the loading on the loaded area is p whilst the loading on the adjacent soil is p_1 (which may of course be zero), the cohesion of the soil is c, the resultant forces on the shearing faces CD and DE are R and R_1 respectively, the opposed horizontal forces on the face BD are H and H_1, and the total loads on the wedges BCD and BED are P and P_1 respectively.

Then resolving at right angles to R and R_1 respectively it will be seen that for equilibrium of the wedge BCD

$$H \cos\beta = P \sin\beta - b\, c\, \mathrm{cosec}\beta \sin 2\beta$$

Therefore $H = P \tan\beta - \dfrac{b\, c\, \mathrm{cosec}\beta.2\, \sin\beta\cos\beta}{\cos\beta}$

$= P \tan\beta - 2\, b\, c$

And from the equilibrium of the wedge BDE

$$H_1 \sin\beta = P_1 \cos\beta + b\, c\, (\cot\beta\, \mathrm{cosec}\beta) \sin 2\beta.$$

(1) "Public Roads", Volume 10, No.3. May 1929.

$$H_1 = P_1 \cot\beta + \frac{b\,c\,\cos\beta \cdot 2\sin\beta\cos\beta}{\sin\beta\sin\beta\sin\beta} = P_1 \cot\beta + 2\,bc\,\cot^2\beta$$

The loads P and P_1 are made up of the superimposed load plus the weight of the soil in the wedge BCD or BED as the case may be.

Therefore if γ is the unit weight of the soil, $P = b\,p + \dfrac{b^2\gamma}{2}\cot\beta$

$P_1 = p_1 b\cot^2\beta + \tfrac{1}{2} b^2 \gamma \cot^3\beta$

Hence putting $H = H_1$ and substituting for P and P_1 we get

$P\tan\beta - 2\,b\,c = P_1 \cot\beta + 2\,b\,c\,\cot^2\beta$

$(pb + \dfrac{b^2\gamma}{2}\cot\beta)\tan\beta - 2\,b\,c = (p_1 b \cot^2\beta + \dfrac{b^2\gamma}{2}\cot^3\beta)\cot\beta + 2\,b\,c\,\cot^2\beta$

$pb\tan\beta + \dfrac{b^2\gamma}{2} - 2\,b\,c = p_1 b \cot^3\beta + \dfrac{b^2\gamma}{2}\cot^4\beta + 2\,b\,c\,\cot^2\beta$

$pb\tan\beta = \dfrac{b^2\gamma}{2}(\cot^4\beta - 1) + 2\,b\,c\,(\cot^2\beta + 1) + p_1 b \cot^3\beta$

$p = \dfrac{b\gamma}{2}(\cot^5\beta - \cot\beta) + 2\,c\,(\cot^3\beta + \cot\beta) + p_1 \cot^4\beta$

TABLE 24.6a

a) BEARING CAPACITIES OF SOILS

Smooth footing, neglecting weight of soil.

$p = p_1 \cot^2\beta\, e^{\pi\tan\varphi} + c\,\cot\varphi(\cot^2\beta\, e^{\pi\tan\varphi} - 1)$ $\qquad \beta = 45° - \varphi/2$

φ	p	
2°	$1.2 p_1$	+ 5.5c
4°	$1.4 p_1$	+ 6.2c
6°	$1.7 p_1$	+ 6.8c
10°	$2.5 p_1$	+ 8.3c
12°	$3.0 p_1$	+ 9.3c
34°	$29.4 p_1$	+ 42.1c

TABLE 24.6b

b) BEARING CAPACITIES P OF SOILS
Rough footing, neglecting weight of soil

$$p = p_1 \frac{e^{(3\pi/2-\varphi)\tan\varphi}}{1-\sin\varphi} + c\cot\varphi \left(\frac{e^{(3\pi/2-\varphi)\tan\varphi}}{1/\sin\varphi} - 1 \right)$$

φ	p
$2°$	$1.2 p_1$ + $6.3 c$
$4°$	$1.5 p_1$ + $7.0 c$
$6°$	$1.8 p_1$ + $7.7 c$
$10°$	$2.7 p_1$ + $9.6 c$
$12°$	$3.3 p_1$ + $10.8 c$
$34°$	$36.4 p_1$ + $52.5 c$

TABLE 24.6c.

c) BEARING CAPACITIES OF SOILS
Terzaghi's straight line formula allowing for weight of soil

$$p = \frac{b\gamma}{2}(\cot^5\beta - \cot\beta) + 2c(\cot^3\beta + \cot\beta) + p_1 \cot^4\beta$$

where ($2b$ = width of loaded strip
(γ = unit weight of the earth. $\beta = 45° - \varphi/2$

φ	p
$2°$	$.08\, b\gamma + 4.3 c + 1.2 p_1$
$4°$	$.17\, b\gamma + 4.6 c + 1.3 p_1$
$6°$	$.29\, b\gamma + 4.96 c + 1.5 p_1$
$10°$	$.61\, b\gamma + 5.77 c + 2.0 p_1$
$12°$	$.82\, b\gamma + 6.24 c + 2.3 p_1$
$34°$	$10.82\, b\gamma + 17.1 c + 12.5 p_1$

If $\gamma = 100$ lbs/cu.ft. $= .0579$ lbs/cu.in., coefficients of "b":-

$\varphi =$	2	4	6	10	12	$34°$
$\gamma N_\gamma =$	.02	.04	.06	.10	.12	1.96

TABLE 24.6d

d) BEARING CAPACITIES OF SOILS

Terzaghi's latest formula allowing for weight of soil

$$p = p_1 \frac{e^{(3\pi/2 - \varphi)\tan\varphi}}{1 - \sin\varphi} + c \cot\varphi \left(\frac{e^{(3\pi/2 - \varphi)\tan\varphi}}{1 - \sin\varphi} - 1 \right) + \gamma b N_\gamma$$

φ	p		
$2°$	$0.4\ b$	$+\ 6.3c$	$+\ 1.2\ p_1$
$4°$	$0.7\ b$	$+\ 7.0c$	$+\ 1.5\ p_1$
$6°$	$1.0\ b$	$+\ 7.7c$	$+\ 1.8\ p_1$
$10°$	$1.7\ b$	$+\ 9.6c$	$+\ 2.7\ p_1$
$12°$	$2.0\ b$	$+10.8c$	$+\ 3.3\ p_1$
$34°$	$34.2b$	$+52.5c$	$+36.4\ p_1$

24.6 FIGURES FOR BEARING CAPACITIES

It will be seen that in each of the formulae given above the value of the bearing capacity consists of a term comprising the surcharge multiplied by a coefficient depending only on internal friction, plus a term comprising the cohesion multiplied by another coefficient depending only on internal friction. These coefficients are worked out for various values of the angle of internal friction in tables 24.6a. to c. from which it will be seen that Terzaghi's straight line formula is a good deal out compared with the logarithmic spiral formulae.

The latter, however, neglect the weight of the soil, upon which in the absence of cohesion and surcharge, the bearing capacity will entirely depend. Terzaghi has more recently developed graphical methods of assessing the component of bearing capacity due to the weight of the soil and as it is rather laborious we will be content with including coefficients of width of loaded strip multiplied by unit weight of soil estimated from his curves. (1) These are included in Table 24.6d. together with the same coefficients of p_1 and c as in Table 24.6b. Table 24.6d. accordingly gives what are believed to be the best values for bearing capacity of a long strip.

Assuming there is no surcharge or cohesion it will be seen that the bearing capacity is directly proportional to the width of the loaded strip, whereas with a cohesive soil the bearing capacity is more nearly independent of the width of the loaded strip.

Figure 24.6e. shows the bearing capacity (as obtained from the coefficients of Table 24.6d.) plotted against the width of the loaded strip for various typical soils.

It is impossible to say how far these reults, worked out for a uniformly loaded strip, will apply to a writhing track loaded at certain points, but it is believed that the general tendency will be the same, namely that on a cohesionless sand the bearing capacity will increase with increased width (the total load varying as the square of the width) whilst on a clay or other cohesive soil the bearing capacity will be indepedent of track width (and total load will be directly proportional to track width)

---

(1) Terzaghi K. "Theoretical Soil Mechanics". Chapters 7 and 8.

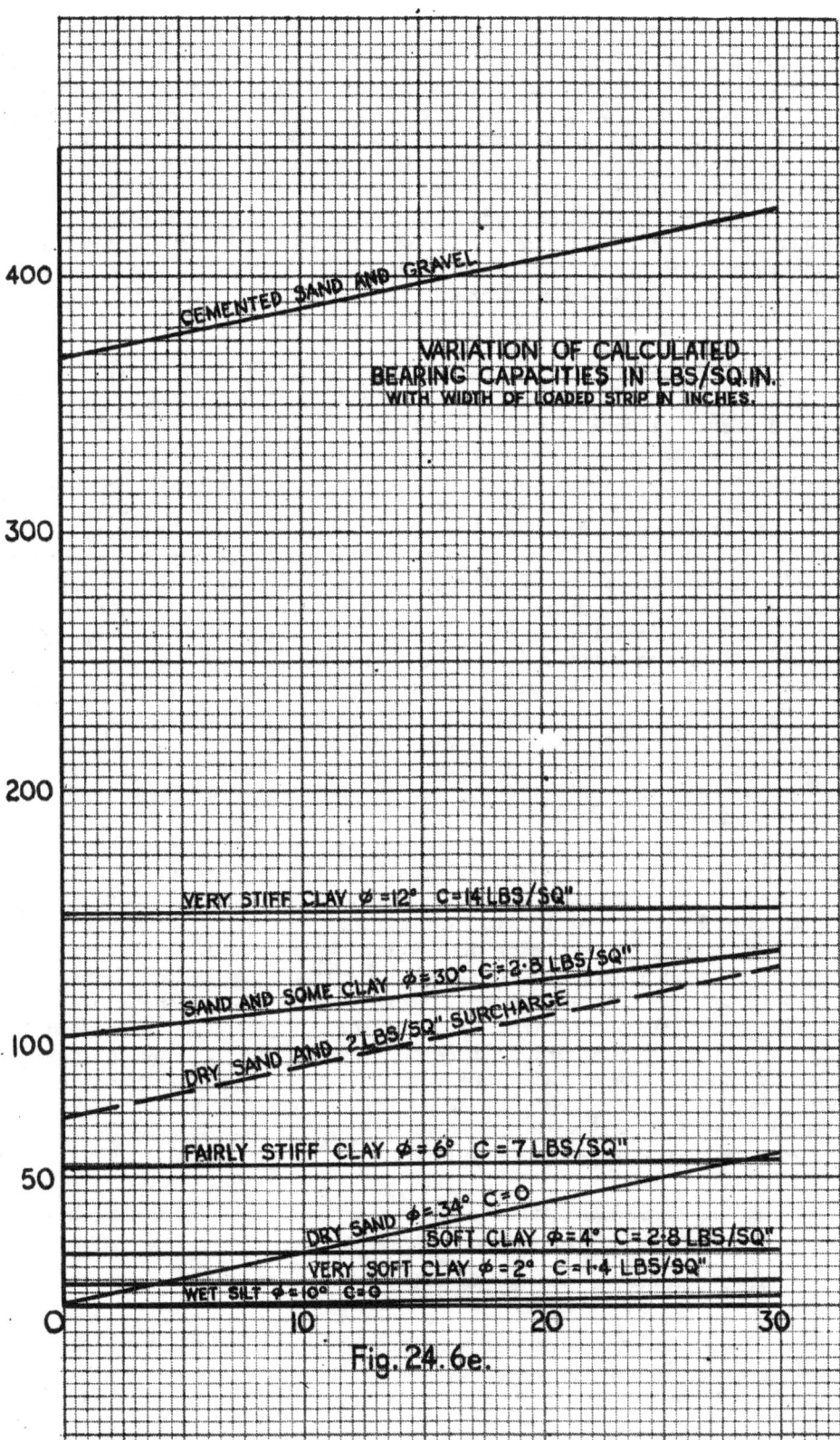

Fig. 24.6e.

CHAPTER 25

GROUND PRESSURE

25.1. MEAN GROUND PRESSURE. THE SO-CALLED SOFT & HARD GROUND PRESSURES

It has hitherto been customary to determine the width of track required by specifying that the mean ground pressure, that is to say the total weight of the tank divided by the total area of track resting on the ground, is not to exceed a certain figure. In general, the so-called ground pressure for soft ground should not exceed 12 lbs. per sq. in. and if possible should be rather less. The so-called hard ground pressure is obtained by dividing the weight by the area of the track which would rest in contact with a hard surface such as a road. For a spudded track the area concerned is that of the faces of the bars or spuds which would rest in contact with a hard surface. It is generally considered that this pressure should not exceed some 70 - 80 lbs. per sq. in.

During some trials made on Cruiser tanks, A.10 and A.13. in the early days of the present war, it was observed that although the track of A.13 was an improved type, the performance of the A.10 was better in certain conditions. This was attributed to the fact that the A.10 (with a 6-wheel suspension like the Valentine) had 50% more bearing area than the A.13) (with a 4-wheel suspension like the Covenanter). Apart from the arbitrary assumption that the bearing area must increase directly as the number of wheels, this statement, and the experimental result on which it was based, throw grave doubt on the practice of relying too much on the mean ground pressure. Again in shingle trials Carriers dug in while Churchills, with a so-called soft ground pressure nearly double that of the carrier, proceeded unhindered. In this connection we have already quoted Merritt's statement that "as a basis for calculating track pressure (i.e. a drawing-board comparison) the theoretical length of the track profile in contact with the ground can be quite misleading. The actual ground pressures are probably but little different from those which would result if a length of track were wrapped round each wheel......" (1)

In studying the actual distribution of the pressure of tracks on the ground it is necessary to rely very largely on calculations since the amount of experimental data available is extremely scanty, and, without a theoretical skeleton upon which experimental results can be hung, it is generally found that such experimental results as are available omit essential figures. In any tests concerning sinkage or adhesion the condition of the soil is likely to have such a preponderating effect as to mask any differences that may be made by the design of track, unless the state of the soil is quite accurately recorded. Such details as "wet grass", or "good firm going", or "average cross country", are little use for applying a quantitative correction to render different results comparable.

Let us apply the ordinary laws of mechanics to examining how the wheels of a tank are actually supported.

25.2. GROUND PRESSURE WITH SLACK TRACK

If a wheel with a smooth continuously flexible slack track wrapped round it descends vertically on to a level piece of ground the first contact will theoretically be a line contact and if a finite load is applied the pressure will be infinite. (Fig. 25.2a).

---

(1) Merritt, H.E. "The Design of High Speed Track Vehicles"
Proc. I.A.E. Jan. 1939, p.15.

25.2

Assuming the wheel and track are rigid the ground will be squashed down, and the area of pressure will increase until the pressure which the ground is capable of resisting produces the required supporting force. It is important to bear in mind that the supporting force is only produced when sinkage occurs, without sinkage there would (in the conditions presupposed) be no supporting force, because the pressure would be exerted only on a negligible area.

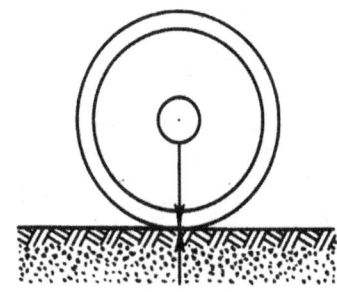

FIG. 25.2a.

The bit of ground under the lowest point of the wheel is pushed down furthest and the sinkage gradually decreases round the wheel to the points where contact with the ground ceases. (Fig. 25.2b).

The total supporting force will be found by integrating or adding up the pressure at each point multiplied by the area upon which it acts. But before attempting to assess what this supporting force will be it is necessary to recollect that we are concerned not with stationary but with moving vehicles. As a wheel moves along, each point in the ground (or in the track lying on the ground) is pressed down until the lowest point of the wheel passes over it. When this point has passed, it is free to rise again gradually to its original level, but in general it does not do so and even if it does the pressure it exerts at a given level will be very much less when it is being allowed to rise than when it is being forced down.

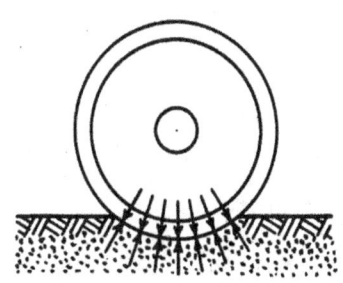

FIG. 25.2b.

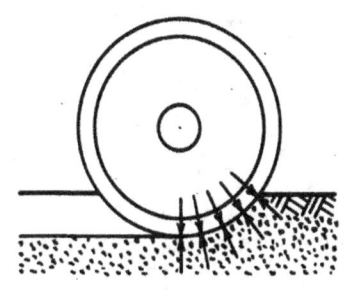

FIG. 25.2c.

Hence we have to integrate the pressure exerted on a piece of track wrapped round the wheel from the foremost point in contact with the ground to the lowest point, and make the result equal to the total weight the wheel has to support (determined by the suspension). To do this we need to know how the pressure varies with the depth. We saw in Section 24.3. that up to the yield point the pressure is approximately proportional to the sinkage whereas above the yield point the pressure is approximately constant. We also agreed that it would be too complicated to try to take into account sinkage both below and above the yield point, and that the simplest plan seemed to be to consider separately the case in which all the sinkage is above the yield point and the case in which it is all below the yield point.

The investigation of sinkage which occurs above the yield point is simpler to investigate, and yields more clear cut results so this case will be considered first.

25.3. MAXIMUM GROUND PRESSURE AND SINKAGE. ABOVE THE YIELD POINT.

In this case it will be assumed that the soil has a definite bearing capacity in lbs. per sq. in., and that, when the loading exceeds this pressure, sinkage will occur and continue without further rise of pressure, whilst any sinkage occurring at a lower pressure can be neglected.

Actually the sinkage causes the load to be distributed over a greater area and this reduces the pressure until the bearing capacity is no longer exceeded.

The assumption referred to is of course more or less an approximation and the results obtained can at best only be regarded as indicating the general trend of how ground pressure varies with different factors and what its order of magnitude is likely to be.

If r is the radius of the wheel, z the sinkage and x the horizontal length of the track pressing on the ground then it is clear from Figure 25.3a. that

$$z = r - \sqrt{r^2 - x^2} \quad \ldots \ldots \ldots (i)$$

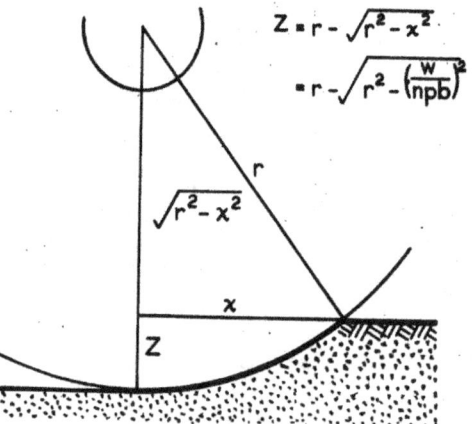

FIG. 25.3a

If b is the breadth of the track and p the ground pressure which in this case is assumed uniform and equal to the bearing capacity of the soil, then the area acted on by the pressure is bx and the total supporting force is pbx

Finally if the total weight of the tank is W and the number of loaded wheels is n, so that the load per wheel is W/n then

$$\frac{W}{n} = pbx$$

whence $x = \dfrac{W}{npb}$

putting this instead of x in the equation above

$$z = r - \sqrt{r^2 - \left(\frac{W}{npb}\right)^2} \quad \ldots \ldots \ldots \ldots \ldots \ldots \ldots (ii)$$

This formula is convenient for calculating particular examples but to see how the sinkage varies with different factors it seems clearer to express the relationship by plotting z against $\dfrac{W}{npb}$ in a series of graphs one for each value of r. This has been done in Fig. 25.3b. from which it will be seen that each graph is a circular arc of radius r.

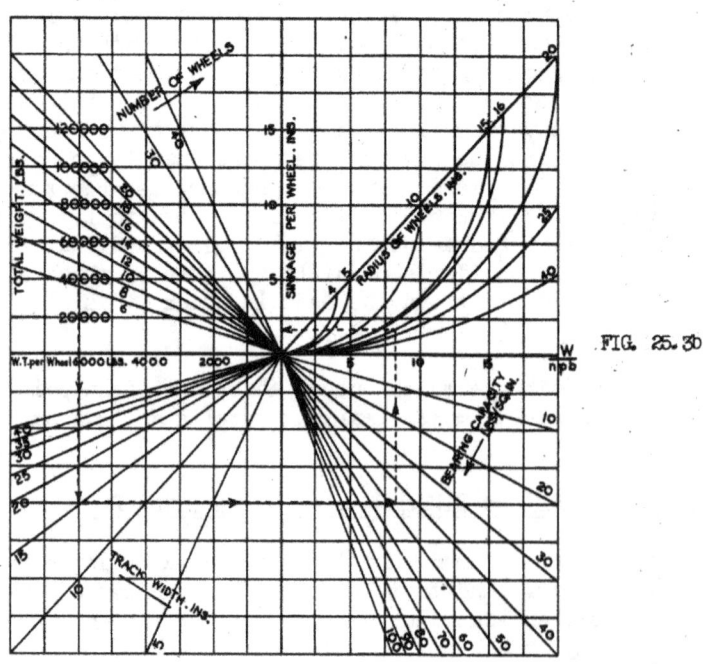

FIG. 25.3b

25.4

The above remarks apply equally to the first wheel and to subsequent wheels so that to get the total sinkage we multiply the sinkage per wheel by half the number of loaded wheels i.e. $n/2$.

Values of $\dfrac{W}{npb}$ can of course be calculated and the corresponding values of z read off using only the upper right hand portion of Fig. 25.3b. Some readers may however get a clearer idea of the influence of each factor if the calculation is done graphically by the radial lines in the lower and left hand portions.

For example the dotted line shows an example where $W = 60,000$ lbs. $n = 10$, $b = 15"$, $p = 50$ lbs/sq.in., $r = 16"$. Starting on the left at the level of 60,000 lbs. we travel to the right to the radial line 10 wheels, thence downward (crossing the axis at 6,000 lbs. per wheel) till we get to the radial line for track width $15"$, thence to the right to the radial line 50 lbs/sq.in. thence up to the arc $16"$ radius, and from this point we can read off on the vertical scale $2.14"$ sinkage per wheel. The total sinkage is therefore about $11"$.

The figures taken are fairly typical for a heavy cruiser tank and suggest that if the track is flexible and slack the bearing capacity of the soil must be very much greater than the mean ground pressure quoted for the vehicle. Figures for mean ground pressure range from about 10 to 15 lbs/sq.in., but the above example indicates that if the bearing capacity, and hence the ground pressure, is only as low as 50 lbs/sq.in. the wheels will sink in to the quite excessive depth of 11 inches.

We have of course neglected the tension in the track. Let us examine what the effect of this will be.

25.4 EFFECT OF TRACK TENSION ON SINKAGE

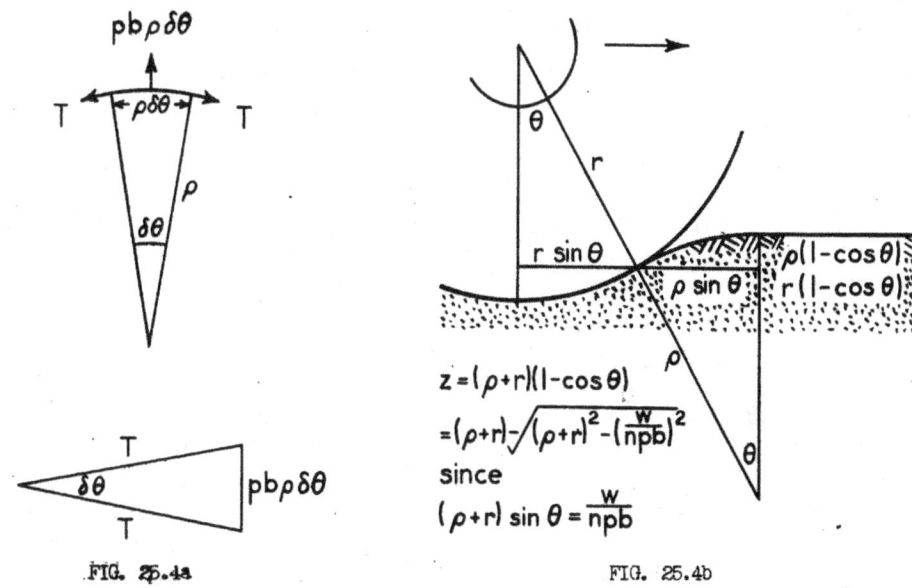

FIG. 25.4a   FIG. 25.4b

It is essential to recollect that even a track must obey the ordinary laws of elementary mechanics. So it is worth glancing at the relation between tension, curvature and lateral loading.

We saw in Section 12.4 that a flexible band freely stretched between two points can only exert or withstand a lateral pressure if it is curved. Hence it is only when a wheel sinks in that the tension in the track can have any effect on distribution of pressure.

If, in Figure 25.4a p is the lateral pressure and b the width of track the lateral load per unit length will be pb, and the lateral force on an elementary unit of radius of curvature ρ subtending an angle $\delta\theta$ will be $pb\rho\delta\theta$

From a triangle of forces it is clear that

$$pb\rho\delta\theta = T\delta\theta.$$

or $\quad pb\rho = T$

Where T is the track tension. Hence the effect of tension in the track will be that it can only take a curve when it is acted upon by a lateral load per unit length inversely proportional to the radius of the curve, i.e. $p = \dfrac{T}{\rho b}$ where ρ is the radius of the curve, T the track tension, p the lateral pressure and b the width. If we consider how a tension in the track will modify Fig. 25.3a. it is clear that the effect will be as it were to chamfer off the corner where the track engages the wheel. This is indicated in Fig. 25.4b.

On the assumptions made the track will be flat and will rest lightly on the ground as far as a certain point since it cannot become curved without sinking in and it cannot sink in without exerting a pressure equal to the bearing capacity of the soil. Beyond this point the pressure is equal to the bearing capacity and as this is assumed uniform, the curvature must be uniform, i.e. $\rho = \dfrac{T}{pb}$. Where the track is in contact with the wheel, obviously its curvature is equal to that of the wheel of radius r.

From Fig. 25.4b. it will be seen that the horizontal length of track exerting pressure on the ground is equal to

$$(\rho+r)\sin\theta = \frac{W}{npb} \qquad \therefore \cos\theta = \sqrt{1-\left(\frac{W}{(\rho+r)npb}\right)^2}$$

while the total sinkage z is equal to

$$(\rho+r)(1-\cos\theta)$$

$$\text{or } z = (\rho+r) - \sqrt{(\rho+r)^2 - \left(\frac{W}{npb}\right)^2} \quad \ldots \ldots \ldots \ldots 8i)$$

Comparing this with equation 25.3 (ii) it will be seen that the effect of track tension on the sinkage of a soil of constant bearing capacity, is the same as that of increasing the radius of the wheels by an amount:-

$$\rho = \frac{T}{pb}$$

We can work out the same example as before taking track tension into consideration.

We took $W = 60{,}000$ lbs., $n = 10$, $b = 15"$, $p = 50$ lbs./sq.in. $r = 16"$.

If we now take $T = 2000$ lbs., $\dfrac{T}{pb} = \dfrac{2000}{50.15} = 2^2/3$

Whence
$$z = (r+\rho) - \sqrt{(r+\rho)^2 - \left(\frac{W}{npb}\right)^2}$$
$$= 18^2/3 - \sqrt{(18^2/3)^2 - \left(\frac{60{,}000}{10.50.15}\right)^2} = 1.8" \text{ per wheel}$$

The total sinkage is therefore reduced from $11"$ to $9"$ by a track tension of a short ton.

If the sinkage is worked out in the same way for a tension of 5 short tons it is found to be reduced to $5\tfrac{1}{2}"$.

Actually of course the sinkage of the front wheels would not be reduced by the track tension as the track approaching them is inclined. This has been ignored in the above calculations, as has the lifting effect of track tension on the front and rear road wheels. These effects, though complicated and tedious, could no doubt be worked out but enough has been said to indicate the main effects of tension. Tension in the track does improve the distribution of pressure and reduce the sinkage as would the fitting of larger wheels. But even with considerable tension the sinkage will be quite excessive unless the bearing capacity of the soil is far greater than the mean ground pressure.

In fact each wheel will sink in until a sufficient length of track is exerting a pressure equal to the bearing capacity to support the load. We have seen how far it has to sink in certain cases, and it is an easy matter to calculate what length of track is then being usefully employed per wheel. This length in Fig. 25.4b. clearly is

$$(\rho+r)\sin\theta = \frac{W}{npb}$$

Hence in the example given if the bearing capacity is 50 lbs/sq.in. a length $\frac{60,000}{10 \cdot 50 \cdot 15} = 8"$ is used per wheel.

This indicates that with relatively widely spaced wheels only a small part of the length of track on the ground is actually helping to support the weight even when the total sinkage is quite considerable. In the particular example, with wheels spaced 40" apart 80% of the track ground contact area would be supporting no weight.

25.5 EFFECT OF SIZES AND NUMBERS OF WHEELS

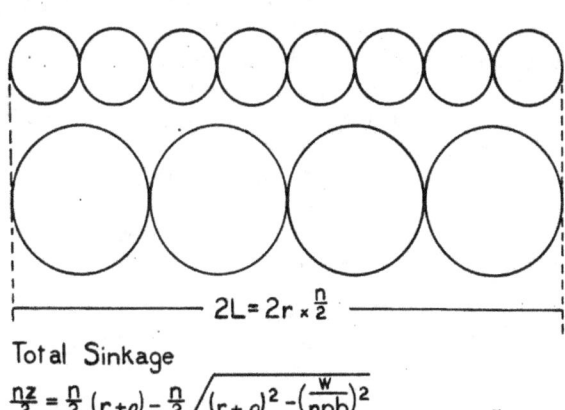

$$2L = 2r \times \frac{n}{2}$$

Total Sinkage

$$\frac{nz}{2} = \frac{n}{2}(r+\rho) - \frac{n}{2}\sqrt{(r+\rho)^2 - \left(\frac{W}{npb}\right)^2}$$

but as $r = \frac{2L}{n}$ & $\rho = \frac{T}{pb}$

$$\frac{nz}{2} = L + \frac{nT}{2pb} - \sqrt{\left(L + \frac{nT}{2pb}\right)^2 - \left(\frac{W}{2pb}\right)^2}$$

If T=0 sinkage is independent of n

FIG. 25.5a

With regard to wheels the choice is often between having a large number of small wheels or a smaller number of larger wheels. If, in Fig. 25.5a we assume that we have a given length $2L$ which we are at liberty to fill with wheels whatever their size then

$$\frac{n}{2} \times 2r = 2L \qquad \text{Whence} \quad r = \frac{2L}{n}$$

and, remembering that $\rho = \frac{T}{pb}$ the formula for sinkage becomes:-

$$\frac{nz}{2} = L + \frac{nT}{2pb} - \sqrt{\left(L + \frac{nT}{2pb}\right)^2 - \left(\frac{W}{2pb}\right)^2} \quad \ldots \ldots \ldots \ldots (i)$$

25.6

With zero tension it will be seen from this that with a slack track the sinkage is unaffected by the number of wheels provided the number of wheels multiplied by their radius remains unaltered. With tension in the track the advantage lies with a large number of small wheels.

On the other hand if the number of wheels can be increased without reducing their radius, i.e. increasing L, the sinkage is decreased in either case. In other words an arrangement like the German Tiger and Panther having overlapping wheels can be expected to perform better on soft ground than comparable arrangements having smaller or fewer wheels.

25.6. THE EFFECT OF TRACK LINKS OF FINITE LENGTH

One of the assumptions made was that the track is flexible so that it can be bent to a smooth curve. In actual fact, of course, all modern tank tracks consist of a series of rigid links and the whole of the flexing must be concentrated in the hinge joints between these links. Consequently the track will not accurately embrace the wheel in the manner supposed, and in fact, may not embrace it at all.

If one imagines a rectangular board resting on a piece of soft ground and a load applied to one extreme edge of it, it will be clear that the board cannot remain in equilibrium, but must tilt up, as no matter what may be the distribution of pressure on the underside of the board this pressure is bound to exert a turning moment about the edge to which the load is applied, and there is no balancing moment.

In the case of a track the tension exerts some restraint on this tilting or rocking of track links but a little consideration shows that although it may limit its extent it is virtually impossible for it to prevent it entirely. On the other hand if the pitch is so long as to be comparable with the spacing between the wheels the tendencies to rocking may be made to cancel out between neighbouring links, (with the possible exception of the links in the neighbourhood of the end wheels).

An example of this is the French Char B arrangement where the wheel spacing was one and a half times the pitch

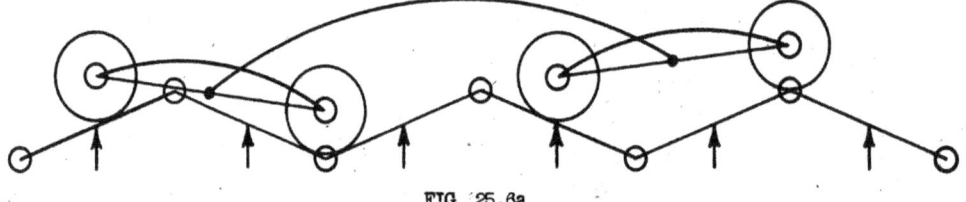

FIG. 25.6a

Fig. 25.6a. indicates that if all the links rock about their centres so that one wheel goes down the next wheel but one will go up a corresponding amount and it will be seen that this is the case whatever the position of the wheels. Hence from energy considerations there will be no tendency for rocking of this sort to occur. The distribution of ground pressure should be remarkably complete.

In fact this machine had a track with a spud in the middle of each link, each side of the spud being radiussed about one pin joint so as to enter and leave the ground with a minimum of disturbance.

Such an arrangement is, however, rare and on most modern tanks there is nothing to prevent rocking or snaking of the track links on soft ground. In order to prevent just the sort of tilting referred to, at all events on hard ground, the spuds are arranged at the ends of the links so that each link can be regarded as a bridge spanning the space between a pair of spuds.

Clearly, when a wheel is directly over a spud on hard ground such as a concrete road the whole weight of the wheel is applied to the spud. As the wheel moves along, the weight on the spud is progressively reduced whilst that on the next spud is progressively increased, until, when the wheel is halfway between two spuds, the weight is equally divided between them, and when the wheel has reached the next spud the weight on the spud first considered has dropped to zero.

Hence in this case the maximum ground pressure under each spud is equal to the weight applied to the wheel, divided by the area of ground contact of the spud. For example, in the case of a spud of area 2" by 15" and an applied pressure of 6,000 lbs. the ground pressure would be 200 lbs. per sq.in. This may be regarded as a maximum figure since it does not rely on any compression of the earth beyond what is required to form it to a flat surface. Moreover, as the earth is formed to a flat surface by a particular spud that same spud remains in contact with that same piece of earth throughout the passage over it of all the wheels, and no change is required in the shape of the earth if it can withstand the pressure of 200 lbs. per sq.in.

If however, the spud sinks in, the whole area of the link will help to bear the weight but the latter will travel across each link in turn and there will be little or nothing to prevent snaking. When the weight is on the middle of a wide long pitched link the pressure may be quite low, for example 3 tons on a link 8" x 24" would be a pressure of only 35 lbs/sq.in. But when the weight is on a joint the concentration of pressure would be much higher until the ground yielded to the rocking tendency and sheared away from under that particular joint.

It would be extremely tedious to attempt to assess the exact ground pressure at each point as each link rocked fore and aft under each wheel and it is thought that the figures given will give an idea of the general trend of results subject to making allowances for the tread of the tracks.

The conclusion that (neglecting track tension) many little wheels or few big wheels of the same aggregate diameter produce the same maximum ground pressure probably needs qualification in the case of long pitched tracks.

Obviously if each link were a flat plate of pitch equal to the spacing between the wheels the ground pressure would be completely uniformly distributed. Although modern tank suspensions do not approach this condition the tendency will be for long pitched tracks with closely spaced wheels (which generally means small wheels) to give a distribution of ground pressure of a different character to that of short pitched tracks with bigger and therefore more widely spaced wheels, which latter would probably more nearly resemble the continuously flexible track assumed in the foregoing calculations.

Until recently the tendency of modern design has been to use a long pitched track and small closely spaced wheels for slow or heavy tanks requiring good soft ground performance, but, owing to their low speed, a suspension of only limited absorption. For fast tanks requiring big absorption it is difficult to provide springing for a large number of wheels and the clatter of long pitched tracks (see Section 15.9) is objectionalbe, so a few big wheels and a relatively short pitched track tend to be used. This distinction applies mainly to British tanks with their division into Infantry and Cruiser types. On U.S. and German Medium types medium sized wheels have been used with track of moderate to short pitch. The latest German heavy tanks Tiger and Panther have in some respects more the characteristics of cruiser tracks and suspensions.

25.7. TRACK SLACK DUE TO BOWING ON SOFT GROUND

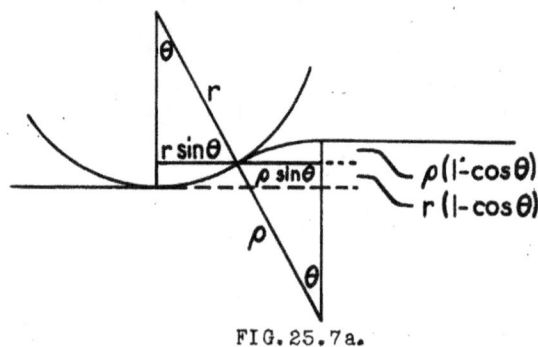

FIG. 25.7a.

From Fig. 25.7a. it is clear that the slack s absorbed by sinkage $= (\rho+r)(\theta - \sin\theta)$.

Now $\rho = \dfrac{T}{bp}$ $(\rho+r)\sin\theta = \dfrac{W}{bpn}$

In the example we have previously considered

$W = 60,000$ lbs., $n = 10$, $b = 15''$, $p = 50$ lbs./sq.in. $r = 16''$

If $T = 0$, $\rho = 0$ $\quad 16\sin\theta = \dfrac{60000}{15 \cdot 50 \cdot 10} = 8$

$$\sin\theta = .5000$$

$$\theta = .5236$$

$s = 16 \times .0236 = .3776$.

Hence total slack in 4 spans $= 1.5104''$ say $1\tfrac{1}{2}''$

---

if $T = 12,000$ lbs. $\rho + r = 16 + 16 = 32$

$$32\sin\theta = \dfrac{60,000}{15 \cdot 50 \cdot 10} = 8$$

$$\sin\theta = .2500$$

$$\theta = .2528$$

$s = 32 \times .0028 = .0896$.

Hence total slack in 4 spans $= \underline{.3584''}$

25.8 MAXIMUM GROUND PRESSURE AND TOTAL LOAD BELOW THE YIELD POINT.

The next thing we have to do is to examine in the same way what the maximum ground pressure is likely to be if the yield point is not exceeded.

This investigation is more cumbersome than the preceeding sections and appears to be of less importance as it seems likely from the results obtained that the yield point will be exceeded except on very hard or well consolidated ground. Also the qualitative conclusions are the same, for example that increasing the number or radius of the wheels lowers the ground pressure, but increasing one and proportionally reducing the other makes very little difference i.e. wheels can be sold by the yard.

It will however, be desirable to include the examination for the sake of completeness.

25.9. THE FIRST WHEEL

We now assume that the relation between ground pressure and sinkage follows a straight line law such as:- $p = kz$ where z is the sinkage, p the pressure and k a constant having some resemblance to the stiffness of a spring.

If in Fig. 25.9a. x is the horizontal distance of any point forward of the lowest point of the wheel and b the width of the track, the supporting force W/n afforded by the part of the ground being pressed down is:-

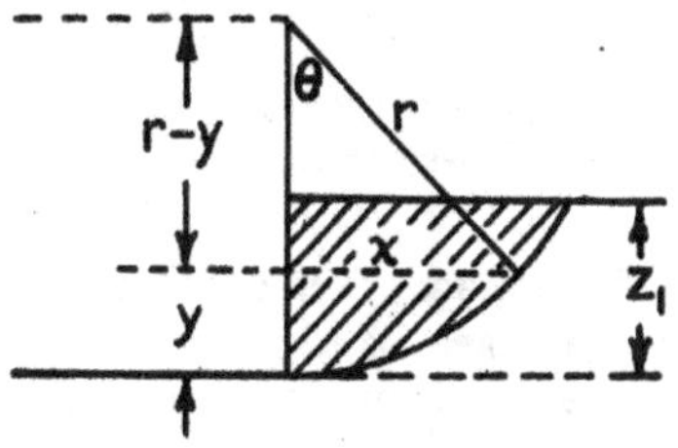

$$W/n = \int p \, b \, dx$$

but since $p = kz$ and k and b are constants

$$\frac{W}{n} = bk \int z \, dx$$

FIG. 25.9a.

but clearly $\int z \, dx$ is the area between the periphery of the wheel and the original ground level, shown shaded in Fig. 25.9a. Hence $\frac{W}{bkn}$ is the shaded area.

We can actually express this area mathemtically in terms of r and z_1, where z_1 is the maximum sinkage of the first wheel, but it seems rather cumbersome.

$$\frac{W}{nbkr^2} = \tfrac{1}{2} \arccos\left(1 - \frac{z_1}{r}\right) - \tfrac{1}{2}\left(1 - \frac{z_1}{r}\right)\sqrt{2\frac{z_1}{r} - \left(\frac{z_1}{r}\right)^2} \quad \ldots \ldots (i)$$

It is more conveniently expressed in terms of the angle of contact θ, thus:-

$$\frac{W}{nbkr^2} = \tfrac{1}{2}(\theta_1 - \sin\theta_1 \cos\theta_1) = \frac{2\theta_1 - \sin 2\theta_1}{4} \qquad z_1 = r(1 - \cos\theta_1) \quad (ii)$$

25.10. THE NEXT WHEEL

Let us assume that when the pressure is relieved the ground stays at its original level and when the pressure is applied again it builds up to its previous level before any further sinkage occurs after which it continues to sink in accordance with the original law. Curves taken with apparatus similar to that described in Section 24.2 tend to justify this assumption.

Hence the supporting force on a following wheel will be shown by the depressed area measured from the original level as in the case of the previous wheel except that there will be no contact and hence no pressure on the portion of the wheel above the level to which the ground was rolled down by the previous wheel.

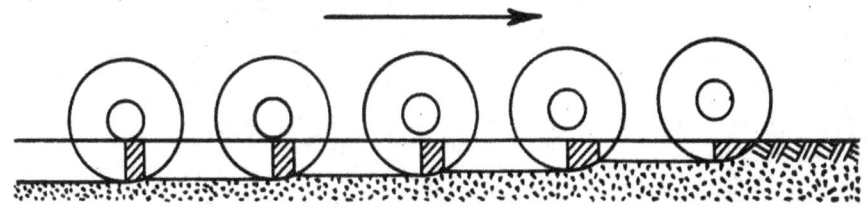

FIG. 25.10b.

The pressure diagrams for successive wheels will then be of the form shown in Fig. 25.10b from which it will be seen that:-

1) The ground pressure increases from each wheel to the next.

2) Each wheel sinks down lower than the previous one giving a stern down effect. In fact this stern down effect can often be observed when a tank is travelling on very soft ground.

25.11 EFFECT OF NUMBERS AND SIZES OF WHEELS ON MAXIMUM GROUND PRESSURE BELOW THE YIELD POINT.

We now want to see how the maximum ground pressure and therefore sinkage would vary with factors such as the number of wheels and their size.

From equation 25.9 (ii) for the first wheel:-

$$\frac{W}{nbkr^2} = \frac{2\theta_1 - \sin 2\theta_1}{4} \qquad z_1 = r(1 - \cos\theta_1)$$

In the case of the next wheel as indicated in Fig. 25.10b. the shaded area is measured from the original level and hence in this case there is an additional rectangle equal to $z_1 r \sin\theta_2$

That is to say $\frac{W}{nbkr^2} = \frac{1}{4}(2\theta_2 - \sin 2\theta_2) + z_1 r \sin\theta_2 \ldots \ldots (i)$

For subsequent wheels a similar equation will apply but in place of z_1 it will be necessary to write (z_1+z_2), $(z_1+z_2+z_3)$, etc.

These equations have been worked out graphically to see how the total sinkage Z varies with $\frac{W}{nbkr^2}$

		WHEEL no.						
$\frac{W}{nbkr^2}$		1	2	3	4	5	6	k assuming $W/nbr = 7.25$
.4	θ z/r Z/r Z $p=kZ$	66½° .60 .60 9.6 30	34° .17 .77 12.3 38½	28° .12 .89 14.2 44½	25° .094 .99 15.8 49½	22½° .076 1.06 16.9 53	22° .073 1.13 18.1 56½	3⅛
.2	θ z/r Z/r Z $p=kZ$	51° .37 .37 5.9 37	27° .11 .48 7.7 48	22° .075 .56 9.0 56	19° .055 .61 9.8 61	18° .05 .66 10.5 66	17° .045 .70 11.2 70	6¼
.1	θ z/r Z/r Z $p=kz$	39½° .23 .23 3.7 46	21½° .07 .30 4.8 60	17½° .047 .35 5.6 70	15½° .037 .39 6.2 78	14° .030 .42 6.7 84	13° .025 .45 7.2 90	12½
.05	θ z/r Z/r Z $p=kZ$	31° .143 .143 2.3 57.2	17° .045 .188 3.0 75.2	14° .030 .218 3.5 87.2	12° .022 .240 3.8 96.0	11½° .020 .260 4.2 104.0	10½° .018 .278 4.4 111.2	25
.025	θ z/r Z/r Z $p=kZ$	24¼° .09 .09 1.44 72.0	13.45° .0275 .1175 1.88 94.0	11.19° .0185 .1360 2.18 108.8	10.00° .0150 .1510 2.42 120.8	9.1° .0125 .1635 2.61 130.5	8.50° .0110 .1745 2.79 139.5	50
.01	θ z/r Z/r Z $p=kZ$	17.9° .0485 .0485 .78 97.0	10.0° .0150 .0635 1.02 127.0	8.3° .0104 .0739 1.18 147.8	7.4° .0084 .0823 1.32 164.6	6.8° .0070 .0893 1.43 178.6	6.35° .0062 .0955 1.53 191.0	125
.005	θ z/r Z/r Z $p=kZ$	14.0° .0296 .0296 .47 118.4	9.2° .0128 .0424 .68 169.6	6.2° .0058 .0482 .77 192.8	5.8° .0052 .0534 .85 213.6	5.2° .0041 .0575 .92 230.0	4.9° .0035 .0610 .98 244.0	250

TABLE 25.11a.

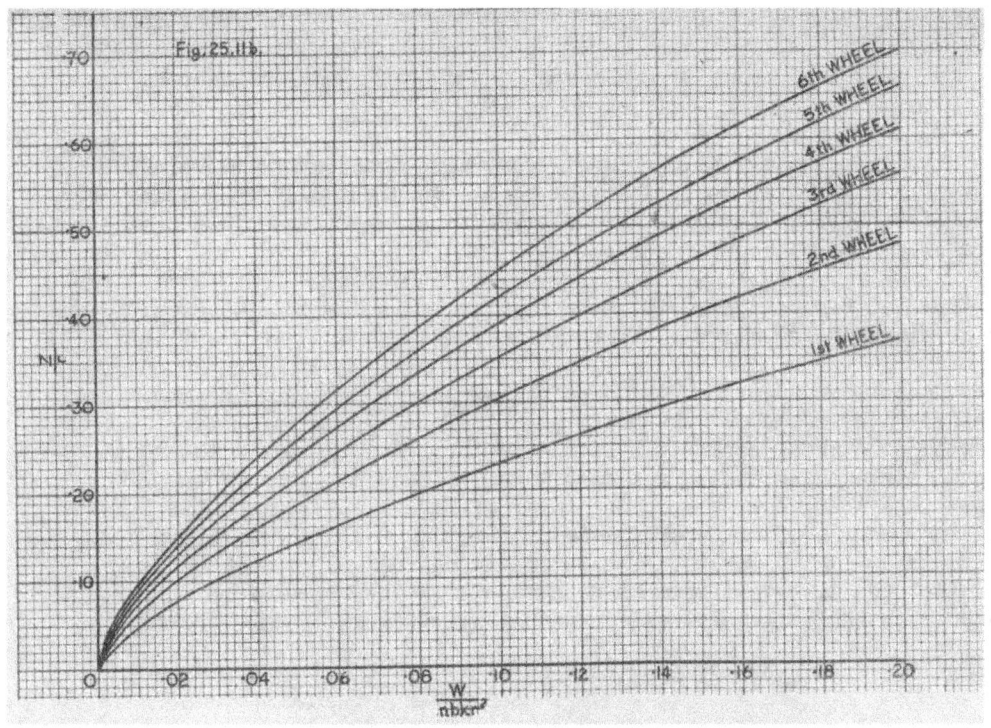

Fig. 25.11b.

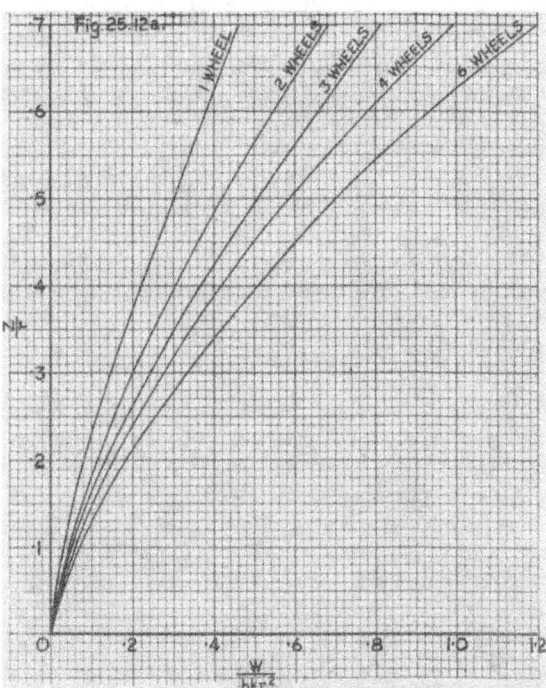

Fig. 25.12a.

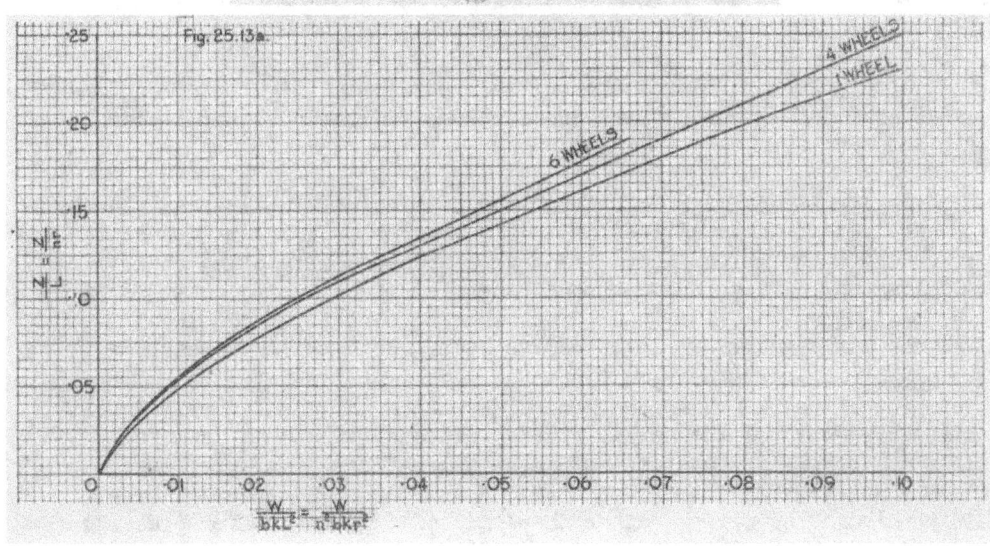

Fig. 25.13a.

Table 25.11a. shows the values of θ, z/r and Z/r obtained in each case for 6 wheels for a number of values of $\dfrac{W}{nbkr^2}$. From these figures it will be seen that in almost every case the sixth wheel sinks to about twice the total depth that the first sinks although the actual increase of sinkage is far greatest with the first wheel, and gets less and less with each subsequent wheel.

From the figures given in Table 25.11a. it is possible to plot curves relating the relative sinkage Z/r to the value of $\dfrac{W}{nbkr^2}$ and this has been done in Fig. 25.11b. which shows six curves representing the six wheels. These curves show the general points mentioned above, namely that each wheel sinks in a little further than the last, the additional sinkage decreases from each wheel to the next, and by the time the sixth wheel has passed, the total sinkage is about double what it was when the first wheel passed. So much for the relationship between curves. As regards the shape of any one curve, it will be obvious that the sinkage increases with the weight per wheel, and decreases with the width of tread or with the stiffness of the ground.

25.12 VARYING THE NUMBER OF WHEELS KEEPING THE TOTAL WEIGHT CONSTANT

From Fig. 25.11b. it is obvious that increasing the number of wheels (keeping the weight per wheel constant) tends to increase the sinkage, whereas decreasing the weight per wheel tends to decrease the sinkage. As an increase in the number of wheels would normally be accompanied by a decrease of the weight per wheel, it is of interest to see which of these two effects is the more important, and this is shown fairly clearly in Fig. 25.12a. in which the relative sinkage is plotted against $\dfrac{W}{bkr^2}$. From this set of curves, it will be seen that the sinkage is considerably reduced by increasing the number of wheels. This, of course, assumes that the wheels remain the same size.

25.13. VARYING THE NUMBER AND RADIUS OF WHEELS INVERSELY.

Often, however, the choice is between a certain number of wheels of one size, and a larger number of smaller wheels. If we assume that the number of wheels multiplied by their radius is the determining factor i.e. that we have a given length $2L$ which we are at liberty to fill with wheels, then $Z/L = Z/nr$ and $\dfrac{W}{bkL^2} = \dfrac{W}{nbkr^2}$. These two quantities are plotted against one another in Fig. 25.13a., from which it will be seen that under these conditions the number of wheels makes very little difference.

25.14. "SQUASHED EARTH", ROLLING RESISTANCE. POWER BELOW YIELD POINT. AN EXAMPLE.

There appear to be no comparative experimental figures of rolling resistance on soft ground, but there are some indications that it may be fairly substantial.

S.J. Wright quotes 500 lbs. per ton as a normal rolling resistance for a wheeled agricultural tractor and in a paper by T.R. Aggs there is a picture of a car in road conditions that produced a tractive resistance of 700 lbs/ton. This indicates that the resistance due to soft ground may be many times that due to all the other components of rolling resistance put together. It therefore seems worth while to consider how much rolling resistance must necessarily be produced by the action of pressing or rolling down the ground, even though this figure may fall considerably short of the actual figure, especially where a tank is sinking in very deeply and its action is a complicated mixture between that of a dog digging a hole, and that of a blunt nosed barge pushing its way through the water, rather than that of a garden roller pressing the ground downwards flatly, in a gentle and economical way.

On the basis of preceeding sections it is a simple matter to calculate the energy or work that must of necessity be expended to squash down a given area of a given ground to a given depth, assuming the yield point is or is not reached.

For example, assuming the yield point is not reached, let us take the case in Table 25.11a where $\frac{W}{nbkr^2} = .025$, $k = 50$, $Z/r = .175$. Suppose the radius r is 15 inches, b, the width of each track is 14 ins. and the speed of the tank is 44 ft/sec. or 44 x 12 ins./sec.

Then the area rolled per second by two tracks is 44 x 12 x 14 x 2 sq.ins. The work done per square inch is:

$$\int p\,dz = \int kz\,dz = \frac{kz^2}{2}$$

Hence the total work required will be

44 x 12 x 14 x 2 x ½ x 50 x .175² x 15² inch pounds/sec.

$$= \frac{44 \times 12 \times 14 \times 50 \times 49 \times 225}{12 \times 550 \times 1600} \text{ HP} = 386 \text{ HP}.$$

For a tank weighing 30 short tons, this, from Section 15.1 is equivalent to a rolling resistance of 161 lbs/short ton.

25.15, "SQUASHED EARTH" POWER BEYOND THE YIELD POINT, AN EXAMPLE

Assuming that sinkage occurs beyond the yield point we saw in Section 25.3 that the sinkage per wheel is equal to:-

$$r - \sqrt{r^2 - \left(\frac{W}{np b}\right)^2}$$

so that if $p = 100$, $\frac{W}{n} = 6000$ lbs., $r = 15$ ins. and $b = 14$ ins., then:-

$$z = 15 - \sqrt{15^2 - \left(\frac{6000}{1400}\right)^2} = 15 - \sqrt{15^2 - (4.3)^2}$$

$$= 15 - \sqrt{206.64} = 15 - 14.37$$

$$= .63$$

Total sinkage is 5 x .63 = 3.15 ins.

In this case the work done per square inch is equal to pZ (since p is a constant) = 100 x 3.15 = 3.15 inch pounds per sq.in.

Hence the total work required will be 44 x 12 x 14 x 2 x 315 ins. lbs/sec.

$$= \frac{44 \times 12 \times 14 \times 2 \times 315}{12 \times 550} \text{ HP} = 705.6 \text{ HP}.$$

This, for a 30 short ton tank is equivalent to 294 lbs/short ton.

The above is merely putting into figures what the tank commander knows as heavy going. It is in fact a common experience that on soft ground the engine simply is not powerful enough to maintain high speeds. This is not surprising when it is seen that even when the maximum sinkage is no more than a modest two or three inches, several hundred horse power would be required to squash the ground down at 30 m.p.h. in the most economical way possible. Bearing in mind that a considerable proportion of the engine power is lost before it gets to the tracks and a further fraction goes in the other components of rolling resistance, it is easy to understand that even going all-out progress is bound to be very slow on really soft ground.

This cut in speed goes hand in hand with a cut in mileage per gallon and the range of action suffers correspondingly.

25.16 AVAILABLE TEST RESULTS, FOR SOFT GROUND

Test results for rolling resistance of tanks on soft ground seem to be almost non-existent. In a memorandum discussing the possibilities of applying a rigid girder track to tanks, Col. Johnson of Messrs. Roadless Traction makes a comparison between the rolling resistance of the rigid girder track and that of the conventional pin jointed type. He states that tests with a reliable dynamometer have shown that the rolling resistance of a rigid girder track is about 80 lbs/ton on a hard surface (a good road), about 100 lbs/ton on a comparatively soft surface (wet sand) and about 120 lbs/ton on an exceedingly soft surface (soft dry beach above high water mark). He goes on to compare the range and power of such a track taking an average figure of 100 lbs/ton, with those of a conventional pin jointed track which he assumes would have a rolling resistance of about 200 lbs/ton over an average cross country route.

TABLE 25.16a

Report No.	ROLLING RESISTANCE ON GRASS FIGURES FROM M.E.E. REPORTS Vehicle	Rolling resistance lbs/ton
F.T. 23/3	Light M2 A4.	113.1
A.12/2	Tractor Medium Experimental	130.1
A.45	A.11.E.1.	142
A.99/1	Praga T.N.H.P. 8 ton tank	153
A.27/7	Light Dragon V.8	159
A.7/6	Light Tank Mk.V.	160
A.27/7	Light Dragon Mk. IIC.	164
A.30/2	Light Tank Mk. VI.	177.8
A.30/20	Light Tank Mk. VI.	180
A. 30/15	Light Tank Mk. VI. "very soft grass".	250

Table 25.16a. corresponds with Table 15.5b but gives figures for grass. The latter is described in some cases as "damp firm grassland" and in others as "very soft grass", but the results do not even indicate how deep the tracks sank in (if at all) and hence do not enable any quantitative comparisons to be made.

If the figures we calculated above are of the correct order for the work required to squash the ground, they must be added to the figures for hard ground to get an approximation to the rolling resistance on soft ground. On this basis it would seem that Col. Johnson's guess of 200 lbs/ton would be none too high on average cross country routes in wet weather and the figure would probably be much more if the going were really heavy.

What this means in power/weight ratio is clear from Section 15.1.

25.17 SQUASHED EARTH POWER FOR RIGID GIRDER TRACK

To show there is no discrepancy in the above figures we can calculate the squashed earth power for a rigid girder track assuming it is equivalent to a single wheel of radius 60 ft. (= 720 ins).

25.17

Assuming the yield point of 100 lbs/sq. in. is reached

$$z = r - \sqrt{r^2 - \left(\frac{W}{npb}\right)^2}$$

$$= 720 - \sqrt{720^2 - \left(\frac{60,000}{2 \times 100 \times 14}\right)^2}$$

$$= 60\left(12 - \sqrt{144 - .357^2}\right)$$

$$= 60\left(12 - \sqrt{144 - .1274}\right)$$

$$= 60 \left(\frac{.1274}{24}\right) = 60(.0053)$$

total sinkage .318 inches

Hence total work required will be

$$\frac{44 \times 12 \times 14 \times 2 \times .318 \times 100}{12 \times 550} \qquad H.P. = 71.2 \; H.P.$$

This is equivalent to 29.7 lbs/short tow.

This agrees reasonably well with Col. Johnson's figure of 20-40 lbs/ton extra rolling resistance for soft ground. It will be noted that the increase of power and rolling resistance due to soft ground are only about a tenth of the corresponding figures for the conventional tank track.

25.18 DIAMETRAL PRESSURE, EFFECT OF SHAPE OF TRACK GROUND CONTACT AREA, ABOVE YIELD POINT.

In Section 25.5 we saw that above the yield point

putting $L = \frac{n}{2}r$ we got:-

$$\frac{nz}{2} = L + \frac{nT}{2pb} - \sqrt{\left(L + \frac{nT}{2pb}\right)^2 - \left(\frac{W}{2pb}\right)^2} \qquad 25.5 \; (i)$$

It is of interest to see how this expression works out in terms of what may be termed the diametral pressure p_d i.e. the total weight divided by the sum of the diameters of the road wheels and by the width of the track.

It is clear that $p_d = \frac{W}{4bL}$ $\qquad L = \frac{W}{4bp_d}$

$$\therefore \frac{nz}{2} = \frac{W}{4bp_d} + \frac{nT}{2bp} - \sqrt{\left(\frac{W}{4bp_d} + \frac{nT}{2bp}\right)^2 - \left(\frac{W}{2bp}\right)^2}$$

$$= \frac{W}{2bp}\left\{\frac{p}{2p_d} + \frac{nT}{W} - \sqrt{\left(\frac{p}{2p_d} + \frac{nT}{W}\right)^2 - 1}\right\} \qquad 25.18 \; (i)$$

With regard to rolling resistance

Work done = $p \times 2b \times v \times \frac{nz}{2}$ ft. lbs/sec.

Rolling Resistance $F \times v$ = work done

$$F = 2bp\frac{nz}{2}$$

$$\frac{F}{W} = \frac{p}{2p_d} + \frac{nT}{W} - \sqrt{\left(\frac{p}{2p_d} + \frac{nT}{W}\right)^2 - 1} \qquad 25.18 \; (ii)$$

whence $\frac{p}{2p_d} + \frac{nT}{W} = \frac{1}{2}(F/W + W/F)$

Equation 25.18 (i) shows that for a given diametral pressure p_d, a given bearing pressure, weight, tension and number of wheels the sinkage is inversely proportional to the track width. In other words a wide short track gives less sinkage than a corresponding narrow long track. Put another way if the choice is between putting wheels side by side or in tandem the side by side arrangement gives less sinkage.

This of course assumes a soil of constant bearing capacity in which case the conclusion is really not surprising. For example if instead of six wheels

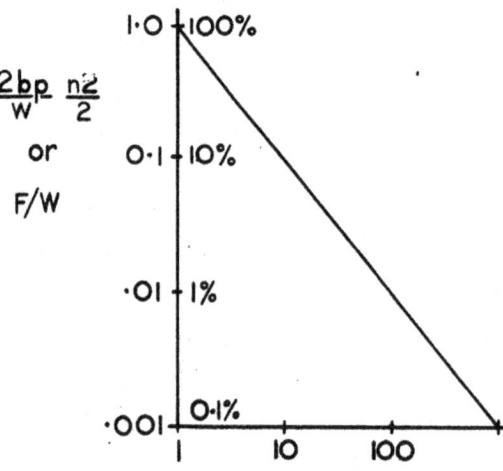

FIG.25.18a.

and a 10 inch wide track we substituted four wheels and a 15 inch wide track, the sinkage per wheel would not be altered so that the total sinkage would only be two thirds of what it was before. (Actually to get this we should have to raise the track tension in the same proportion as the track width.)

The rolling resistance, however, is independent of track width and the reduced sinkage theoretically obtainable by adopting a wide short track area is offset by the extra area of ground squashed down in travelling say a mile.

For moderate values of rolling resistance (i.e. if F/W is negligible compared with W/F) this resistance is approximately inversely proportional to

$$2\frac{p}{p_d} + \frac{nT}{W}$$

For example, with 10, 32" dia. wheels and a 15" track on a 60,000 lb. tank

$p_d = \frac{60000}{10 \cdot 32 \cdot 15} = 12\frac{1}{2}$ lbs/sq.in. $2p_d = 25$ lbs/sq.in.

Hence unless the bearing capacity of the soil is a good deal more than this, this component will do little to reduce rolling resistance. If it is say 100 lbs/sq.in. the value of $p/2p_d = 4$ and rolling resistance would be about 25%.

As to the tension factor on a 10 wheeled 30 ton tank one ton tension would only make $nT/W = \frac{1}{3}$ but 12 tons would make $nT/W = 4$ which with the 100 lbs/sq.in. bearing capacity would bring the rolling resistance down to about $\frac{1}{4+4} = 12\frac{1}{2}\%$.

The corresponding sinkages are

$25\% \times \frac{W}{2bp} = \frac{60000}{4 \times 2 \times 15 \times 100} = 5"$

and half that amount i.e. $2\frac{1}{2}"$.

Thus on soft going the track tension, if adequate, can come to the rescue.

25.19. THE SHORT WIDE TRACK AND THE LONG NARROW TRACK.

We have already remarked on the need for data as to what soils are typical and what are not, and it is believed that this is the key to the controversy between long narrow tracks versus short wide ones.

One extreme condition, the most favourable to the long narrow track, would be a layer of softish mud on a rock hard bottom. Assuming the mud to be penetrated in either case the sinkage is the same for each. Hence the work done in squashing a unit area is the same for each and as the area squashed is greater for the broad track the rolling resistance is greater in direct proportion to the width.

On the other hand with a soil of constant bearing capacity we saw in Section 25.18 that, under comparable conditions, the sinkage is proportional to the length, and hence the effects on rolling resistance of the increased area and reduced sinkage cancel out. Thus the short wide track gives less sinkage than the long narrow track but the same rolling resistance.

It is believed that the load sinkage curves of most typical soils will be somewhere between these two extremes in which case the short wide track will give less sinkage but more rolling resistance than the long narrow track. This would be the case with a homogeneous soil below the yield point.

On some types of bog the bearing capacity might even decrease with depth in which case the short wide track should give less rolling resistance as well as less sinkage than the long narrow track. This would also be the case if the increased sinkage resulted in bellying and bulldozing.

In the above remarks we have neglected the effect of area on bearing capacity. If on non-cohesive soils the bearing capacity increases with track width, as the formulae of Section 24.6 indicate that it does with the width of a uniformly loaded strip, then it would appear that on a homogeneous non-cohesive soil such as dry sand, the short wide track would give lower rolling resistance and much lower sinkage than a long narrow track.

It would be unwise to arrive at any dogmatic conclusion without a great deal of experimental data in view of the complexity of the problem. For example increased rolling resistance will demand increased adhesion and this may tend to promote shear and reduce the bearing capacity which in turn increases sinkage and rolling resistance. In other words a cumulative effect or vicious spiral may arise. But on the whole it does appear that the advantage rests if anything with the short wide track on fairly soft soils where the question begins to be of importance. This of course is quite apart from considerations of general design, steering etc.

www.ingramcontent.com/pod-product-compliance
Lightning Source LLC
Chambersburg PA
CBHW081919090526
44591CB00014B/2396